Women Volunteering

WENDY KAMINER

Women
Volunteering

The Pleasure, Pain, and Politics
of Unpaid Work from 1830 to the Present

ANCHOR PRESS
DOUBLEDAY & COMPANY, INC.
GARDEN CITY, NEW YORK
1984

I have used pseudonyms
to identify all the women volunteers interviewed in this book,
in order to preserve their anonymity.

This is the first publication of
Women volunteering.
Anchor Press edition: 1984.

Library of Congress Cataloging in Publication Data
Kaminer, Wendy.
Women volunteering.
Bibliography: p. 227
Includes index.
1. Women—United States. 2. Voluntarism—United States.
3. Women volunteers in social service—United States.
4. Women—Employment—Social aspects—United States.
I. Title.
HQ1426.K35   1984   305.4′3

Library of Congress Catalog Card Number 84-3119
ISBN: 0-385-18423-9
Copyright © 1984 by WENDY KAMINER
Printed in the United States of America

First Edition

To Miriam Gold and Sam Kaminer

ACKNOWLEDGMENTS

Perhaps I would have written the same book without the help of my friends and my editor. But it would have been a much more painful process. It would have been excruciating without The Writers Room, an inexpensive work space in the middle of Manhattan, where writers can write in good company. So, thanks a lot to all the people who support The Writers Room. And thanks as much:

To my editor, Laura Van Wormer, for giving me good advice and seeing me through. To Betsy Moore, my old friend and a kind of partner to me in this endeavor, from the beginning. She conducted nearly half of the interviews that comprise the research base for this book. I have sounded out ideas on her and benefited from her support more than I can say.

To Esther Cohen, for reading my manuscript and listening to my tales of woe. To Debra Franco and Skip Shepard, for always finding time for putting up with me. To Jane and Paul Knopf, for putting me up; their house has been a haven for me. To Mary Bleiberg, for taking an interest in my book and for always reading everything I write and always liking it. To Charles Bleiberg, for his free legal advice. To Jerry Goldfeder, for always being good for a laugh.

To Meri and Selma Lobell, for talking to me and helping me find such interesting women to interview. To all the women I interviewed, for telling me their stories, over coffee. To Leonora Morgan, a wise and loyal friend and the best artist I know.

CONTENTS

PREFACE

You have to wear white to march in the Smith College Alumni Day Parade. You wear a class ribbon across your chest and may or may not carry a sign making a gentle joke about your age. Undergraduate women in white dresses and long-stemmed roses line up in attendance along the way.

It is a reunion parade, led off by the oldest returning alumnae who graduated from college before women won the right to vote. I like to imagine them marching on the White House in 1917. I like to imagine them angry—and wonder about them. Do they vote? Did they marry, have children, earn their own livings, or were they volunteers?

I last saw the parade the weekend of my tenth reunion, in the spring of 1981. I wasn't marching in it, and neither were my friends. We didn't parade around in white dresses, we didn't work for free, and we resented the women who did. They took something away from us; they were not respected. Mention volunteering to a member of the class of 1971 and you are likely to remind her of what she doesn't like about her mother.

It was different for the first generation of college-educated women, a century ago. The ideal middle-class woman of their day was supposed to be kept fashionably idle, and strictures against her earning money were strong. "Real" paid work was the exclusive province of men, and a woman shamed herself and the men in her family utterly by engaging in it. Going to work meant that she was not enough of a woman to secure a male protector or that the one she had was a failure. At a time when marriage and motherhood were a woman's only true calling, volunteering was a bold and liberating step out of the home and into a working role in the community. We forget that volunteers were once troublemakers and pioneers.

Many of the first college volunteers followed Jane Addams into social and settlement work. Addams opened Chicago's Hull House in 1889 after graduating from a women's seminary, with no useful occupation to engage her. She had nothing but a "sense of futility, of misdirected energy," and a "moral revulsion" to an "unnourished, oversensitive" life of too much leisure. She wanted to test out the ideals she had talked about in school; she wanted to do something about urban poverty, and needed to feel that she lived by her own "common labor." Settlement work became a consuming passion for her, and Addams believed fervently, throughout her life, that in work lay salvation. The settlement movement she envisioned would not only serve the progressive cause of social justice; it would restore a "balance of activity" to the lives of college women like herself who were "smothered and sickened" with advantages.[1] Volunteering would be an antidote for femininity.

The volunteer tradition remained strong in women's colleges, from the late 1800s into the 1960s; they turned out generations of volunteers, fulfilling a tradition of "social responsibility." Smith alumnae quarterlies today are still filled with news of them. They volunteer in libraries, museums, courtrooms, hospitals, and schools. They serve in political office, as commissioners, councilwomen, and mayors. Or, like Helen O. L., class of 1918, they "jog along, working for local Friends of Music and Historical Society . . . fight[ing] weather, weevils, black spot, bird malnutrition."[2]

By the time I went to college in the late sixties, career expectations for women had, of course, changed considerably, along with our approach to problems of social welfare: Volunteers would never provide adequate care for the people who needed it; government was responsible for the delivery of social services. Women had a right to be paid equally for their work and would only be free when they were. We were trained for professional success; it was the mandate of our generation. We would not have to break any rules to get there. In ten years, most of the women in my college group built very respectable careers for themselves, with a minimum of struggle. We were not rebels, only a model group of new women. The class of '71 automatically produced professional women with graduate degrees, and an overwhelming number of lawyers.

I had been one of them, but by the time of my tenth reunion was easing out of the practice of law and into free-lance writing, and barely supporting myself. I was obsessed with money. I dreamed of finding money on the street. I walked with my head down. I spared change to the homeless woman on the corner so that it would never happen to me. If you want to be a writer, someone said, marry money.

I got about as far as smiling almost graciously when a man paid for my dinner—and wondering what "serious" married women did with their time when they didn't have to make "serious" money. Most of the ones I met were volunteers, and they were anxious to go to work at "real," paying jobs, not just because their families "could always use the money," but in response to new work patterns and pressures for women. In the mid-1970s, women who had spent ten or fifteen years raising children and volunteering entered the paid work force in record numbers.[3] Volunteering was no longer enough for them. It didn't give them the recognition or respect they felt they deserved or the security and independence that comes from earning your own money. They wished they were lawyers like me. I wished that, like them, I could afford to work for free.

The politics of our situations were murky. They needed the status and satisfaction of earning money and were willing to give up "socially responsible" jobs for the sake of it. I needed money and wanted to be paid for my work but didn't want to do the kind of work that paid. I considered coming full circle and declared that anyone who wanted to pay my rent was welcome to it. Still, I felt like I was falling; there was something almost sinful about being supported; at the very least, it would be terribly embarrassing. The correct course for any one of us to take wasn't clear to me. Should we work for love or money?

It was naïve to expect that the world would give us both— love and money in our work. Yet this was precisely the expectation with which so many volunteers were entering the work force. It was reflected in a strain of popular feminism that emerged in the mid-seventies. Paid work was glamorized. It

was said to be "fulfilling." It would provide a woman not only
with financial security but also with a strong, new, autonomous
identity for herself, and the pressure to get a job was tremendous. "I remember friends of mine jumping to get the most
menial jobs," says Marcia Pollack, who volunteers four days a
week on the staff and board of a national religious voluntary
organization. They would take any kind of job for money they
didn't need, she recalls, just to be able to say they were working
and not staying home with their children. Charlotte Andrews, a
community volunteer for fifteen years, remembers the typical
young married woman of the seventies "hiring sitters to work as
a receptionist in some crummy office and saying that was liberating." Charlotte volunteered, while her children were young,
on the boards of several community agencies and for the PTA
and found her volunteering far more satisfying than the edito-
rial job she'd held before her marriage. "I liked my job, but . . .
it was a job."

Volunteering has always offered women something they will
rarely find in the most prestigious paying jobs—freedom and
flexibility and the chance to do the work of their choice. Even
the professionals of my generation may rediscover the pleasure
of doing their own work, in their own time, particularly when
they start to raise children. It is clear that a new phase is beginning for many of my college classmates. They are taking sabbat-
icals from their jobs or working part-time, having babies, and
settling into their communities. If they are not careful, they
may wake up one morning and find themselves volunteers.

At reunion, my friend Laura admitted to me, rather sheep-
ishly, that she had joined the League of Women Voters. She is a
classicist, now working only part-time, teaching at a local college, while she raises two preschool children. Having made me
promise not to make fun of her, please, she delivered a short
speech explaining why she'd joined the League. She was new in
town and wanted to meet other women who didn't just play
tennis or bridge. Volunteering is an interesting and relaxing
change for her after ten years of university life. She was, she
says, beginning to "burn out."

Ten years out of college, others are ready for a similar change,
a shift in focus from professional to family life. At reunion,

everyone is talking about babies. In a group of eight women, comprised of three lawyers, a social worker, a scientist, a librarian, a college professor, and a business woman, babies are the primary topic of conversation.

I haven't gotten to babies yet; I'm still trying to figure out work. So, I escape for a few hours to the inevitable Saturday afternoon panel on "Choices, Challenges, and Commitments" for women in the eighties. The panelists, five Smith alumnae, are all successful "career women." They tell us their stories. Meg Greenfield, of the Washington *Post*, class of '52, says she has always made decisions by letting one of her options disappear. Lucy Benson, class of '46, former president of the League of Women Voters and a former Under Secretary of State, says that if there is a rational plan to her life she hasn't discovered it yet. Everyone wonders what new patterns will emerge for women today. Meg Greenfield, in talking about young women and work, mentions Janet Cooke, the former *Post* reporter who faked a story that almost won her a Pulitzer Prize. What troubled Greenfield about the incident was that Cooke wanted to win a Pulitzer Prize but didn't want to write a Pulitzer story. Her career meant much more to her than her work. If she took so little pleasure in her writing, for its own sake, the prize would not have saved her.

It is not that women should abandon the quest for success and recognition for their work, paid or not. In talking about volunteering, the panelists are careful to point out what's been in it for them. Pamela Plumb, class of '65, is the unpaid mayor of Portland, Maine; she likes her work, and she likes her status as mayor. Lois Stair, class of '41, National Fundraiser for the Episcopal Church, stresses the professional training she received as a volunteer and tells us how she turned her work into a paid career. She knows volunteering is passé and wants to give us a good, hard reason to do it. "Volunteering is fine," mutters the woman sitting next to me, class of 1911, "but not everyone can afford it." "Some can," answers her friend, "and someone has to do it."

This is why Beth Haller volunteers, at a community crisis center for teenagers and for the League of Women Voters. She is the thirty-four-year-old mother of two and a full-time volunteer who says she feels like a throwback to an earlier time. But she will continue to volunteer as long as her children are young, as long as her family can manage on one income. She likes her work, believes she is developing professional skills, and feels obliged to be a volunteer. She doesn't need to be paid and there is so much that needs to be done. "We need volunteers. If I've got the time, I'm going to do it . . . Somebody has to."

You cannot dissuade Beth from working for free by reminding her that it is important for women to take their place alongside men in the paid workplace or that we should pay people to deliver social services. She is concerned about social welfare cuts, she says, but would "rather see the programs survive than worry about who should be paid with money that's not there." She agrees that women may have been held back by volunteering but doesn't want to see it die "while we're out there becoming a major part of the corporate structure." She hopes we can have both—volunteering and economic power—and is sometimes a little wistful about her own status. Perhaps one day, Beth says, she will go out into the world like other women she knows "to become somebody . . . somebody important, and leave this other life behind."

Sylvia Mallow is the paid director of the community center at which Beth volunteers. She worked as a nurse before her children were born and volunteered for about fifteen years until they were on their own. She is not sure whether volunteering is, in the long run, good or bad for women or for the state of social services. She has "a lot of conflict" about the volunteer tradition, because it is important for women to be paid for their work and "no one will pay you for what you give away for free." But she does not believe that "all the measure of our worth is money." And she does not want "to allow all the things that need doing to go undone because there's an administration that won't support it . . . there's a lot of pain and things that need doing." She does not want to "step over bodies" while we are out there fighting for social justice, and social justice "will be a long time in coming."

It is hard for women who grew up in the sixties to know how to respond to this. We were supposed to live up to our political theories. We were supposed to war against poverty. We were

supposed to advance the status of women. And we were supposed to be volunteers. Whether you marched for peace or
social justice, for a simple sense of belonging, or because you
didn't want your boyfriend to be drafted, you marched for free.

*Elizabeth L. Moore, M.S.W.,
assisted in planning and conducting interviews.
I have also relied on her unwavering support
throughout the process of researching
and writing this book.*

Women Volunteering

ONE

WOMEN, WORK, AND MONEY:

Social Service and Social Change (An Overview)

When we talk about volunteering we tend to choose sides. "Are you for or against," people ask, when they hear I am writing a book about it. "Is it good or bad for women?" We are proud of the volunteer tradition: It is the heart of a humane, compassionate society in which not everything has its price. Or we are infuriated by it: It is an unholy blend of sexism and Reaganomics that keeps women powerless, dependent on men, and collaborating in the cutoff of public funds to pay for social services. We have reduced volunteering into a code word—for "sharing, caring, and community service" or the "exploitation of women." It is a way of responding to it reflexively, to let everyone know where we stand and whether or not we are feminists.

I never did come up with a short answer to the question of volunteering; perhaps that's why I wrote this book. Because for me volunteering is not a religion or an ideology or a test of my feminism. It is a work experience, as complex and multifaceted as paid work or motherhood and as difficult to label. So my purpose is to dispense with volunteering as a symbol—for the domestic enslavement of women on the one side or their domestic bliss on the other; it is not to answer the question of whether I'm for or against but to persuade people to stop asking it.

Why do they? The trouble is that in the 1970s volunteering became a battleground for the war between feminists and antifeminists over the nuclear family and the proper priorities for a woman. What must come first for her—family, or work and her place and power in the world? Volunteering as a career choice came to stand for the primacy of the family—the two-parent, one-income dream family. For generations it was posited as the ideal alternative to paid work for married women, because they had husbands to support them and because volunteering was the only job in the world that need never conflict with marriage and motherhood. A volunteer wouldn't take a "real" job away from anyone's husband and she could be home at three o'clock to greet her children. She could work outside the home without ever redefining her role within it.

This was the tradition that has become such anathema to feminists, and rightly so. It is the tradition Ronald Reagan evoked when he praised voluntarism and blamed unemployment on the ladies in the work force.[1] In applauding community service and self-help, it was clear that he was not only advocating federal budget cuts but also promoting an irksome ideal about women's proper place.

But this notion that they belong at home or within the confines of their communities is an anachronism that is finally losing its hold over women. Today the career volunteer looks and often says she feels like a dinosaur. Over one half of all the women and over one half of all the wives in this country work for money. Women head over nine million of America's families and comprise 43 percent of the paid labor force.[2] Economic hardships and the emergence of a popular feminist movement have made paid work a cultural norm even for married women, for the first time, and made equal pay and equal employment opportunities for all women matters of right as well as necessity.

Economic equality and the restructuring of the family have been primary goals of the contemporary feminist movement; volunteering had to become one of its primary targets. It represented a tradition of public housewivery; women would serve their communities out of love and duty, as they served their families. Volunteers might be proud of this capacity to work from the heart, but it made it impossible for them to fend for themselves in a world in which every relationship is commercialized and every act measured in dollars. Career volunteering denied women their capacity to be self-sufficient and also their right to run things. Social policies, often carried out at the lowest levels by women volunteers, were usually set by men. The power to establish a community service center lay with the men who had the power to fund it; the power to write and enforce laws with the men who had the money to run for office or were well enough connected to others who did. The political cost of volunteering has become especially clear in recent years now that women are finally in the running themselves, no longer licking envelopes. With campaign costs soaring, women candidates have a much harder time than men raising money—because they don't have the same access to corporate funds and because the individual women voters who support them have less and give less in campaign contributions than their husbands.[3] As a tradition of women providing support services in politics and social welfare, volunteering was participation without control.

It was also participation at a price that can be said to have been borne by women in the paid work force along with volunteers. Women have always been shunted out of management and into clerical and pink-collar jobs, where a majority of all paid women workers are still concentrated today. The only professions traditionally open to them have been low-paying, low-status service professions—teaching, nursing, and social work. The minority of women counted as professionals by the Labor Department today "are believed to consist mostly of teachers and nurses earning relatively low pay."[4] It can readily be argued that this lowers the state of social services as well as the status of women. Not only is a woman a second-class worker; a social service job is second-class work.

There was good reason then for a twofold feminist attack on service volunteering: it was not just bad for women but bad for the people it purported to serve; social services would never be adequately funded as long as women provided them for free. In 1971 the National Organization for Women issued a resolution telling women they should only volunteer to effect social change, not to deliver social services. Lobbying for funds to establish a public welfare program was permissible; working for free with needy individuals within the program was not. The new woman of the 1970s could be an activist; she could work for free to change an inequitable system but she could not be a volunteer. Money was power, and women had to earn and control their own money in order to control their own lives and the institutions that control society.

It was a neat equation that made its point; women had to stand up for themselves in the professional marketplace. It has renewed relevance today; in 1981, Reaganomics clarified the usefulness of voluntarism as an excuse for withdrawing government support of social services and a way of keeping "ladies" in the home or at the service end of the paid work force. Typical of the Reagan administration attitude toward women and work was a remark by Secretary of Education Bell blaming the crisis in the schools and a dearth of quality teachers on the fact that women had abandoned the classroom for higher-paying professions[5]—an attitude that is, arguably, one legacy of volunteering. But only one; the volunteer tradition is a much more complex phenomenon than Reaganomics, and early feminist approaches to it factored out the complexities of volunteering—its history, its relation to the role of women in the family, and the contributions made by volunteers to social reform. The moral was clear, but the story was only half-told.

It began a hundred and fifty years ago, when middle- and upper-class women ventured out of their homes and into their communities for the first time by volunteering. The ideal nineteenth-century woman did not work for money; many had to, and many did—by 1850, women comprised about one fourth of the nation's paid labor force—but working women were not "ladies." "Ladies" were active in voluntary associations dedicated to charity and service work and the moral elevation of society, which first emerged in the 1830's. Through their associations, "ladies" learned to organize and became involved in public affairs and, eventually, progressive movements for social reform—settlement work, consumerism, and even trade unionism. They forged new roles for themselves and new goals for society by working for free. The rank and file of the nineteenth-century suffrage movement was comprised of traditional volunteers.

Volunteering was hardly a daring choice for modern American women, but it still represented a conscious attempt to balance domestic life with work. By choosing a volunteer career, a woman was not simply choosing home and family; she was acknowledging that, although it came first for her, family life and the social activities that went with it were not enough. "I couldn't be one of those bridge-playing ladies," is a common refrain from a woman who volunteers because she has free time and is not looking to just fill it. For her, volunteering has been a kind of halfway house between the family and society. It may not have gained her the world, but at least it made her a part of it.

As a service volunteer, she could also be a force for social change. Service work introduced women to social welfare problems a hundred and fifty years ago, and it continues to do so today. "There's never been a time when advocacy and service volunteerism didn't go hand in hand," observes Winifred Brown, Director of the Mayor's Voluntary Action Center in New York. "People who've been there and smelled the smells and seen the sights and become part of it become your strongest advocates . . . They talk for the staff of the agency they're in; they talk to the problem at hand, and they talk for the client who needs the service." They may not organize the rally at City Hall, she says, but they will "step forward" and become part of it. "They will vote . . . they've become aware there's something to vote for . . . if those volunteers are predominantly middle-class, we change the system by the voice of the predominantly middle class." Brown believes it was "cruel" and counterproductive to distinguish social change from service work. "If you tell people that service work is not advocacy, it won't be." Sometimes, you have to show volunteers to themselves as agents for change, "shake them and remind them of the purpose and push them ahead." You have to make sure that the service volunteer "never loses sight of the fact that it's wrong to have to do this and as soon as we can create a better system, [she] can take [her] volunteer job and move it someplace else."

By moving where they choose, volunteers can also focus public attention on "low visibility" issues, adds Brown. "Fifteen years ago, what legislator would have put a penny into rape prevention?" Volunteering gives individuals a voice in establishing and changing public welfare priorities. They come into the Voluntary Action Center with priorities of their own sometimes, saying, "Nobody thinks this is important. Nobody else cares about it but I think this is the most important thing in the world and this is where I want to put my time." We would not want the bureaucracy setting forth an exclusive agenda of "important" social issues, and we should not presume to set one forth for each other. Ruth Berger is a career volunteer who has always been active in peace work, because peace "was always *the* issue to me. I just didn't see how people could talk about lesser issues so seriously." But, she adds, her mother has always volunteered in hospitals; she had wanted to be a nurse and feels that helping people who are sick is "the only serious work for women." She also makes recordings for the blind, because she suffered from eye disease as a child. People choose their own issues based on their own experiences, and, says Winifred Brown, "they move to change systems by a combination of intellectual and emotional drive."

The difficulty of distinguishing between service work and advocacy, in fact, becomes especially clear when you and the members of your community are the people at risk or in need. Even the hardest feminist line against volunteering had to make exceptions for service work in a battered women's shelter or rape crisis center—because it helped other women whose needs were not being met by the system and promoted a kind of public consciousness raising: By providing shelter alternatives for battered wives or guiding rape victims through the criminal justice system, volunteers would begin to change prevailing attitudes toward sexual violence while they assisted its victims.

Traditional service volunteers could carve out similar exceptions for their work, within their own chosen communities. If counseling women in need is productive and politically correct, so is teaching a disadvantaged child to read: Literacy programs make people aware of a crisis in the public schools while they help individual children get on with their lives.

There was something arrogant and short-sighted about the general feminist prohibition of service volunteering. Even when we are all impassioned advocates, marching on City Hall and demanding change, there will still be large classes of people with needs to be met in the meantime. What if they are members of your own community, people with whom you identify, whose struggles are your own? And what if they're not? Women who have been victimized by sexism and oppressed by this inequitable system of ours are hardly the only people worth saving between now and the day that we change the world.

It is interesting that the attack on service volunteering didn't come from the working-class and minority women for whom problems of equal pay, equal opportunities, and adequate social services were so crucial, but from middle- and upper-class and primarily white feminists, who, in another life, would perhaps have been volunteers. It was as if they were whipping themselves into shape. Sandra Wells, president of an organization of professional black women, regards the controversy that erupted over volunteering in the mid-seventies as a controversy for middle-class white women who had "to holler for the right to work . . . The right to work wasn't a relevant issue to us. We had always been working . . . Black women have always worked, very few of them stayed at home." The volunteer work they did on the side was essential to the health and welfare of their communities; if they didn't take care of their own, no one else would.

Volunteering has always been "very important" to the black community, says Carla Raymond, director of education programs for a national civil rights organization. The black church and "informal networks" of information and service have been crucial to its "survival." Volunteering was simply not the problem for the black community, says Sandra Wells. The problem was the relegation of black women in the work force to domestic service and low-level clerical jobs; the problem was providing for "things like child care and . . . Headstart programs for poor kids."

There have always been even more tangible and immediate problems facing self-supporting working women than the presumed effect of volunteering on employment opportunities and social attitudes toward women in the work force. More to the point, perhaps, is the fact that a majority of paid working women are not unionized. According to a recent congressional report on "Women's Economic Issues," "only 20% of working women belong to labor organizations. These women earn almost a third more than their non-unionized counterparts."[6] The hard economic problems for women are inequities in social security and pension plans, the lack of adequate day-care facilities, the disproportionate effect of federal budget cuts on them, and unemployment and wage discrimination, which is occasioned more by the unwillingness of men to welcome women into a limited job market than the unwillingness of women to enter it.

Perhaps the volunteer tradition contributed to the sexism from which these inequities flow; but while it kept one class of women out of the "real" world of work, it also gave them work experience and skills that might someday be translated into paying jobs. Volunteering can offer untrained women greater opportunities to acquire and exercise administrative and executive skills than paid work. A recent study by the Wellesley Center for Research on Women found that both high school and college educated volunteers spend less time on clerical work and more time on professional or management-level activities than paid women workers. It noted that a volunteer job often serves as a kind of training ground for women seeking to enter the job market for the first time or to advance their positions in it.[7]

Volunteering both eases the transition into the paid workplace and makes the years at home more palatable and productive. It has traditionally been a compromise for women. The professional volunteer who stayed out of the job market to raise her children gave up the kind of career her husband had built in the meantime, but she developed skills and contacts and earned standing in her community that will make her employable, when she's ready. She may miss the other career, given up for the sake of the family; it is, in the words of one volunteer, "a sacrifice," but she is not a likely candidate for tomorrow's displaced homemaker. Charlotte Andrews, who at forty-five has been volunteering for over fifteen years, spent a year in graduate school and two in the paid work force before her marriage, so that she would "always have something to fall back on"; raised by a single working mother who was widowed young, Charlotte knows there are no guarantees. So, she has always sought out volunteer work that would give her professional status and expertise and doesn't doubt her capacity to care for herself, or her children, if one day she must. After so many years of service on so many boards, she can always find a job as executive director of "some agency."

Volunteering has been a trade-off for her—between the demands of work and family. Something has been lost in the process, the "person that would have come from the continuing development of potential" that goes with a lifelong paid career, but, she says, her time has not been wasted:

"I never had the kind of career that starts at twenty-one and is lifetime . . . I did not have that and I will never have that and I gave it up and I regret it. But I'm glad as long as I had children that I did it that way."

She did it automatically. "We were scripted to marry, and once you married you had children." If you wanted to work, you volunteered.

Today, the script is finally changing; women are demanding and beginning to take their rightful place in the paid work force. No longer a reflex, volunteering is not even a fashionable or respectable option for married or single women in a feminist world. It is clear to Charlotte that if she were twenty years younger and starting out today, with a graduate degree and the desire to work outside the home, she'd be starting as a paid professional and not a volunteer. Still, volunteering gave her, at least, a part-time outside job and the chance to enter the paid work force on a managerial level. Given the script, the cultural prescription of her day, the 1950s, volunteering was a little liberation.

Now that her children are grown, Charlotte may even choose to remain a volunteer, as long as she can afford to do so. What she has missed in the past fifteen years is not a paycheck but the time to devote herself to her work fully, to enjoy one career uninterrupted by children, developed over a lifetime. As a volunteer, Charlotte has been struggling with the same problem with which younger women are struggling today, with much ado and a sense of discovery, as if it had never been a problem for an earlier generation: how to raise a family and pursue a career at the same time.

Talking to today's volunteers and reading about the women who have come before them made clear to me the importance of volunteering as an extra-domestic job for women who do not work outside the home for money, and as a community connection for women who do. I had learned much from feminist theory about the economics of volunteering but very little about its past or present place in women's lives. This is what I learned from interviewing volunteers—that there is no one way to characterize what they do and why, to sum up volunteering and state the one and only thing it means for women.

That it is wrong to expect women to volunteer because it keeps them close to home, because it is women's work, does not make it wrong for one woman to decide to do it anyway because, for her, it is the right way to balance the conflicting personal, familial, and social obligations and desires that confront every woman who wants to have a home and also work outside of it. Put very simply, volunteering, like most things in life, is a complex and paradoxical mix of rights and wrongs, strengths and weaknesses. It takes a strong woman to be a successful volunteer, one who doesn't need a job to know how to use her time productively or a paycheck as a measure of her worth, one who can afford to be proud of serving her community for free. But volunteering, alone, cannot provide her with what she needs to get on in the world—professional status and an income she can call her own. It will never fully empower her —to earn as much money as any man and function alongside him as an equal partner.

Is volunteering good or bad for women? It has always been a double-edged sword. No wonder it has been so divisive. As a career choice, it has been used by women and against them—as a way of getting out of the house when they were not supposed to work for money and as a way to keep them there, denying them the power to earn their own livings and with it the chance to live their own lives, outside the institution of marriage. Volunteering has improved domestic life for women and, in doing so, prolonged its hold over them. It has also given women their political life, introducing them to the political process while allowing them only limited access to it and no direct control. It has turned "housewives" into campaign workers, activists, and community leaders, but left them outside, on the sidelines, marching on City Hall and clamoring for reforms by the men within who can afford to run for office and win. A century ago volunteering laid the groundwork for women's suffrage and the emancipation of women by bringing them out of the home and into the world of politics, civics, and social affairs, without ever challenging sex-based divisions of labor and wealth, in the family and the workplace, that have made women the second sex, dependent on men for their keep. From the beginning, volunteering has both liberated women and kept them in their place.

TWO

THE WAY WE SEE OURSELVES:

American Facts and Fancies about Volunteering

America is supposed to be a country of volunteers, in the hardy, helpful spirit of the colonists and pioneers. Grade school stories of men and women "volunteering" to carve new worlds out of the wilderness and images of frontier barn raisings are part of the national consciousness: Americans are good neighbors. We are a team, joiners of social clubs, civic groups, and political parties. We share, care, and cooperate, and do for each other for free.

Some do, and if "volunteering" means any freely chosen, unpaid activity, like doing a favor for a friend, then we are all volunteers, at least on occasion. According to a 1981 Gallup Poll that defined volunteering, broadly, as "working in some way to help others for no monetary pay," 47 percent of the men and 56 percent of the women in this country volunteered between March 1980 and March 1981, notably in areas of health and education and through their churches or synagogues; 31 percent of the population are surmised to have volunteered "regularly."[1] The National Center for Citizen Involvement, a resource center and clearinghouse for volunteering, lauds recent trends in self-help groups, crisis intervention, and grass-roots politicking as evidence of a continuing American commitment to progressive public service and activism. In a 1980 report, it suggests that the "me decade" of the 1970s may have served as "the gateway to a new era in volunteering and citizen involvement," and that Americans, by 1980, had had enough of narcissism and "in record numbers, in new and innovative ways, sought to reach out to one another."[2]

This is the way we like to see ourselves as a country: neighbors holding out hands to each other, instinctively—an image that was regularly invoked and exploited by the Reagan administration in its attempts to justify massive cuts in funding for social services. Budget cuts were characterized not as a retreat from problems of social welfare but as an affirmative quest for "private solutions" to them, packaged as a return to an all-American tradition of good neighborliness. In a 1981 speech to the National Alliance of Business, the President theorized that "the independent spirit of the people and their communities," once "unleashed," would "accomplish far, far more than Government programs ever could." Undaunted by facts and figures indicating that the private sector would never make up in voluntary contributions what was lost with the withdrawal of government support for social services,[3] Reagan reached back into movie history for an anecdote to define voluntarism and prove what was good about it:

"What exactly is voluntarism? I guess Gary Cooper did about the best job of describing it in the movie *Mr. Deeds Goes to Town*. 'From what I see,' he said, 'there will always be leaders and always be followers. It's like the road out in front of my house. It's on a steep hill. And every day I watch the cars climbing up. Some go lickety-split up that hill on high—some have to shift into second—and some sputter and shake and slip back to the bottom again. Same cars—same gasoline—yet some make it and some don't. And I say the fellas who can make the hill on high should stop once in a while and help those who can't.' "[4]

This was not just a simplistic, highly romanticized vision of voluntarism; it was a one-sided, ideological one. Political activism—organized protests against government policy and challenges to its authority—are as much a part of an American volunteer tradition as people helping people up a hill. Volunteering is not just charity but confrontation—between the poor and disenfranchised and their government. It was political, confrontational volunteering that sustained the feminist, anti-war, and civil rights movements and pressured government into creating the poverty programs of the 1960s. That there was no place for it in the Reagan administration was clear in its early attempts to dismantle VISTA[5] (Volunteers in Service to America), the "domestic peace corps," established in 1964. To the proponents of private solutions on the Right, VISTA was not voluntarism but subversion. Like the Legal Services Corporation, it was condemned for seeking to organize poor people "as a group" and empower them. In 1981, Constance Horner, director of VISTA, noted that conservatives were opposed to "community organizing which is designed to elicit a confrontation between poor people as a group and government or nongovernment institutions in their communities."[6]

In the lexicon of the Right, self-help was only a euphemism for Social Darwinism: if you weren't fit to survive on your own, if you couldn't pull yourself up by your bootstraps, you deserved to fall. According to Constance Horner, the trouble with "programs, entitlements, [and] rights" engendered by confrontational organizing, is that they "enhance dependency, not self-reliance."[7] The fact that some people were better equipped for self-reliance than others, not by nature but by class, was conveniently ignored. Cuts in the social welfare budget and retreat from enforcement of civil rights laws denied those at the bottom of the social and economic scale the basic tools they needed to help themselves—equal education and employment opportunities. It was as if poverty were a character defect that hard work would overcome, as if the basic disadvantages to which some were born were only failures of will. The theme of the Reagan administration was that this was America, where anything was possible, and those not strong enough to succeed could always fall back on the generosity of their neighbors: for them there was always voluntarism—10 percent of the rich man's income and the free social services of his wife. To the

extent that it was tied to legal and economic policies that denied disadvantaged classes of people equal rights and opportunities and sought to discourage the kind of confrontational volunteering that shaped the protests movements of the sixties,
the Reagan version of voluntarism was a regressive form of
social control, a way of preserving the status quo. If feminists
had denounced the volunteer tradition of social service, Reagan
did not even recognize the tradition of social change.

It was a lesson in public relations, how saying it can help to
make it so. "If you tell people that service work is not advocacy,
it won't be," said Winifred Brown, Director of New York City's
Voluntary Action Center. The characterization of volunteering
as only social service and not activism is a popular one that can
be self-fulfilling. By reinforcing it, the Reagan Administration
was able to promote voluntarism without necessarily promoting
the social and political unrest it sometimes fuels.

Voluntarism was news in the early 1980s, and the news was
decidedly upbeat. The President created a task force on "Private Sector Initiatives"; he handed out voluntary service
awards, and state and local governments followed suit. Corporate responsibility programs appeared, and corporate employ-
ees were encouraged to devote a percentage of their work time
to volunteering.[8] The volunteer workplace was "professional-
ized," and "life experience" credits extended to volunteers by
professional schools and employers.[9] Service volunteering was
repackaged as a strategy for career advancement for men and
women, a "bridge" into the job market for the disadvantaged
and disabled, as well as a second occupation for the retired.[10]
With the approval of the business community, volunteering was
back in vogue.

New trends in volunteering and its new respectability
brought more good news from the major women's voluntary
associations. Membership levels are relatively high and, for
some, even rising, after the awkward period of the 1970s when
"traditional" volunteering came under attack. Both the Junior
League and Hadassah, two organizations closely identified with
tradition, reported record numbers of members in 1982—
370,000 for Hadassah, as against 318,000 in 1972, and 152,000
for the Junior League, against 107,000 in 1972.[11] Membership

in the General Federation of Women's Clubs has been rising for the past two years, after a loss of some 600 clubs and 150,000 members during the seventies;[12] today, the Federation claims 600,000 members and 12,000 affiliated clubs throughout the country. The National Council of Negro Women estimates that it "represents" 4,000,000 women nationwide, through its network of affiliated organizations. The League of Women Voters, with 110,000 members, has yet to make up for the members it lost during the last decade, but it is now enjoying the services of older women who are turning to volunteering after retirement.[13] The National Council of Jewish Women—a service organization with a relatively traditional membership ("most" of its 100,000 members are married and 80 percent do not work for money)—reports that volunteering is "alive and well," thanks, in part, says a Council spokeswoman, to the "President's promotion of voluntarism" and the fact that "the media has been giving it more coverage . . . It is our hope that the women's movement liberated women to make choices that are best for them . . . whether it be a career in voluntarism, business, or as a housewife."[14]

This would hardly be an unwelcome change; none of the recent reforms in volunteering are unwelcome or simply part of some master plan by the Right to defuse the impulse toward social change. Some—those involving the professionalization of volunteering—were made partly in response to the feminist movement: it was time to recognize volunteer work as *work*, an experience to be recorded on a résumé. But in reviewing the predominant image of volunteering that has emerged in the past few years—good neighboring seasoned with a little good career strategy—it is hard to separate facts from public relations fictions. The President, the private sector, and the press may have revived what has been billed as a proud American tradition, but they haven't taught us very much about it.

For a country of volunteers we have a slim store of facts on volunteering. There are no reliable studies or statistics on the number of volunteers nationwide or the kind of work they do; there is no way to quantify their contributions to American society. The Labor Department keeps no statistics on volunteering, and the 1980 Census included no surveys of volunteers.

There has been no comprehensive sociological research on male and female voluntary associations or on the universe of unaffiliated, individual men and women volunteers. We simply don't have the hard facts on who volunteers for what in America today. All we do have now is the 1981 Gallup Poll, which, again, suggests that about one half of all Americans are occasional volunteers.[15] Independent Sector, the consortium of corporations, foundations, and voluntary associations that commissioned the poll, uses it to estimate the "dollar value of time volunteered by Americans" to be a "record high of 64.5 billion dollars," adding that 84 million Americans volunteer an estimated 8.4 billion hours a year.[16] But the Gallup Poll on which these estimates were based only covered one twelve-month period between March 1980 and March 1981, and counted as volunteers people who had worked for free "on a sporadic basis or for a one-time cause." Volunteer activities noted by survey respondents included taking care of a neighbor's dog when his owner was sick, giving free legal advice to a neighbor, and baking brownies for a cub scout troop.[17]

None of this tells us very much about the people for whom volunteering is still a primary work activity. Helping your neighbor move, or singing in the church choir, two more sample activities noted in the Gallup Poll, are hardly comparable to working three days a week at a community service center or serving as president of your local PTA. Even the people tentatively identified by Gallup as "regular" volunteers, who comprised 31 percent of the survey sample, did not necessarily devote most of their working time to volunteering. To qualify as a "regular," for purposes of the poll, you had only to volunteer a minimum of two hours a week during one thirteen-week period.[18] This too does not compare to volunteering a minimum of two days a week, as so many career volunteers do. The Gallup Poll is the most recent and comprehensive one available on volunteering, and it does not provide us with a reliable estimate or demographic profile of career volunteers. It does note that, in general, the people most likely to volunteer are educated, suburban or rural, upper-income white women who are employed part-time. It also suggests that upper-income women who are not the chief wage earners in their family are more likely to volunteer regularly.[19]

This neatly coincides with the traditional stereotype of a volunteer; it may, in fact, only reflect it. My own interviewing experience indicates that upper-income white women who are not the chief wage earners in their families are the people most likely to call themselves volunteers. Paid working women, minority women, and women who see themselves as radicals or, at least, reformers working to change the system are apt to call themselves community organizers or activists. "What is a volunteer?" I asked Roseann Navarro, a thirty-two-year-old Hispanic woman who works full-time as the paid director of a community health center and as an unpaid "organizer." "Volunteers," she said, "are middle-aged white women coming in to help out . . . They mean well, but they don't know what the hell they're doing . . . That's a horrible image to have, but that's my image." Roseann sees herself as a "community participant." Margaret Porter, a photographer, active in the feminist community and the peace movement, and the "black sheep" of a white, upper-class New England family, has an equally negative image of volunteering: "It doesn't feel real or substantial . . . it feels fluffy; it feels vacuous." Margaret only works for free but she does not say she volunteers: "I think of myself as a person who wants to do service."

It is hard to imagine a volunteer who doesn't serve or participate in her community, but the label "volunteer" when applied to a woman does mean something more to most of us. Despite the recent interest of government and the corporate world in volunteering, it is still commonly considered a housewife's vocation. Roseann Navarro has reason to give herself another name: the fact that she has always worked for money and that the disadvantaged community she serves is her own distinguishes her from the stereotypical volunteer. It also makes volunteering much less problematic for her than it is for the woman who is not sure she can support herself or her family or for a woman like Margaret, who is trying to escape from a family tradition that she associates with Reaganomics—one that, in her view, diminishes women and teaches a wife to volunteer to help the poor while her husband makes money exploiting them. She sees the all-American volunteer tradition —Gary Cooper helping out his neighbor—as an all-American myth. It is not the tradition handed down by her mother and grandmother. For Margaret, volunteering is not simply American men and women helping each other maintain country and community as they have for over two hundred years.

THREE

VOLUNTEERING IN RECENT HISTORY:

A Summary History of Volunteering and the Status and Image of Women in America, from the 1830s through the 1920s

A) There is a volunteer tradition unique to leisure-class women that began not in the colonies or on the frontier but in the cities and factories of the nineteenth century, with the onset of a system of wage labor for men. This tradition has less to do with barn raisings and good neighboring than with a kind of public housekeeping: women support, care for, and clean up after their communities, for free, while men do the "real" and sometimes heartless work of earning money. The notion that women, particularly wives, should volunteer exclusively is a relatively modern one, rooted in post-industrial concepts of work and gender.*

For the pioneer or farm family in agrarian America, domestic life was work, for men and women, and it was not simply measured in dollars. The family worked to produce its own goods, at home, on its own land. Labor might have been divided according to sex: women did most of the manufacturing—spinning and weaving were important home industries—while men were more often farmers. But both sexes worked to one end, to provide for their families, and inhabited one world.[1]

This changed over the course of the nineteenth century with the industrial revolution and the accompanying process of urbanization. The home was no longer the workplace; it was replaced by the factory and eventually the office; private domestic activity was no longer work because it didn't generate capital. Change came first to New England, in the early 1800s, with the growth of textile mills and mercantile capitalism—shipping, banking, and trading. By 1890, even though almost one half of all American families still lived off the land,[2] the consciousness and character of the country had been changed by industrialization. Work was commercialized, taken out of the home and sexualized. It would be the exclusive province of men.

A new cultural model of the "respectable" middle-class family had emerged in the East by the 1830s: man would go out into the world to work for money while his wife stayed home, keeping house, bearing and raising children. Her life was private; his, public; they would perform separate functions in mutually exclusive spheres, because of their sex.

What began as a division of labor hardened into a biological mandate; by mid-century, it was a popular credo—"The Cult of

* What follows is a summary, often secondary history and an analysis of volunteering and the role and image of women in urban American society, from the early 1800s to the present. Several fine, comprehensive histories of the feminist movement and the status of women in the family and the workplace have been produced in the past twenty years and are noted in my bibliography. I have no desire to reinvent the wheel here, only to provide an essential historical context for a discussion of volunteering and women today.

True Womanhood": Woman was said to be the moral guardian of home and family. She was the "nurse" and "educator" of "future man"—and helpmeet to the present. Her domestic chores might not have been work, but they were a preordained and very sacred trust. In one of the many popular treatises on femininity published in the 1840s, a Mrs. A. J. Graves reminded women that their virtues were simply "not of this world"; home was their only "appropriate sphere of action." By leaving it "to mingle in any of the great public movements of the day," a woman was "deserting the station which God and nature have assigned her." Mrs. Graves neatly summed up True Womanhood: "The religion and politics of men have their widest sphere in the world without; but the religious zeal and patriotism of woman are most beneficially and powerfully exerted upon the members of her household . . . when our husbands and sons go forth into the busy and turbulent world . . . their hearts will be at home, where their treasure is and they will rejoice to return to its sanctuary of rest, there to refresh their wearied spirits and renew their strengths for the toils and conflicts of life."[3]

This was the ideal of white middle- and upper-class families, living in cities and towns—and the cultural imperative of the century. But it did not reflect reality for farm women or the hundreds of thousands of urban, working-class women and girls struggling to support themselves and their families with paying jobs.

Throughout the nineteenth century, women, particularly single women, worked for money, primarily in domestic service and manufacturing. In 1850, women comprised nearly one fourth of the nation's manufacturing force;[4] 330,000 were domestics, and about 200,000 were employed in manufacturing.[5] The 1890 census reported 4 million women working outside the home, with 1.2 million in domestic service, at least 1 million in manufacturing, and 75,000 in the relatively new field of office work.[6] By 1900, there were 503,000 women office workers and about 5 million women working outside the home.[7] The only respectable profession open to women throughout the century was teaching; nursing became a not quite so respectable alternative after the Civil War. In 1890 there were a quarter of a million women teachers and 40,000 nurses and midwives.[8]

This was largely a labor force of unmarried, immigrant, and black women. The proportion of black women working at the end of the century was at least twice what it was for whites.[9] Black women were likely to continue working after marriage, and in 1890 about 1 million of them labored, primarily in the South, as field hands, domestics, and laundresses; blacks were not hired for factory work until the early 1900s.[10] The typical factory girl of the nineteenth century was a young, unmarried immigrant or the daughter of an immigrant family. In 1900, three quarters of all women in factory work were under twenty-five, either foreign-born or first-generation American, and less than one in twenty were married.[11] The more genteel, less common occupations for women—office work, teaching, and nursing—were generally reserved for the relative minority of native-born, middle-class, white women in the work force, most of whom were single. In 1890, only one out of every twenty-five teachers and half a million of the total 4 million women in the work force were married.[12]

It is important to note the size and composition of the female labor force and to understand what paid work meant for women in order to understand volunteering. What it meant, very simply, was working long hours, at grueling low-level jobs, for very little and rarely equal pay. In occupations open to both sexes, notably manufacturing and teaching, pay scales for women were systematically depressed, and the more highly skilled, higher-level jobs were reserved for men.[13] Prospects for improvement in the lot of working women were faint; they were relatively unorganized, with no significant union support and no voice in the legislative process. Moreover, women, especially married women, were severely stigmatized for working; they were supposed to be comfortably supported by men. Given working conditions, opportunities, salary levels, and cultural prescriptions for women in the nineteenth century, paid work was not something very many would freely choose to do.

The Cult of True Womanhood became a self-fulfilling prophecy, even for those women who couldn't afford it. It contributed to their limited employment opportunities, low salaries, and questionable social status. If respectable women didn't work, there would be no respectable jobs for those who did. Gentlewomen in need stayed home, sewing and baking, and selling their wares anonymously through "womens' exchanges;" some took in boarders. The sorry, awful fate of poor women in an age when paid work was unfeminine was decried by British journalist Harriet Martineau, who toured the country in the early 1830s:† "One consequence, mournful and injurious of the chivalrous taste and temper of a country with regard to its women is that it is difficult, where it is not impossible for women to earn their bread. Where it is a boast that women do not labour, the encouragement and rewards of labour are not provided. It is so in America . . . the lot of poor women is sad."[14] True Womanhood may have been a middle-class myth, but it had a very real effect on the lives of all women, rich and poor. Femininity can be a very vicious cycle.

Volunteering broke it, for generations of leisured women who created new, unpaid jobs for themselves outside the home. It gave them public lives, ended their domestic isolation, and gave rise to organizations of women dedicated to institutional reform in education, health care, and criminal justice, as well as the cultural and "moral" enrichment of society. If the stereotypical nineteenth-century volunteer was a ladylike friendly visitor or charity worker, and if what she did was "women's work," at least she was doing it in the company of others like her, in the world of the community. By playing her woman's role outside the home, she would begin to change it.

B) The first significant voluntary associations of women were the literary clubs, charity circles, and anti-vice societies of the early to mid-1800s, all of which grew out of the emerging ideal of true womanhood. They championed the feminine virtues—purity, religiosity, and concern for others; even literary clubs reflected, in part, a movement to educate women for marriage and motherhood. These associations represent three primary types of volunteering—cultural activity, moral reform,

† Martineau's three-volume work *Society in America*, published in 1837, includes some valuable and rather caustic observations on the customs and status of American women.

and social service—that organized scores of women into a loose network of associations before the Civil War and gradually coalesced into the nineteenth-century Woman's Movement.

A sexual stereotype of femininity became a rallying cry for nineteenth-century feminism. The Cult of True Womanhood proved to be somewhat subversive. By separating the sexes so completely, it made women a class unto themselves, a sisterhood, with common problems, goals, and sensibilities. By endowing them with all the moral virtues, it gave them a mandate to venture forth into the world, to make it better. As women organized for charity work, to combat commercial vice, or for institutional reforms, they began to realize that in order to effectively exercise their "gentle influence" on the world they would have to have a voice in its political processes.

The nineteenth-century Woman Suffrage Movement was largely comprised of relatively conservative, middle- and upper-class women for whom women's rights were only a means of achieving womanly reforms.‡ One of their leaders, Julia Ward Howe, President of the American Women's Suffrage Association, explained that women were obliged to put their "feminine graces" and "virtues" to use in the world, to check the excesses of men in society as well as in the home. "To keep up the tone of society is part of every woman's duty . . . Religion, peace, purity, temperance, are as much in place at the polls as at the altar or the fireside."[15] By the end of the century, tens of thousands of women were claiming their right to participate, for free, in public affairs, if only to protect their children. Before there were feminists, there were volunteers.

1. Charity and church work were probably the most common forms of volunteering for women in the early 1800s. Religion was "an occupation" for American women, commented Harriet Martineau; aside from marriage, it was their primary "pursuit."[16] Women were disproportionately active in church work, and female converts predominated in a wave of religious revivalism that peaked in the 1830s and 1840s.[17] Women were

‡ Historian William O'Neill has called them "social feminists," as distinguished from the more radical women's rights advocates who demanded equality because they had a right to it, "for its own sake." (William O'Neill, *Everyone Was Brave*, Chicago, 1969, p. 143.)

supposed to be naturally pious and pure and the bearers of Christian benevolence. They had a special mission to help the poor and bring Godliness into the world and, led by their ministers, organized numerous church and charitable societies throughout New England. They raised money for church and mission work, brought food and clothing to the poor, and established and maintained schools and orphanages for them. "Many are engaged in charities," said Martineau, "doing good or harm according to the enlightenment of mind which is carried to the work."[18] Church work was not quite a force for change in the status of women; indeed, it perpetuated sexual stereotypes and was based on a strong commitment to the traditional nuclear family. But it brought women together, gave them an extra-domestic identity, and contributed greatly to what historian Nancy Cott has called the "group-consciousness and sense of sex-identified social purpose" upon which the women's rights movement would be based.[19]

Religion-inspired service work also provided a satisfying and even consuming career alternative for gentlewomen who would or could not marry. One of the most famous and remarkable of these was Dorothea Dix, who, in the 1840s, embarked on a one-woman crusade to change the way society treated the mentally ill. She traveled alone, throughout New England and the South, inspecting prisons and poorhouses, reporting on conditions in them to state legislatures and lobbying for reform. Her efforts led to the establishment of the first publicly funded institutions to house and, it was hoped, care for, the mentally ill. She called these asylums her "children."

Dix's personal and professional history are worth examining in brief; her commitment to public service was the way she solved the problem of being an intelligent, achievement-oriented woman in an age of Domesticity. Born in 1802, she began working as a teacher at fourteen, in a school she opened and managed in her home in Boston. She wrote and published stories (moral tales) and religious verse, and continued teaching until she was a "spinster" in her early thirties, having suffered a broken engagement at twenty-two. She worked compulsively, from dawn to midnight, during the years spent teaching and writing, and finally collapsed in a total nervous and physical breakdown when she was thirty-four. She spent two years recuperating in Europe and five years later, having returned to Boston, began her famous movement for penal reform with a visit to a local jail to teach Sunday school. She devoted herself to this work for fifteen years and then embarked on a third career, when she was in her sixties, as Superintendent of the U.S. Army Nurse Service during the Civil War.[20]

Dix was utterly committed to her work and led a brave and independent life for a woman of her time, but she was no feminist. She thought it was inappropriate for women to engage in organized political actions (although she learned quickly enough how to manage the legislative process to achieve her reforms) and she believed deeply that women, like herself, should not work for pecuniary gain. Instead, it was the duty of her sex to serve society, without expectation of reward or desire for personal advancement. The public interest alone justified her work, by making it a moral imperative. Dorothea Dix lived by a womanly creed of religious service: "No day, no hour comes, but brings in its train work to be 'performed' for some useful end—the suffering to be comforted, the wandering led home, the sinner reclaimed . . . Oh, how can anyone fold the hands to rest and say to spirit 'Take thine ease, for all is well.' "[21]

2. The pursuit of religion gave women a moral right to volunteer and vindicated the most militant of their early voluntary movements—the anti-vice crusades of the 1830s. Spurred on, in part, by the national evangelical movement, they organized moral reform societies dedicated to abolishing prostitution and establishing a single standard of sexual morality for men and women. The New York Moral Reform Society, formed in 1834, led the crusade, with a chain of auxiliary associations in urban and rural areas in the East and the publication of an evangelical, semimonthly journal of national prominence, *The Advocate of Moral Reform*. Moral reform societies fought for legislation that would make it a crime for men to patronize prostitutes, conducted raids on local brothels, and published, in the *Advocate*, the names of men even suspected of "immoral behavior," like visiting a brothel or simply reading pornography.[22]

The anti-vice movement illustrates the complex politics of volunteering—and of liberation—for nineteenth-century women who had no real political or economic power with which to challenge their restrictive domestic roles. They were disenfranchised, with very limited access to the paid workplace, no generally recognized rights to hold or control their own property, and virtually no legal recourse against abusive or neglectful husbands. Moral reformers were hardly feminists; they clung to ideals of True Womanhood and Domesticity. And they were aggressively anti-libertarian; buoyed by the belief that they had a holy mission to legislate morality, they wanted to outlaw "licentiousness" by jailing men who indulged in commercial sex and suppressing pornography, "the literature of the brothel." But in the 1830s the sexual freedom of men was, in fact, a threat to the welfare of women who had no equivalent freedom of their own and were imprisoned in marriage by law, religion, custom, and an economic system that made it almost impossible for them to support themselves. Women sought to sanctify the family structure and the rigid code of sexual morality that went with it in order to protect themselves from its abuses. Their rather reactionary agenda for anti-vice reform was based on a surprisingly radical view of prostitution; they blamed it on men—on the double standard and the dearth of decent jobs for single women: Prostitutes were not evil, seductive harlots but victims of a system of social and economic inequities. There was in this the first glimmer of an understanding that something was wrong with the role of women in society. One hundred and fifty years later, it is easy to say that what was wrong was the basic ideal of True Womanhood, which moral reformers fought to enforce. Beginning from a position of weakness, they needed their grant of moral superiority; True Womanhood looked like their only strength.

3. Not all of the early voluntary associations were dedicated to service or social change; not all involved women in work. Some were social or self-improvement groups, which generally took the form of literary societies. By 1850, New England had achieved nearly universal literacy, and reading was a primary leisure activity for middle- and upper-class women. It became

an excuse for association; they would gather together to read outloud to each other from popular and religious literature and sometimes share writings of their own. The usefulness of these groups was wryly noted by Martineau: "All American ladies are more or less literary, and some are so to excellent purpose, the saving of their minds from vacuity." But, she added, while "readers are plentiful, thinkers are rare. Minds are of a very passive character."[23]

American ladies might have been literary, but they were not very well educated. Private female secondary schools and seminaries began appearing throughout New England in the early 1800s, but their purpose was to prepare girls for marriage and motherhood or teaching—the spinster's alternative. The most famous and rigorous of these were Emma Willard's Troy Seminary and Catherine Beecher's Hartford Female Seminary, both founded in the 1820s. Even Beecher and Willard, pioneers in women's education, dedicated their efforts to preparing women for their only two professions—marriage and teaching; they were not trained for serious scientific, artistic, or intellectual endeavors. The "intellect" of American women was "confined," wrote Martineau, by domesticity and an accompanying educational system that intended only "to make women something like companions to their husbands and able to teach their children."[24]

Literary societies could only be expected to reflect the educational backgrounds and domestic orientation of their members, and, since they were not service or reform societies, they seem like aimless, even foolish exercises in association for its own sake. Reading and writing were only pastimes for True Women who were strong in moral and maternal instinct and weak in mind. A woman's intellectual life was generally quite private and played out in letters and diaries more than in social reading groups. She was not supposed to have an independent life of the mind for its own sake.

One exceptional woman who did, and sought to encourage others to follow, was Margaret Fuller, the leading female journalist and intellectual of early-nineteenth-century New England.[25] Having received an unusually demanding classical education from her father, she took her place among the male intelligentsia of her day, Transcendentalists like Emerson and William Channing, and initiated one of the more notable variations of the New England literary society. This was a series of "Conversations," rather high-minded lectures and seminars for women on philosophy, religion, classical mythology, sociology, and the arts. They were not quite voluntary; Fuller charged for her services and had organized the Conversations in order to earn money. But she conceived them with a grander overall purpose; Fuller wanted nothing less than to change the way women thought. She would train them the way she had been trained by her father "to systemize thought and give a precision and clearness in which our sex are so deficient, chiefly, I think, because they have so few inducements."[26]

Fuller herself never resolved the dilemma of being an intellectual woman at a time when intelligence was not a womanly virtue. She worked most of her life and lived on her work; she edited the *Dial* magazine, wrote for the New York *Daily Tribune,* and produced a major, early feminist treatise on the "woman question," *Women in the Nineteenth Century.* But for most of her short life (she died at forty, shipwrecked) Margaret Fuller was deeply conflicted about her own sexual identity (she associated her intelligence with maleness) and confused about the course she should take as a writer: "I have always thought . . . that I would write not like a woman, of love and hope and disappointment, but like a man, of the world of intellect and action."[27] She struggled to find a form to suit her mind as well as her sex: "I love best to be a woman; but womanhood is at present too straitly bounded to give me scope. At hours, I live freely as a woman; at others, I should stifle . . ."[28]

While intellectual freedom and opportunities for intellectual advancement were limited for white women of Fuller's class, they were practically nonexistent for black women. There was considerable resistance in the North to educating free blacks.* They were denied access to public schools in some states and were not readily admitted into private white schools and seminaries.[29] In the early 1830s, Prudence Crandell admitted black girls into her school for young ladies in Cromwell, Connecticut,

* In the South, it was a crime to teach a slave to read.

and in one year was forced to shut down after she and her students were harassed and assaulted by townspeople and local officials and her school nearly destroyed by vandals.[30] Although several black-administered schools for girls opened in the twenties and thirties (the first boarding school for black girls was founded by fifteen-year-old Maria Becraft in 1820), black communities could hardly support the kind of private school system being built by white America. What black schools there were were likely to be coeducational: maintaining separate facilities for boys and girls was expensive.[31]

Concern for education prompted the formation of a number of black literary societies in the cities and towns of the East and Midwest in the 1830s. Free blacks, men and women, had been organizing into voluntary associations since the late 1700s; they formed mutual aid, church, moral reform, and temperance, as well as antislavery societies. Literary societies were an offshoot of these. They were dedicated to the "moral and mental improvement" of their members, to encouraging reading, and to providing their communities with books and libraries. There were several exclusively female literary societies, ranging from the ladylike to the pragmatic. They included the Minerva Literary Association of Philadelphia, a "school for the encouragement and promotion of polite literature," the Afric-American Female Intelligence Society, dedicated to the "diffusion of knowledge, the suppression of vice and immorality and . . . such virtues as would render [its members] happy and useful to society," and the Ohio Ladies Educational Society, which worked to establish a public educational system for blacks in Ohio who were not allowed to attend the public schools.

Although literary societies did not last much more than a decade, partly because of an overriding concern for abolition, they are said to have provided the "background for the organization of the Negro school. They were among the supporters of the educative life among Negroes in a day when there were few formal instruments of education in existence for their use."[32]

C) Abolition was the primary political imperative for reformist volunteers of the mid-nineteenth century. Men started effectively mobilizing against slavery in the early 1830s; they were soon joined by a small minority of women, many of whom would later go on to lead the fight for women's suffrage.† Abolition not only engaged women in a fight for freedom and equal rights; it made them part of a national political movement, and taught them the rudiments of grass-roots organizing. They formed political associations, spoke out in public on public issues, and went through the painstaking process of collecting signatures on antislavery petitions to present to Congress; fifty years later, they would do it all again in their drive to win the vote.

Female antislavery societies, some of them interracial, began appearing in the late 1830s; with the notable exception of William Lloyd Garrison, male abolitionists did not welcome this addition to their ranks. Women were denied equal participation in the convention of the American Anti-Slave Society in Philadelphia in 1837 and in the World Anti-Slavery Convention in London in 1840. Abolitionists were, in part, scared off by fierce public opposition to the entry of women into the political arena. Abolition was not charity or church work, but political action; for a woman to engage in it was considered an offense against nature. "There were no bounds to the efforts made to crush the actions of women who . . . used their powers in the abolition question," wrote Harriet Martineau. "Newspapers . . . laud [their] exertions in all other charities," but women in the antislavery movement were censured for "casting off the refinement of their sex [and for] the act of duty which [they] had performed in deciding upon their duty for themselves." "The reproach," she added, "is not that the ladies hold anti-slavery opinions, but that they act upon them." Martineau considered the consequent failure of so many women to act, out of the "retiring modesty of sex," as evidence of the moral bankruptcy of femininity.[33]

Speaking out in public was the most daring step undertaken by women abolitionists; it violated an almost holy, sexual code of silence. The first American woman to attempt a public speaking career was Maria Steward. Steward, a freeborn black woman,

† Among them were Elizabeth Cady Stanton, Lucretia Mott, Sojourner Truth, Sarah and Angelina Grimké, and Susan B. Anthony.

teacher, and abolitionist, delivered several public addresses in Boston in the early 1830s. Her speaking career was brief; soon after it commenced, she ended it and retreated to teaching, in part because of the opposition she encountered from black men.[34]

A few years later, abolitionists and women's rights activists Sarah and Angelina Grimké became the first white American women to speak in public, to the great consternation of the clergy. The Grimkés began quietly enough, delivering antislavery lectures to small groups of women, but soon embarked on what became a notorious speaking tour of New England: they started addressing large, mixed groups of men and women, and it was this that aroused the ire of the Church and of proslavery groups as well: "Then they were adjudged immodest, and their conduct denounced as unwomanly and demoralizing . . . Clergymen denounced them from their pulpits, especially warning women members against them. Municipal corporations refused the use of halls for their meetings and threats of personal violence came from various quarters."[35] In 1837, the Congregationalist ministers of Massachusetts excoriated the Grimkés, although not by name, in a widely publicized "Pastoral Letter." The letter was an ominous reminder to the supposedly weaker sex that "the power of woman is her dependence, flowing from the consciousness of that weakness which God has given her for protection . . . When she assumes the place and tone of man as public reformer, our care and protection of her seem unnecessary . . . and her character becomes unnatural." Women reformers were warned that they would forfeit their place before God and the Church and "fall in shame and dishonor in the dust."[36] With her immortal soul apparently at risk, political volunteering was a dangerous job for a woman.

But she persisted, and by mid-century a small minority of women had been politicized by the antislavery movement; many more were bound together in a loose network of voluntary associations. Notable abolitionist women were becoming feminists; in 1848, Elizabeth Cady Stanton and Lucretia Mott organized the first Women's Rights Convention in Seneca Falls, New York, and a core group of feminists began demanding reform of marriage, divorce, and property laws, as well as the right to vote. Service volunteers were becoming interested in public affairs, at least in the social welfare, and, in the decades after the Civil War, they would fill out the ranks of the Woman Suffrage Movement: "For every active suffragist there were a hundred women engaged in club work, education, charity and various reforms . . . When suffragists spoke of the 'woman movement,' therefore, they meant . . . all women who were engaged in non-manual, extra-domestic pursuits."‡[37]

D) The fight for women's rights, briefly displaced by the Civil War, intensified in its aftermath. Extension of the vote and due process rights of citizenship to black men—and not to women—deeply embittered militant suffragists and split the suffrage movement. Elizabeth Cady Stanton and Susan Anthony broke from their abolitionist allies, male and female, and founded the exclusively female National Women's Suffrage Association in 1869; months later, their more conservative rivals formed the American Women's Suffrage Association, and it was not until 1890, twenty years later, that the two camps would reunite. The enfranchisement of black men, along with a steadily increasing rate of immigration, also introduced an ugly element of racism into popular arguments for suffrage: it was said that native-born white women would vote with their class and offset the power of the new black and immigrant male electorate. The elitism of the late-nineteenth-century suffrage movement has been frequently noted; it was led by privileged white women and found its constituency among similarly privileged, newly energized volunteers and, to a lesser extent, newly educated college women.

The Civil War had mobilized service volunteers and left them with a heightened sense of purpose. Women who had been

‡ There was relatively little organized feminist activity in the South, which does not necessarily mean there was absolutely no feminism. For an illuminating study of white and free black women in the antebellum South, see Suzanne Lebsock, *The Free Women of Petersburg: Status and Culture in a Southern Town, 1784–1860* (New York, 1984). Ms. Lebsock found that, between 1784 and 1860, the women of Petersburg, Virginia, managed to increase their personal and economic independence, within the limits of their conservative, slaveholding society, despite the absence of an organized feminist movement.

involved in relief work and the unladylike job of nursing wounded soldiers lost some of the debilitating modesty of their sex and expanded their own definitions of women's work.[38] In the North, women had already been volunteering for at least thirty years; now they'd participated in a victorious national war effort. That they had a mission in the world—to safeguard its morals and care for its casualties—was no longer a matter of controversy; that there was work to be done was clear.

In the closing decades of the nineteenth century, industrialization and the influx of single working girls and immigrants into the cities created a new population of urban poor and new problems and needs that women could meet. Volunteers were ambitious, and they had a mission: to improve slum housing, health care, public education, and help turn prisons into penitentiaries devoted to rehabilitation; to elevate the moral tone of postwar life and protect women and children—by ending child labor and prostitution and closing down the saloons. Like their predecessors of the 1830s, volunteers in the late 1800s formed associations dedicated to social service, moral reform, and self-improvement; but they organized with greater confidence and ease and in far greater numbers, nationwide.

1. The largest and probably most provocative of the postwar associations was the evangelical Woman's Christian Temperance Union. The WCTU, founded in 1873, claimed over 150,000 members across the country by 1890. Under the leadership of Frances Willard, it fought for social reforms and suffrage, as well as temperance and an end to commercial vice.[39]

The WCTU was the spiritual successor of the moral reform societies of the thirties, and it was at the forefront of a "social purity" movement that swept the country in the years after the Civil War. Dedicated to the moral cleansing of society, the WCTU made votes for women one of its first priorities, carrying the cult of domesticity to its logical and most frenzied extreme. According to Frances Willard, "government [was] only housekeeping on the broadest scale."[40]

The goal of the WCTU was quite simply to remake society in its own image of virtuous womanhood. Women were by nature "the less tainted half of the race," wrote Willard. They purified all they touched and had a holy mission to "go forth into the world" and make it "homelike": ". . . not that the world [would] come into the home, but that the home, embodied and impersonated in its womanhood, [would] go forth into the world."[41] To carry out this mission, Frances Willard involved her organization in improving education by organizing kindergartens and Sunday schools, in reforming penal institutions for women, and in a crusade to rid society of pornography and prostitution, along with alcohol, the root of all evils.

Like the early moral reformers, women of the WCTU were militant anti-libertarians—and for similar reasons. They fought for temperance and the suppression of pornography (and contraception) to protect wives from their drunken, abusive husbands, and single women and girls from the debauched males who would lead them into prostitution. They approached problems of sexual violence and exploitation from a position of legal and economic powerlessness that underscored their fanatic belief in the power of womanly virtues. They fought to protect the family that, in its ideal state, protected women and gave them their much-exalted mission in the world.

2. The mandate for women to domesticate society was pervasive; it shaped postwar service as well as moral reform societies and helped make the plight of single working women and girls in a new, urban industrial age a popular cause for women volunteers. In their ideal world, an unmarried girl stayed home, under the care and protection of her family. By migrating to the city, to live and work unprotected, she threatened to destroy the future of virtuous womanhood. Alone and earning her own living, a girl would lose either her virtue or, at best, her femininity. The specter of prostitution and the sacrificing of womanly virtues to work prompted the first postwar voluntary efforts to help the working girl. A voluntary association would serve as her surrogate family, continuing her moral education and protecting her from corruption.

This naïve and condescending view that the problems of working women were primarily moral ones would give way, for many volunteers, to the pragmatic teachings of the progressive era. By the turn of the century, upper-class women had developed more sophisticated, less patronizing approaches to reform and were beginning to focus on improving wages and conditions for workers instead of providing them with moral guidance. The evolution of these efforts reflected, in part, the education volunteers received from their work, which contributed to the increasing responsiveness of the feminist movement to the problems of working-class women.

The first associations for working girls were the Young Women's Christian Association and the Association of Working Girls Societies. The YWCA was the first and largest of these; founded in Boston in 1868, it soon spread to cities throughout the country. "Y" chapters provided religious and moral guidance, shelter, and assistance in finding jobs to country girls in the big cities. Working girls' societies began forming in the 1880s, following a model originated by heiress Grace Dodge. They affiliated in 1885 into a network of clubs in the East and Midwest. The business of these societies was to supervise the moral, spiritual, and social lives of single girls and to educate them in the middle-class ways of virtuous womanhood.[42]

A more practical approach to helping working women was adopted by the National Consumers League, another affiliated organization founded in New York in 1890. It began by harnessing consumer buying power to pressure retail businesses into improving wages and conditions for women workers; in later years, it would become an important advocate of protective legislation for women (and opponent of the ERA).

The League was led, in its beginnings, from 1890 to 1896, by Josephine Shaw Lowell, a wealthy and prominent volunteer whose own career began with traditional service work and culminated in progressive reform. Lowell, who was widowed young, during the war, started with war relief work and then devoted herself in the 1870s to charity work, particularly friendly visiting to public institutions and the homes of the poor; in 1876, she was appointed to the New York State Board of Charities and became involved in the reform of penal institutions and almshouses. By 1890, she had lost faith in charity and prison work and, having resigned from the Board of Charities, assumed the presidency of the Consumer's League, with the conviction that "if the working people had all they ought to have, we should not have the paupers and criminals."[43] The problem, she now said, was not so much that the poor lacked moral fortitude but that they worked under "dreadful conditions for starvation wages." She also became increasingly aware of the need to educate upper-class women in the ways of the working world, particularly those wealthy young women who worked for pin money, "taking a clerk's place but refusing to accept half a clerk's salary because she does not need more. She should think of the women who do need more and whom her unselfish selfishness is helping to starve."[44]

The next and most progressive step in the efforts of volunteers to improve the lot of women workers was the founding of the National Women's Trade Union League in 1903. This was an unusual cooperative association of leisure-class volunteers and working-class, trade-union women. Both groups served together on the executive board; although volunteers dominated the organization in its early years, working women eventually assumed an equal role in it. The purpose of the WTUL was to help organize women and bring them into the union movement, as equals, to upgrade their status and increase their power as trade unionists. In the first decades of this century, with chapters in New York, Boston, and Chicago and smaller cities in the East and Midwest, the WTUL became an important source of support for women strikers, particularly in the garment industry.[45]

The WTUL was unique: "It was the only early 20th century women's organization that attempted to build such an egalitarian, cross-class alliance."[46] That it existed at all was, in large part, due to the previous experiences of its founding volunteers, who had been disillusioned by traditional charity and service work. Many WTUL volunteers had been settlement workers; they had had their collective consciousness raised.

3. The settlement movement, led, notably, by Jane Addams and Lillian Wald, was the most famous and daring experiment in progressive volunteering and the most influential in shaping the new, turn-of-the-century college women. The settlement house was intended to serve as an urban community center, to encourage the formation of voluntary associations among the

residents it served, and to provide them with social services, including health care, education, and vocational guidance. It was also a sort of graduate center for social work, a life experience school for college women who volunteered to live in the settlements, administering social services to the poor, for free.[47]

In the 1880s and 1890s, college itself was still something of an experiment for women. Equal higher education for them began after the Civil War with the opening of women's colleges in the East. Vassar College was the first, in 1865; it was followed over the next twenty-five years by Mt. Holyoke, Wellesley, Smith, Bryn Mawr, and Radcliffe and Barnard, which opened as respective adjuncts to Harvard and Columbia. Several midwestern colleges had been admitting female students since Oberlin opened its doors to them in 1837, but in the mid-1800s coeducation did not mean equal education for women. At Oberlin they were restricted to a less rigorous course of study and had been admitted, in part, to provide a more balanced atmosphere for males.[48] It took the creation of exclusively female colleges to begin to establish a tradition of scholarship and professional training for women, divorced from marriage, maternity, and teaching.

Providing women with equal education was, of course, highly controversial: it brought them uncomfortably close to what was considered the inherently masculine sphere of life and encountered strong opposition from the medical profession, as well as from other defenders of virtuous womanhood. Women were said to be, by nature, too frail for strenuous intellectual endeavors: college would ruin their health, and possibly their reproductive capacities.[49] It would also, it was feared, make them unwilling or unable to marry, and, in fact, turn-of-the-century surveys of college women indicated that they tended to marry less and to marry later than the general female population.[50]

Women's colleges themselves were respectful of most feminine behavioral stereotypes. With strong, traditional religious leanings, they maintained strict ladylike codes of conduct for students, functioning, in the beginning, like extended versions of the Victorian family. At Vassar, a Lady Principal supervised the deportment and even conversation of students "to guard against coarse or insipid frivolities of rustic and fashionable talk." At Smith, an "unwritten code" of well-bred womanhood outlawed such pastimes as walking "merely for pleasure." Wellesley students were prohibited from attending the theater or opera, even during school vacations.[51]

The eastern colleges were ladylike enclaves for young white women of "solidly bourgeois" backgrounds.[52] By the turn of the century they had together graduated a grand total of four blacks. Higher education for black women meant coeducation, generally at one of the black universities that opened in the 1860s—Howard, Fisk, or Atlanta. The very small minority of black women who did attend college were likely to be trained to be teachers.[53]

Professional opportunities for all women graduates were severely limited at first: college naturally preceded the entry of women into the professional world. In 1890, there were only 360 women medical students and 200 women lawyers,[54] nationwide; as late as 1872, the U.S. Supreme Court had refused to compel the admission of women to state bar associations.[55] Colleges turned out some librarians, lady journalists, novelists, and editors; but, apart from teaching and nursing,[56] the primary profession open to college women at the turn of the century was professional volunteering, primarily in the social services. The fact that settlement work was unpaid was of small consequence to privileged, educated women, for whom it was a welcome escape from the family parlor.

It was also a demanding and often enlightening full-time job that involved women in electoral politics, legislative reform, and trade unionism, as well as in the delivery of social services. Settlement workers were both social change and service volunteers, and their experiences underscored the connection between the suffrage movement and the fight for social reform. It was clear that women would have no appreciable effect on social problems until they had a voice in social policy, and they had a responsibility to make sure their voice was heard.

The settlement movement didn't abandon the ideal of virtuous womanhood; it simply made the most progressive use of it: The primary goal of the volunteer was not to make society virtuous but to make it fair. Poverty was not the result of some moral failing; it arose, rather, from economic and political inequities that women were uniquely suited to address. They would humanize the slums and clean up local government. They owed it to their families as well as their communities to do so, said Jane Addams: ". . . as society grows more complicated it is necessary that woman shall extend her sense of responsibility to many things outside her home if she would continue to preserve the home in its entirety." Addams believed that city government was, after all, women's work; it "demand[ed] the help of minds accustomed to detail and variety of work, to a sense of obligation for the health and welfare of young children, and to a responsibility for the cleanliness and comfort of others."[57] Although at the other end of the scale of virtuous womanhood from moral reformers, settlement workers essentially agreed with Frances Willard of the WCTU that society was just one large house for women to keep.

4. Progressivism and moral reform were two extremes of virtuous womanhood; it found its middle ground in the women's club. The popular club movement began officially in 1868, when journalist Jennie Croly, having been refused admittance to an event at the New York Press Club, founded Sorosis, an exclusively female club designed to promote the intellectual development of women and to provide them with a community of their own, outside the home. Women's clubs, dedicated variously to self-improvement, socializing, and community service, soon proliferated throughout the country, carrying on the tradition of literary societies on the grand scale. The General Federation of Women's Clubs was founded in 1890 by a coalition of sixty-one clubs; by 1896, it had an estimated one hundred thousand members nationwide.[58] The club movement had become the center for both the leisure and volunteer work activities of middle-class women.

What distinguished clubs from other voluntary associations was that they brought together women who had nothing in common but the simple desire to associate. This was underscored by sociologist Sophonisba Breckinridge in her landmark 1933 study *Women in the Twentieth Century*. Breckinridge noted: "It was the appearance of women's clubs all over the country which represented the general, unspecified leisure time activity of women for which no prerequisite in the way of education, belief or male relationship was required. Clubs began to appear in the sixties and their growth marked the emergence of the middle aged and middle class woman from her kitchen and her home."[59] Clubs may have been justly described as a "body of women banded together for the purpose of meeting together,"[60] but they did play an important role in organizing middle-class women, bringing them into their communities and eventually the suffrage movement.

The typical club of the early 1890s was primarily social and cultural, according to constitutional prescriptions of the newly formed General Federation of Women's Clubs. But by 1896 the Federation was admitting philanthropic clubs and beginning to address questions of social welfare. In 1910, with eight hundred thousand members nationwide, it had taken up a few progressive causes of the day, with established committees on Civics, Social Service Reform, and Industry and Child Labor, as well as Art and Household Economy.[61]

The club movement was not feminism; it was a way for conventional women to become active outside their homes. Individual affiliated clubs tended to be relatively conservative, more so than their national organization, said Breckinridge, adding that in the early 1900s local clubs were still addressing questions like "Is housework incompatible with the higher life?"[62] But many were also actively engaged in community work, often centered on children, education, and the arts. They founded and maintained public libraries and arts societies and worked to improve local school systems, juvenile courts, and "humane institutions" for children. Even these relatively ladylike volunteer activities worried the more strident defenders of virtuous womanhood, like Grover Cleveland. He denounced the "club habit" as a threat to "the integrity of our homes and the benign disposition and character of our wifehood and motherhood . . ." Cleveland proclaimed that "the best and safest club for a woman to patronize is her home."[63] But the typical clubwoman extolled the "womanly virtues" and followed a familiar credo of volunteering that managed to be both assertive and self-effacing. She declared her right to leave the home, in order to be a helpmeet to man in the world: "Since the time

when Adam's rib was removed and . . . mysteriously wrought
into . . . woman, to quite recent times, man has looked upon
her as an unnecessary and meaningless thing, whose sometime
charm was the only reason she should be allowed to trespass
upon the earth which was barely large enough for himself. But
gradually man is outgrowing this primitive idea of woman's
limited share in . . . the universe. In the hospital she may be a
nurse; in the school she may be a teacher; in the office a stenog-
rapher; in politics a follower . . . She does not ask to manage,
to direct, but only to be allowed to help . . . The heart of the
[club] movement is opportunity for greater usefulness and unselfish service."[64]

The services provided by women's clubs were particularly
important in black communities, in which welfare needs were
less likely to be met by the state and general public. Black
women began organizing beneficial societies, to improve education and health care and provide support for the destitute in
their communities, in the decades after the Civil War. From
their beginnings these clubs tended to be more service-oriented than social, and their membership, on the local level, was
likely to include working as well as middle-class women.[65] For
them, the purpose of a club was not to fill leisure time or to get
out of the house, but to insure the survival of their communities.

At the national level, the tone of the club movement was
more middle-class; national leaders were often college-educated, middle-class women. The clubs affiliated in the 1890s,
with the formation of the Colored Women's League of Washington, D.C., and the National Federation of Afro-American
Women, founded in Boston; in 1896 the two groups merged into
the National Association of Colored Women.[66] The NACW was
organized into departments, which reflected a concern for cultural enrichment as well as economic and social advancement
and civil rights. The "leading" departments included Women's
Suffrage, Patriotism, Education, Conditions in Rural Life, Music, Literature and Art, Gainful Occupation and Business, Better Railroad Conditions, Mothers' Meetings and Night School,
Health Conditions, Child Welfare, and Public Speaking.[67] Education and early child care were among the first priorities of the
federated clubs; in the 1890s the Colored Women's League

organized a day-care center for poor working mothers,[68] and Mary Church Terrell, first president of the NACW, dedicated herself to the establishment of a kindergarten system, noting that "it was the duty of colored women to do everything in their power to save the children during the early impressionable years of their lives."[69] Children, as always, were a primary concern.

The national club movement also served needs unique to a new population of middle-class black women, not just to be of use to their communities but to elevate the image of black women popularly held by whites. In white racist mythology, black women were not admitted into the enclave of True Womanhood; they were, instead, presumed to be bereft of all the womanly virtues—promiscuous and, even, mentally deficient. Disproving these "audacious" accusations was "the strongest reason" for the club movement, said Josephine Ruffin, one of its most prominent national leaders: "If an estimate of the colored women of America is called for, the inevitable reply, glibly given, is 'For the most part ignorant and immoral, some exceptions of course, but these don't count.' " It was the duty of black women to "stand forth and declare ourselves and principles, to teach an ignorant and suspicious world that our aims and interests are identical with those of all good aspiring women . . . All over America there is to be found a large and growing class of earnest, intelligent, progressive colored women, women who, if not leading useful lives, are only waiting for the opportunity to do so, many of them warped and cramped for lack of opportunity, not only to do more, but to be more." They would organize "for the sake of [their] own dignity and the dignity of [their] race . . . Too long have we been silent under unjust and unholy charges . . . Now with an army of organized women standing for purity and mental worth, we in ourselves deny the charge and open the eyes of the world . . . by a dignified showing of what we are and hope to become . . ."[70]

Volunteering helped all women become something—more than domestic or sexual adjuncts to men. It gave them work to do in their communities and a sense of usefulness. It loosened the bonds of True Womanhood and showed privileged women the inequities that prevailed outside the four walls of their homes; even the most traditional service volunteers became aware of the need for social change. If many ventured into the slums like Lady Bountifuls, some were radicalized by what they found. Service volunteering helped mature the Woman's Movement and heal the rift between leisured and working-class feminists—by making volunteers aware of the problems of their chosen ministry of working and non-working poor. It also turned mainstream, middle-class women into suffragists, and the efforts of progressive volunteers, like the women of the National Women's Trade Union League, helped extend the suffrage movement to the working class. After the turn of the century, the Woman's Movement embraced a coalition of women that crossed class boundaries; and, it was this coalition—of social reformers, clubwomen, service volunteers, paid workingwomen, and ladies—that would finally win the vote in 1919.

E) This was the first women's movement, begun in 1848; it lasted seventy years, ending with passage of the suffrage amendment. Feminism didn't survive the Jazz Age; not many progressive reform movements did. The story of the twenties is familiar; in the aftermath of World War I and the Russian Revolution, it was, like the 1950s, a time of "Red scares" and "normalcy." The reformist zeal of the Progressive Era was replaced as the cultural ideal of the decade by the private pursuit of pleasure and personal fulfillment. Sexual mores changed drastically, with the popularized teachings of Freud and Havelock Ellis and the emergence of a successful birth-control movement, led by Margaret Sanger.

A new image of the ideal woman took hold—what historian Sheila Rothman has called the "wife/companion." Women were now supposed to be loving and romantic sexual companions to their husbands. Marriage was still their highest calling, but its emotional focus had shifted from maternal to romantic love.[71] While model married women were loving wives, single ones, still young enough, were flappers—early versions of the "*Cosmopolitan* woman," hardly feminists. The modern "feminine mystique," later identified by Betty Friedan, was born, or at least foretold, in the 1920s.

It was accompanied by a significant increase in the marriage rate among college women (which by the end of the decade had risen to about 70 percent[72]) and a relative decline in the rate at which women were entering the paid work force and the professions.[73] A greater percentage of professional women were married, and even the rigorous classical curricula of the women's colleges began to include courses like "Marriage and the Family," in keeping with the revival of an old trend to educate women to be wives.[74]

It shouldn't surprise us that service and reformist volunteering waned in popularity among the white middle classes along with feminism and paid careers. The ideal new woman of the 1920s was interested in volunteering that served purely social needs or was directly related to her own children or family life. Two of the most significant voluntary associations to emerge in the twenties were the college sorority and the PTA. The PTA, of course, continued a tradition of women volunteering for their children, in the public schools. The sorority was a new and noteworthy development that reflected the tone of the decade: Sororities flourished while an interest in settlement work among college women declined drastically.[75]

The shift from public service to private, social volunteering was also reflected in the agenda of the General Federation of Women's Clubs, which reverted "to the literary program"[76] of its early years, and in the drop in membership suffered by the newly formed League of Women Voters. The successor organization to the National American Women's Suffrage Association, the League was formed in 1920 to "promote non-partisan political education" and the "participation of women in government."[77] Sociologist Sophonisba Breckinridge noted that because the League was political and service-oriented, it had a limited appeal for the woman of the 1920s. "The fact that the League is a hardworking organization has discouraged the casual 'joiner'; that it has eliminated social features rather generally has disappointed some women; the fact that it occasionally espouses unpopular causes has served to alienate still others." Precisely because it was hardworking, the League was distinguished from more popular associations like the General Federation of Women's Clubs in another very important respect—

most of the women who joined and rose to leadership positions in it were not married.[78]

Although work, paid or unpaid, was becoming an acceptable option for single women, it was still a daring and questionable one for a wife. A demanding, professional volunteer job was put in the same corner as a paid job and considered a too consuming "outside" activity that threatened the family. The problems of combining marriage and an outside job became major concerns at the women's colleges during the 1920s.

A look at Smith College alumnae quarterlies from these years is instructive: The suitability of marriage as an exclusive career for an educated woman is a recurrent topic of debate. Articles about new paid and unpaid jobs for women—in business, politics, and social service—are juxtaposed with stories like "The Country Minister's Wife: How College Fitted Me for My Job."[79] Letters from alumnae discuss the propriety and possibility of combining marriage with paid or unpaid work. One writer praises the "art of housekeeping" as a "creative" and satisfying occupation for a woman. "Marriage is more than a job," she says. "It becomes the fullest expression of ourselves and the opportunity it offers is quite without limit."[80] Another, who signs herself "the Quack," disagrees: "Save where the children are many and young and the income small, most . . . householders have more leisure than they think [and] it is a poor leisure that does not look out of its windows beyond the end of the street." She worries that younger women will insulate themselves in marriage and be lost to domestic busywork; she urges them to work outside the home, for money or for free, to contribute to their communities and save themselves from the emptiness and "fecklessness" of a life without work. An "outside job," she reminds them, "is not a thing to be dropped with a thud at the altar."[81]

This identification of volunteering with paid work, in terms of its effect on the family, is remarkable. It serves as a reminder of the importance of volunteering as a work experience for married women, particularly in periods when their roles were very narrowly prescribed. This was underscored by Betty Friedan in *The Feminine Mystique,* in her review of women's lives in the 1950s. In 1957 she conducted a survey of 200 college women,

fifteen years after their graduation, and found that a strong
commitment to community work helped many of them "grow
up within the framework of suburban housewivery." For those
self-directed volunteers who were working not simply to advance their social status or "escape" the house but in pursuit of
their own interests and ideals, volunteering was "an act of ma-
turity, a commitment that used and renewed strength of self."[82]

Yet volunteering was one of the first targets of the contemporary women's movement, led by Friedan herself. Volunteering
became identified with the feminine mystique and the patriar-
chal family that made women no more than wives and mothers.
So long as they remained at home, raising children and working
for free in their communities, they would remain the weaker
sex. The virulent feminist attack on volunteering in the early
seventies was unavoidable; it accompanied a long overdue cri-
tique of the traditional nuclear family.

An earlier generation of feminists had been ambushed by the
family, when marriage and femininity won out over the vote.
Perhaps it was inevitable. William O'Neill has suggested that
the first women's movement self-destructed, by allying itself
with the traditional family and prevailing concepts of femininity.[83] Social feminists like Julia Ward Howe and Frances Willard
sought not to free women from domesticity but to domesticate
society. They never addressed, and even exacerbated, the un-
derlying problem—the notion that men and women were des-
tined to inhabit separate spheres and perform mutually exclusive functions in society and at home. The problem was a family
system based on immutable sex roles—paid work for men; unpaid housework, community work, and economic dependence
for women. Instead, social feminists made the electoral system
the problem, and votes for women became their primary goal:
women's suffrage would purify, pacify, and change the world,
and by fighting for it in the name of virtuous womanhood they
made sure that suffrage was all they would get. It wouldn't free
women who still believed in their own femininity, who believed
they deserved the vote precisely because they were wives and
mothers. Indeed, it took sixty years and the emergence of a
second women's movement for women to begin to use their
votes effectively, to advance their own interests as a class; the

first significant "gender gap" in the national electorate appeared in 1982, when women crossed party lines to cast their votes as women. The vote is, arguably, only an effective means of feminist reform in the hands of an organized group of feminists or "women-identified" women, and, in the 1920s, the coalition that had successfully fought for suffrage fell apart. The first women's movement ended when the ideal woman went home.

It may not be fair to blame this on volunteering or to fault early feminists for failing to challenge the family, but the temptation to do so is strong. Today we can hardly reconcile a family system that trained women for a life of domestic service and a volunteer tradition that extended her domestic responsibilities into the community with feminism; certainly in the 1960s and 1970s volunteering looked, not like an escape from the home, but like a retreat from the world that was bound to end badly for women. But women in the nineteenth century began from a position of utter powerlessness; they were disenfranchised and uneducated, with virtually no economic rights, much less opportunities, and subordinate to their husbands, as a matter of law and divine destiny. Sexual stereotypes were dictated by God and there was no place in society for the women who broke them. It is doubtful that nineteenth-century feminists could have successfully taken on the family, which was supposed to protect women, or that anything but an appeal to the womanly virtues would have successfully mobilized middle-class women and enlisted them in the fight for suffrage. They weren't about to go to work for money, but they might volunteer if it would make the world more virtuous.

So they did—and were half-liberated in spite of themselves. The most traditional clubwomen and service volunteers were enlivened and even radicalized by work undertaken in the name of the most regressive notions of femininity. Charlotte Perkins Gilman, one of the most radical turn-of-the-century feminists and one of few to trace the subordinacy of women to domesticity and the economic dependence of wives, called the club movement "one of the most important sociological phenomena of the century." It marked, she said, "the first timid steps toward social organization of these so long unsocialized

members of our race." In her view, club work, church, and
service volunteering saved scores of women from slowly dying
within their domestic cages, by giving them "outside" social
lives and an opportunity to "labor together . . . for other
needs than the family relation." If volunteering was a function
of femininity, it was also the first social movement to release the
"struggling human soul in woman."[84]

FOUR

THE VOLUNTEER
HERSELF:

Interviews

An unscientifically mixed sample of women volunteers were interviewed for this book. Some volunteer exclusively; some are former full-time volunteers, now in the paid work force; some combine volunteering and paid work. They volunteer in community-based and national organizations, in politics, the arts, social services, through their churches or synagogues, or for their favorite causes. They vary in age, ethnicity, and race, but virtually all the women who volunteer to the exclusion of paid work are white, middle- and upper-class; full-time volunteering is primarily a white middle- and upper-class tradition. Virtually all of the black women interviewed work at paying jobs while they volunteer. The majority of women in the entire sample are middle-class and many are married, because the volunteer tradition is so closely associated with middle-class marriage, family, and community life. They are all living in cities and towns in the Northeast.

This is not intended to be a survey of the volunteer world today, nationwide, or a statistically sound analysis of current trends in volunteering. Nor are these interviews presented as moral tales—of "good" or "bad" volunteer jobs and "good" or "bad" life-styles for women. Most of the experiences described in the book are mixed; most of the women interviewed will make their peace with these mixtures without any help from me. This is not a lesson or a "how to" book on volunteering. It is a collection of stories of women volunteers that takes a look at the volunteer work ethic and the interrelations of volunteering, paid work, and family in the lives of women today.

The decision to volunteer is, ultimately, an individual one. There are no rules or dogmas to guide you through it. But it helps to understand the history of volunteering; it helps to hear from women volunteers. And, after so many years of being analyzed, categorized, and lectured at, it is, I think, their turn to talk and ours to listen.

The Ideal:
Service as a Holy Calling

"You don't just think about yourself. Think about other
people and make your life useful."

Ann Geller, volunteer

Ask a woman why she volunteers and sooner or later she is
bound to recall the "feeling that comes from helping out." But
if she is sincere about it, if it runs deep, it is a feeling she is likely
to find difficult to describe. Talking about it may embarrass her;
the satisfaction of helping her neighbor is personal and seems
rather unsophisticated. She doesn't want to present herself as a
do-gooder. "It sounds corny," women tell me; it sounds "trite,"
even "sanctimonious" to say you volunteer "to make things
better," or because "you have to give something of yourself to
your community."

Their embarrassment is, in part, a response to the feminist
work ethic; women who now understand the importance of
putting a price on their work, just like men, are self-conscious
about playing out traditional, seemingly self-effacing feminine
roles. Twenty years ago they could have proudly, even smugly,
declared they volunteered in order to serve their communities.
Today, even in the most peripheral of feminist circles, it is more
fashionable to say they are on a career track, developing professional contacts and expertise.

This has left women somewhat confused about their motives
for volunteering. If they have been encouraged, even pressured
by the feminist movement to demand something for themselves from their work, many still have a residual impulse to
apologize for doing so. Their tendency is to distinguish between

the desire for a professional career and the impulse to serve a community as "selfish" and "unselfish" reasons for volunteering.

It is a distinction that makes no sense at all to me, because it suggests that there is something wrong with looking out for yourself and that there are saints among us who don't—who choose work that satisfies none of their own needs or desires. It suggests that helping yourself is incompatible with helping your community, and it both reflects and reinforces the common misconception that feminism, which on this value scale stands for "selfishness," cannot be reconciled with the impulse to volunteer, which stands for "selfless," "nurturing" femininity.

But the volunteer tradition is an article of faith as well as one of femininity; not every woman volunteers on account of her sex; some believe that service is a holy calling, for men and women alike. The first woman I interviewed spoke freely, simply, and directly of her own desire to "do things for people," because for her it derives not from socio-sexual conditioning but from a commitment she made years ago to God. The will and talent to volunteer, she says, is simply "the Lord working inside a person." For her it is a kind of blessing.

I liked her simplicity, the way she looked me in the eye and talked about "doing good" without pretension, complacency, or embarrassment. She was clear about her own need to volunteer —and about the enjoyment she derives from volunteering. Many women have told me that they would not want to be paid for their volunteer work: doing it for free is part of the pleasure of it; but it is not a worldly pleasure, and the women for whom volunteering does not have to be a worldly endeavor sometimes describe that pleasure best. For them there is nothing self-sacrificial or selfless about a life of service; it has been freely chosen, it is "self-satisfying," and if they feel somehow compelled to volunteer, it is by faith and not by femininity.

So I begin with four women for whom volunteering is a spiritual quest—not because their motivations are better, or purer, or even different than anyone else's, but rather because, on some level, they are the same. For me, these women clarify an ideal of volunteering that many share but few are able to express without fear of sounding starry-eyed or silly or like just another woman born to serve. This is not to suggest that volunteering can or should be clear and simple for all of us or that a spiritual commitment to work is the answer. Indeed, the last woman interviewed in this section doesn't quite know how to answer her own call to volunteer, because she is angry and confused about what the volunteer tradition has always meant for women. But there is still "something" in her, she says, that "wants to serve" in spite of that tradition, something that I think is shared by most of the volunteers in this book. There is, after all, a dimension of volunteering, even for women, that transcends the politics of sex and social service. It is not an answer, but it seemed to me a place to begin.

ANN GELLER

Ann Geller says her husband hates to go to New York with her because she looks so friendly. People on the street stop her just to talk: "I have that kind of half-smile."

I suspect she doesn't mind being approached by strangers: it has been her mission to help people in need since she was fifteen and "made a kind of commitment to God." It began with a church-sponsored youth conference and Bible study group of high school girl friends:

"We started to get together . . . to help each other in our lives . . . What we were gonna do was read a chapter from the Bible and discuss it . . . My mother, who was really very active in church, said, 'Well, this will last three weeks' . . . We met . . . and it worked for thirty years, and through it all we began to get a vision of doing things for people."

It was "amazing," Ann agrees, that "all the people in the original group stuck" for thirty years, but the notion of service they developed together became "the guide, the touchstone for everybody's life . . . in their marriages, in their bringing up of their children, in the kind of jobs and the kind of volunteer work they did."

Ann has been volunteering steadily and exclusively since

then for nearly forty years. She is now in her mid-fifties, with two grown children and a husband who has always been able to support the family by himself in middle-class comfort in suburban New Jersey. Ann has been "lucky," free to devote all her time away from home to volunteering, and "it has been a satisfying kind of life." Much of her work has been centered in her church—both she and her husband have been active members of the local Presbyterian church for years—and much has involved teaching—in Sunday school and youth groups. She also served as president of the board of directors of a home for teenage girls, worked as a "friendly hospital visitor" for many years, and has been an active member of her local Christian women's club. Ann prefers working with women: "I mean, I like men and I'm flirty and all that"; but she has better, "more balanced" relationships with women. Now her primary volunteer activity is leading Bible study groups of women in neighboring suburban communities. She has four groups this year, including one that meets in the evening for paid workers. None of her groups have been self-initiated. Women who know of her work have organized and asked her to lead them.

I have no experience with Bible study groups and imagine them to be a series of Sunday school classes. But Ann describes what I recognize as consciousness-raising or support groups, framed in the language of faith. She prepares lesson plans based on the Bible and inspirational literature to provide a context for discussions of "whatever's concerning them . . . their personal lives, their children, their families . . . their jobs, their relationships, their ambitions . . . their guilts, anxieties, and, then, the nation and the world. It starts out and it ripples." She tells me stories about the "girls" in her group. One who was too shy to talk for three weeks has turned into a "jabberer." One who was "trying to grow" posted a list of "immature emotions" on the refrigerator. "She has four kids at different stages and she told her kids, now here is where I'm weak and here is where I'm trying to grow . . . Well, that brought a certain camaraderie, sometimes kids think parents don't see themselves as they are . . . there was a kind of respect and interest in the fact that she was working on these things . . . and she was interested in changing herself."

Working as a group leader has been easy for Ann. Her special "gift" is teaching. She has known this since she was a teen-ager. When she stood up in her Bible group or in church to lead a discussion, people responded—and told her she was a natural. "It wasn't only that I was comfortable doing it; they recognized it. A gift, I feel, a real gift, is a two-way thing, doing it and people recognizing it. That's a gift." But she doesn't want to "brag" about it. "It isn't anything I do particularly. It's a gift I'm given and I'm responsible for using it and I enjoy using it . . . If I could choose, I would just teach until I was old and could no longer tie my shoes."

She hopes her groups will continue that long, but "I never know from year to year," she says, because attendance is voluntary. "Those people don't have to come. If you are teaching in a paid situation, [and] they took your class, they have to come." But the women in her groups "have to want to come and keep coming. They have to want to bring up other people. They have to want to be there."

But this is what makes her work so pleasurable. She wouldn't want people coming just because of the money, and she wouldn't want to be paid because then she would have to come too, for the money. She wouldn't feel free.

Volunteering has been uncomplicated for Ann, because of her faith and because she has never felt a need to pursue a paid career: it would be too "confining." "If the Lord wants me to do something, it's okay;" but she would feel "fenced in" by a salary. Although Ann travels as far as fifty miles for her groups and attends them when she is distracted by problems of her own, she says she is too undisciplined to hold a paying job and shudders when she thinks of working nine to five.

Ann looks so traditional. She married at nineteen, had two children in her early twenties, and has not worked for money since she was a teen-ager. She has lived the proper life for a middle-class, married church woman. Yet she sees herself as a "rebel," undisciplined, a little flighty, and always breaking rules. By volunteering, she is only doing what she wants to do. She has never wanted a paid career and never wanted to be a housewife, and, she says, has always resisted doing what was expected of her because she was a woman:

"A long time ago, when I was growing up, I was very convinced that men don't have to do the same things and be good at the same things. They can be good at all kinds of different things and have all these options—jobs—according to what their abilities are. And I didn't see why women all have to be housewives and take care of kids and cook and sew. I didn't see that women were any different than men and why would they have to have a very prescribed role. Suppose they're not good at those things. So I . . . was not going to be pushed into conformity. I just didn't buy that . . . You are who you are."

Ann, for one, has always been a terrible housewife. "I mean, I clean," she assures me, laughing. (It is a reflex; we are both surveying the room a little furtively, looking for dirt.) "But I don't cook . . . I was never any good at cooking and all that." She has always been "active on the outside," even with "a house and two kids." Everyone helped out and her husband was "very supportive."

Ann admits she may have abdicated a responsibility to earn money; volunteering feels a little self-indulgent to her. She was raised by a single working mother and a single working grandmother.

"My mother was a career woman . . . Her mother was a Swedish immigrant and her father had died when she was six months old, so her mother had worked . . . My grandmother married later when she was in her thirties (to a younger man); her husband was only twenty-nine when he died and she lived to be 93 . . . She was a strong woman who had a hard life, very hard, and made out." Ann's mother was also a "self-made kind of person." She worked until her thirties (as a private secretary). "She got married at 34 . . . her husband lived only fourteen years . . . so she went back to work . . . She worked at our church for twenty-six years, running the office . . . and she ran around and did a whole lot of things that were not required of her because she wanted to . . . So I was with women who were very self-sufficient, had to make it on their own 'cause they didn't have any husbands and they were workers and I'm not of that same character . . . Everybody takes care of me and I try to contribute what I can.

"I've always felt that I had a very good world . . . I arrange my world. I'm faithful to it; when I say I'm going do it, I'm there always. But I've made that commitment myself."

It was sometimes a commitment made in spite of herself. Ann never liked hospital work, especially friendly visiting; she worried about "imposing" herself on people. Serving as president of the board of directors at the home for girls was a little scary because she wasn't sure she could handle fiscal matters. But with the help of the Lord, and a hospital administrator who sat with her on the board, she managed.

Volunteering has always been a kind of ministry for Ann, and she has felt "guided" in it by God. She hasn't chosen her work so much as allowed it to choose her, by "keeping her eyes open" and responding to whatever needs presented themselves. Some of the work was a trial for her, but she is glad she did it. She has learned from all her jobs, one thing has always led to another, and now, for the past five years, she has been doing the work she loves. "It's good to do some things that are hard to do, along the way, 'cause you get so specialized that you don't have any feel for anything else . . . I would do these things like hospital work because I felt there was a need, and I wanted to do them; but it was hard—it wasn't bad, it was just hard . . . and then I had the opportunity (as board president) to speak to big groups, maybe a thousand, maybe a couple of hundred, and you go do that and you sit and eat the dinner and you give the talk and it's alright; I don't mind it; it's alright . . . But what I really like is the living room, you know, talking back and forth together, informally . . . If you ask me what I like, that's what I like."

There are a few regrets, and although Ann believes she has volunteered because it was what she wanted for herself, not because she is a woman, she wonders what her life would have been like if she'd been born a man. She should have gone to college; not going was partly her own fault and partly the fault of her mother, who didn't "press" her. Now Ann does not consider herself a professional—not because she is unpaid, but because she has received no formal training for her work. She is self-taught and has picked up things "here and there." "If I had been a man, maybe I just would have been a pastor." But it probably would not have worked, she adds. "I wouldn't have been any good, man or woman, as a pastor. Because I had a lot of growing up to do and I made mistakes." (Yes, she knows that pastors make mistakes.) But "I was not a compliant person, and I think being free and able to do it the way I did it—[the way] I do it . . . is the best thing."

Ann is sure about the work with her Bible groups because "it hasn't anything to do with my ups and downs." She had a cancer scare last year and tells me as an aside how she managed to lead a group while awaiting her test results, consumed with fears for her health. God gave her strength to do it, and it helped her "telling them about hope and faith." No matter how upset she is about something in her personal life, she can always focus on her work. She knows it is the Lord in her. "I can be very upset about something at home . . . and I'm going to a group and I say, 'Lord, I'm a mess and I don't know how I'm going to do anything here; would you please fill me up with yourself and help me to gather the fragments of everything I know about this and be helpful,' and He has never let me down."

I think she is describing what I would call a creative process. It is just that, to her, intuition, talent, and will are gifts from God. A creative inspiration is divine. I want her to take credit for her work. She gives it to God. To me it is only a semantic difference. Not to her, and not, I imagine, to God.

Ann Geller describes a work experience that, if not divine, transcends her sex, her class, and her generation. Still, I know she could not have enjoyed this same uncomplicated life had she been poor—or middle-class and born twenty years later, into my generation. What form would this pure ideal of service have taken for her then?

LYNDA GELLER

Lynda Geller, Ann's thirty-four-year-old daughter, has always combined volunteering with paid work. She needs to earn money, but it is important to her to serve and do the work she enjoys; so she has always earned just enough "to get by"—and is living at her parents' home in New Jersey when I interview her mother because she cannot afford an apartment of her own. She is comfortable there; it is only temporary, and living with her parents doesn't feel to her like failure. It is simply what happens to you when you don't earn very much money. Lynda has made her career choices freely, does not regret them, and believes she will work it out.

One year later she is living on her own again in New York and working part-time as an administrator and program planner at a home for girls sixteen to twenty-one years old. It is the same home her mother served as board president over ten years ago. Lynda has worked here since then, in a variety of paid and unpaid positions. She recently resigned as vice-president of the board to assume her present staff job. "It is a nice situation," she says. "I don't make a lot of money, but it's adequate . . . I can work my own hours and I can call my time my time, and that's nice." Lynda still volunteers at her church in New Jersey, still serving on the board of elders; she was the first woman appointed to the board in the history of the church. She also performs, for free, with a liturgical dance group, and writes short stories she is not yet ready to show the world.

Living a life of service is a little more precarious for Lynda than it has been for her mother, primarily because, at thirty-four, she is unmarried and self-supporting. She has an equally strong religious commitment to serve and has always known she would volunteer, but since graduating from college Lynda has earned her own living—primarily in the field of social services. It is interesting: her volunteering is based on faith, not femininity, she says, but her professional life has been shaped by her sex:

"I had always planned to go into social work . . . it fits in with my upbringing. It was something that women did . . . I certainly never thought about being a doctor or lawyer or any of those things because I didn't come out of a background where women did that. So the very choice of social work was tied in with my view of myself as a woman. The service is different."

I am a little confused about the difference; her choice of social

work obviously reflects a credo of service—if the paid work has
something to do with being a woman, why not the volunteering? I think she is telling me that in society only women are
supposed to be social workers; in her church, everyone is supposed to serve.

"Growing up in a church community . . . the backbone of
your belief is that you would serve . . . you're called to serve
and you're accountable for your time and your energy . . . for
your life."

Lynda embarked on her own path of service as a student at a
small evangelical college in New England. She began by visiting
a woman inmate in a nearby state prison. "It sounds kind of
innocuous," she says now, but she was just nineteen at the time
and "felt like it was something I ought to do . . . I felt a little
calling to it, I suppose; it just struck me . . . It was hard to do
because she was not always receptive to my coming . . . but I
figured I was going to see it through . . . Later it paid off,
because when she was getting out she commented that she was
so surprised that I kept coming and that it had really meant a lot
to her."

Lynda's next volunteer job was in a crisis intervention program for teen-agers, which sometimes entailed taking girls off
the streets into the apartment she shared with a classmate,
sometimes for periods of several months. She did this for the
same reason she volunteered at the state prison: "It was just
meeting a need that was right there in front of us."

Volunteering in college led to her first "professional" job in
an art therapy program at a state mental hospital. It was hard
work which would never make a significant difference, but
Lynda believed it was worthwhile. She thought a lot about her
role in the institution because people always asked her about it.
What could she hope to accomplish? Was she depressed by her
work?

"People used to ask me that a lot . . . It never dawned on
me to get depressed. They would ask me, so I'd stop and think
about it and I'd say, 'Well, no, because it's going on anyway
whether I'm here or not, and not being here doesn't do anything at all. All it does is protect me from what's going on. I
didn't feel that by being there I had to save everybody's life and

make it all different. You were just trying to humanize the place a little bit, bring a little dignity in whatever corner you could, and it was a losing battle and you knew it, but that didn't mean it wasn't worth doing."

The money she made doing it had very little effect on the way she felt about her work. It didn't "validate" her; apart from its practical importance, the paycheck was only a novelty: "Nobody had ever paid me to do this kind of thing before . . . I just did it and there was the paycheck and that was nice."

The paycheck had nothing to do with the "service piece of it" or even with Lynda's sense of herself as a "professional," and after three years at the hospital she decided not to pursue a paid career in social work. She liked it, believed it was important, and knew she would always serve; but she wanted to "develop other parts of [her]self," and went back to school in New York for an academic graduate degree, instead of a master's in social work. She had always been interested in the arts and in writing, and spent several years in New York studying, trying to write, working part-time at a bookstore, and volunteering at her church and at the home for girls. Lynda has remained in the social work profession—working at the home as a staff person and volunteer, because they needed her and asked her to stay on—and because it is the only field in which she has professional standing. Even as a social service volunteer, she feels like a professional; unlike her mother, she needs to have a "professional identity."

"When I was in school and I was running out of money and I worked in a bookstore . . . I came back on the board . . . it was very important for me to keep my hand in over here just for my own sense of myself as a professional. 'Cause I was a student and I was a bookstore clerk and it wasn't satisfying. So I could come over here and be vice-president of the board and sit in on the meetings and be an executive and feel that I knew what I was doing and that I was doing something valuable and important and something that not everybody could do."

Now she is paid for her work at the home, no longer has to work at the bookstore, and carries on her other activities, dancing, writing, and church work, for free. But it doesn't matter to Lynda which of her activities earns money: "I'd be doing these things no matter what . . . I know I need a certain amount of money to live on . . . one of my activities has to bring me an income; it's important . . . Right now I'm getting money from this particular program, but if I were getting money from my writing, yes, I would still be here in this program . . . I'll always have social service in my life somewhere."

It has nothing to do with being a woman, Lynda repeats: not for her. In her commitment to service, she feels "like a mixture of both [her] parents." "I do a lot of what my mother did, but I do things my mother didn't do that my father did, like being on the board of elders; that was never an option for women . . . So when I come home from meetings, it's my father and I who talk about it. Because that's the role he's always played, and she's never been on any of the boards. So I feel very much like I'm doing both things."

Lynda is an optimist and a believer. (She is lucky; at thirty-four she can say, "I have never questioned my faith.") She believes volunteering "is a good thing for men and women." And although she realizes that women have been "exploited" by it in the past—even the church expected women to serve more than men—she thinks the future will be different:

"What I see in my church with the women in my mother's generation . . . who never grew up having any political positions in the church, never serving on any boards . . . but they taught the children . . . they taught the classes, they were always allowed to teach and they served all over the place and the men went off and worked all day and they went to board meetings in the evenings, and all day the women were working, serving, volunteering in the church, bringing food . . . and that was how the community was structured."

Now, she says, there is finally a new group of women joining the board of elders. Nobody was surprised when Lynda went on, because she is a single working woman, "not the housewife type." But the woman who followed her onto the board was a "classic housewife," a young woman with small children. "It was a really good step. Now all these women who have been working for years in that church and never been on the board, they're coming on en masse. That's a real change."

It has changed, at least, for Lynda. But if she will never

volunteer in quite the same way as her mother, she volunteers for some of the same reasons: "I'm only doing what I should be doing, and I'm only doing what's expected of me and we all have to account for our lives."

ALTHEA COWLEY

Althea Cowley invites me to her church on a Sunday afternoon. She wants to show me around and introduce me to her sisters. It is important for me to hear about their work, as well as hers; they serve church and community together. It is a Pentecostal church in Harlem, where, she reminds me, the needs of the community are great. The church runs schools and shelters, programs for drug addicts and support groups for single parents. Althea has asked five or six women to join us and encourages them to tell me about their missions. She will not let me tape our conversations; she just wants me to see and hear for myself and to understand that she is part of a family.

Althea is a devout, impassioned Christian; she has accepted the Lord into her life and He has given her a clear and simple ethos of volunteering. It is a "sharing" of His love and part of a process of spiritual healing—"You are being helped by helping someone else." She has been "blessed" by her "sharing": "I always got what I put my heart to because of my belief." It has given her the "strength that's needed to achieve," and she has been achieving for thirty-five years now. (Althea is fifty-one and proud of it, she says, because "I think I am so beautiful.") She built a satisfying career for herself at a major insurance company and raised a teen-age daughter alone—her husband "left" twelve years ago, when her daughter was twelve. Thanking God, she says, "I have always been able to make it."

"Making it" began when she came to New York at seventeen from her home in the Bahamas, "frightened to death." "Nassau is so small and secluded and here I am coming into the big city." She moved in with an aunt, got her high school equivalency diploma, and found her first job in a factory. She felt "mis-

placed" there and believed she "could have done better," even
though "there was much prejudice in those days"—and few
white-collar jobs for young black women. The phone company
wouldn't hire her because, they said, she had high blood pressure. Schrafft's wouldn't give her a job as a candy wrapper
because she was "overqualified" and refused to accept her ap-
plication for a clerical position—"the prejudice again. So, one
day I decided I would take off from . . . the factory . . . I
would walk every street that day to find me a job . . . a little
better than the factory job and a job with some security." She
walked into the lobby of an insurance company, asked the
guard if they were hiring, and walked out with a clerical job.
She was one of six black clerks in the entire company; they
hired her, she says, because she was young and naive—she
didn't even know how to smoke. "I believed they took me
because they saw my innocence . . . and I lied and talked myself into the job." She has been there ever since, having "moved
up the ladder very fast" from clerical to managerial positions.
She likes her job; she is an administrator and, when she is not
volunteering, she likes to be running things.

Volunteering is different; she prefers service to administrative work, although she has done both. Althea has prepared a
list for me of her volunteer activities. She supervises her
church's hospital ministry, serves as president of its women's
auxiliary, which runs support groups for the "oppressed, depressed" women in the community, and is active generally in
the church's mission work. She also answers calls on a crisis
hotline (a telephone ministry) and is a board member of a long-
term residence for girls. She likes organizing and coordinating
activities, but that is not why she volunteers: ". . . sitting on
the board . . . it's just rules and regulations . . . It's not like a
ministry." Serving "one to one" is better. "I get better joy out of
it."

Althea began her volunteer career with the most traditional
of service jobs—friendly visiting at an orphanage and a V.A.
hospital with a group of churchwomen she met at her job. She
doesn't question the efficacy of this work; it was a "sharing" of
simple pleasures that brought joy to her and the people she
visited. The visits meant "so much," she says, to the shut-ins at

the hospital. "If no one had gone to visit them they wouldn't be able to walk on the grounds . . . People were so happy when someone came. They were all looking to see—was someone coming." Althea doesn't expect to "solve all the problems," and just "being there" for someone in an institution or serving food to a homeless woman on a soup line is better than doing nothing. "You were there . . . you smiled and said how are you today . . . that was helping." It was "touching" someone else's life, she says, and enhancing her own.

Service work, for Althea, is inextricably linked to her own spiritual health. She stopped volunteering once, for a few years after her marriage, in her late twenties, because she wanted to devote all her spare time to her husband. "I was so busy trying to be a good wife and I felt that every moment with my darling husband was very important and that Sunday was our only time together, and most of my volunteer work was done on Sunday. But she missed the work, felt a "void" in her life, and went through a physical and spiritual crisis shortly after the birth of her daughter:

"I was ill. I was paralyzed for a couple of months. I had a kind of illness, I don't know what it was. It had paralyzed my whole side . . . I woke up one morning and I had a pain . . . and after the pain went away I found that I had no life in the arm and after that there was no life from [the shoulder] down . . . for ten months exactly . . . They didn't know what it was. I went through a series of treatments at the hospital . . . electrical treatments . . . to try to restore life to the arm and the side, and nothing happened. And then it was during that period that I accepted the Lord as my personal savior, and I experienced a spiritual healing . . . And healed physically.

"That's kind of deep," she says, looking me over, "so we'll skip over that."

Not so fast, we won't. How did she come to accept the Lord? How did she find her faith?

"I seeked it through prayer and meditation . . . It's only through prayer and meditation that you can arrive at that . . . that you believe that something's going to happen when all others are saying it's not. The prayer came first and after the prayer came the belief and from the belief it went into a trust

. . . you begin to trust in God and then there was faith and hope."

Did she have it before, this saving faith of hers?

"That's a good question . . . I believe I had it but I never had to exercise it . . . Perhaps it was there but I never had to put such a thrust into the faith. When you're in good health and everything is going nice, good health and a job, everything is going for you. But when you find yourself with no job, paralyzed, no friends, then that's the time you really have to trust. When sometimes you say what am I trusting in or trusting for, you still have to trust and there's still that faith that has to be there . . . you keep building on it and you reach that peak where you rest."

She supposes she always had a "reserve" of faith. The doctors had wanted to operate on her, but she refused to let them, against the advice of friends and family: "I stood alone not to take that surgery; there was something in me . . . I might add that I don't think I have ever been motivated to exercise such faith again . . . I believe if I would, something else would happen, but I never did . . . So maybe I'm off balance, I don't know."

Althea has been "resting" since then in her faith and exercising it through volunteering. She would not want to be paid for her service—"It wouldn't be the same." She doesn't care if men don't volunteer as much as women—"They'd rather watch the baseball game, it doesn't bother me at all." And she has always ignored what feminists have said about women and volunteer work. "It had no bearing at all . . . I never gave it a second thought . . . I know why I'm doing this, and it doesn't matter what people say."

Volunteering has not been a source of conflict for Ann or Lynda Geller or Althea Cowley—because of their faith and because of their circumstances and the ways in which they have integrated service into their lives. Full-time volunteering was easy for Ann Geller; it was the accepted pattern of her class and generation, and she has never been troubled by her economic dependence on her husband. She can smile when she says, "Everybody takes care of me." Lynda Geller and Althea Cowley take care of themselves. Volunteering is a "piece" of their lives, along with paid work. It is not a symbol of dependence or incompetence. They have to earn their own livings, and they do.

Their paths of service have always been clear. They do what they can to ease whatever problems come before them, without agonizing over the political correctness or long-term effect of their actions: Sometimes it is enough just to "be there," doing your best. You can't save the world and don't have to try. You have only to do what you can, day by day. You are accountable for every day and every act is sanctified.

MARGARET PORTER

Margaret Porter believes she has been called to serve and has always been free to do so. She was born rich and, at thirty-four, enjoys an independent income of about twenty-five thousand dollars a year from the family trust. Because of her aristocratic background and what she calls a "social conscience," and because she is a feminist, volunteering is a problem for Margaret: it is a family tradition—her grandmother did it, her mother did it—and a family curse. Service work makes Margaret uncomfortable; it feels like charity and, she says, "somewhere along the line" charity supports the arbitrary divisions of wealth that she would like to help eradicate. It feels dilettantish and reminds her of the devaluation of women's work as well as the failure of upper-class women to demand their rights, assume full responsibility for themselves, and acknowledge the unsavory ways in which their husbands earn their money. Margaret wants to share her wealth, her "resources and skills," but, she adds, only in a way that will help change the system from which she has benefited so unfairly. It is hard for her to serve "one to one," day by day, to take her work as it comes; she worries about the ultimate consequences of every action: how is her energy being used? Whom or what is it finally serving?

I have been friends with Margaret for about ten years, but it was only recently that I began thinking about her as a volunteer. It is not the way she presents herself or the way others see her. She is a talented photographer who, at her own expense, is putting together a book of portraits of lesbian women she has photographed in her travels. Margaret is a lesbian and hopes that her book will somehow serve her community. She is an activist in the peace movement and has compiled a cross-country arrest record, marching against nuclear power and defense spending. And, she is a gypsy, an adventurer, who has lived with the Berbers in North Africa, studied with Grotowski in the Polish woods, and takes off on a solitary pilgrimage to some wilderness, somewhere, once or twice a year. Lately she has been going off on periodic retreats to an ashram. She studies Yoga and hopes it will illuminate her path. Margaret is always on some quest or other, trying to figure out how to serve.

She has known something was wrong with the world, she says, since she was seven years old and first became aware that not everyone in it was rich:

"When I was seven years old, my parents got divorced and my mother took us to Nassau. We lived in a big house on the hill. Our neighbors were poor whites; they were my best friends. They lived in this little shack down the road . . . the schism was just so evident there. You go there, you can't help but see it. Living in Connecticut, you don't see much of the poor . . . there was not much of it around to see. So when we moved to Nassau I became aware that there was this houseful of people down the road from us and when they had Christmas, they got ball-point pens, and basically nothing . . . And everyone lived in two, maybe three rooms . . . We had this big house, filled with rooms, and they had this little teeny place and I knew it was wrong."

After a year in Nassau, she went to live with an aunt in Mississippi. "She owned a string of movie theaters, and they all had 'colored' entrances and 'colored' water fountains. And the first time I saw this entrance and was able to read it, 'cause I had learned to read . . . I stood outside it . . . and the feelings that I had standing outside of it—I just knew that it was wrong. I knew my family was wrong. I knew there was something evil in it . . . And I didn't trust my family from that day on, from the time I was eight years old and went to the movie theater and read the sign."

When she was twelve and thirteen and back in Connecticut, service work looked like the answer. She volunteered at a low-income housing project in Stamford, "taking care of children." "We'd be with them, we'd play with them . . . I felt this was a good thing to do. I grew up with the notion that people must do service. People of means supported people who had less; the rich gave to the poor."

She is cynical about that tradition now. "You tithe a certain percentage of your income so that you'll go to heaven . . . Somehow there was a magical quality in it . . . If you did it, you would be taken care of and you would go to heaven—and you would earn more money. You know, it's an old biblical concept, really. You give 10 percent away to the less fortunate . . . the law of the tenfold return and you get 100 percent back."

Disillusionment set in early, she says, at fifteen, when she was living in New York and volunteering at a Headstart program on the Lower East Side. "I would go down to the center every morning to try to be with little children. Every day I would experience these children all day long—maybe a little headway, maybe a little closeness . . . But it gave me a very queasy feeling . . . I remember feeling very strongly that it was useless." It was a disappointing experience; she had hoped to be rewarded "at least metaphysically" for her work. "I had an expectation that . . . at least I would feel good about doing it. And I didn't. I felt shitty about doing it."

Today, she thinks she knows why. "It was wrong that these children had to suffer in this way . . . it was the system that gave us the discrepancies and the discrimination that made Headstart necessary." Working for Headstart was only another form of tithing.

Margaret's next job was in a laundry. She had decided it was important to earn money and be paid for her work. It had to do, she says, with self-respect. There had been something else wrong with her Headstart job: the salaried teachers didn't respect her. It might have been "the age thing": but she began to

feel that "a volunteer was just someone to do the dirty work."
At least in the laundry she would be paid for it.

Since then she has worked at a variety of odd jobs, as a cock-
tail waitress while she was in college, and, later, as a receptionist
in a squash club, a substitute teacher, a photographer's assistant,
and an actress and dancer with an experimental theater group
in New York. Working for money, earning her keep, was important to her: "There's something self-respecting about being
paid to do your work. You know, 'Here, go buy your food, maintain your apartment.' " Working for money made Margaret like
everybody else. "It was easier to be with people and be able to
say, 'I have this job, this is what I do.' "

She stayed away from volunteering for over ten years. Most of
her work time in college and the few years after she graduated
was spent earning money at odd jobs. It wasn't until she was in
her late twenties, after redefining herself as a lesbian feminist,
that Margaret began, once more, to want to volunteer. It was
different then; she was part of a larger community of women
who needed each other. "It was a whole different ball game
going in to help women." It didn't feel like "noblesse oblige" to
serve what she identified as her own community. She volunteered to teach photography classes in a women's prison.

This led to her first paid job in social service, in an expanded,
publicly funded arts program in mental hospitals, nursing
homes, and prisons. It was "nice being paid," and this was the
"best job" she has ever had—"the most dignified and humane."
But she still doubts the value of the work: "I came away feeling
that it was useless . . . I felt that I reached some people . . .
helped them to know they were more than the sum total of
their physical predicament." But there were still too many
"contradictions" bound up in working within an institution.
"The institutions were so horrifying and horrible . . . They
were wrong; they were ugly; they were inhuman, deranged—
the prisons, the nursing homes, the mental hospitals . . . the
institutions themselves need to be changed, not supported."

What confuses her is that "at the same time, there's people
there . . . trapped in those institutions . . . The butt end, the
by-products of the system—they're people, they're human beings." She would like now to believe there is "room for every-

thing," service and social change work. You just have to be careful, she adds, not to be "manipulated by the powers that be." You can't go in "thinking the system's hunky-dory and here's your little niche in it." Margaret is still trying to serve within institutions today. She is learning to do hospice work and goes into hospitals to talk with people who are dying. She is, after all, a friendly visitor.

Margaret hasn't held a paying job since she came into her inheritance on her thirtieth birthday, four years ago. She tells herself now that she is "just doing exchange on a larger level." "I'm exchanging, for free, goods and services that come to me every month. It might not come directly, but I'm getting paid for my work." It looks to me like she is earning her inheritance. She says it is a matter of giving it back; the money is not really hers, and she is bound to return it, either in the form of services or by paying other people for their work. She gives away about one quarter of her yearly income, "primarily to women artists who are also doing political work," and toys with the idea of simply giving it all away. She is not sure if she should hold on to her inheritance and direct its use or renounce it completely. "Sometimes I feel if I let go of the money, my path of service will be clearer." Sometimes, she thinks her path is to take responsibility for her wealth and make sure that it "serves." Perhaps she should use it to buy land and set up a land trust for a community of women.

Margaret knows she is set apart by her money; in some ways, she enjoys her status and likes being in control. But it is also a barrier between her and other women that she has to struggle to overcome. Much of her political work is done with working-class women and, sometimes, she says, "they hate me . . . They have so much anger for their deprivation, for what they had to see their parents do, and it's very hard . . . They've spent their whole life hating the rich. And now the rich is in their circle, giving them money. It creates a tremendous amount of conflict, within me and within them . . . Some of my friends wear buttons that say, 'Eat the Rich' . . . They hate the rich . . . I'm one of them. What do they do when they hate the rich and I'm there?"

The majority of Margaret's close friends and almost all of her lovers have been "privileged women." "I'm going to get called on this," she admits. "I call myself on it . . . but, on some level, they're the only women I can trust . . . They're the women I can feel okay about going out to dinner with. I don't have to feel guilty. They've got it too."

For all her guilt about being rich, Margaret is at home with her money and relishes the freedom it gives her. It might have been "nice" being paid a regular salary; working at a job, like everyone else, relaxed her. But she is glad she doesn't have to do it. She has never looked for "fulfillment" in the marketplace and has few illusions about the joys of paid work:

"Volunteerism made me feel a little sleazy, but it ain't nothing compared to working for money . . . I get this feeling inside, like being tired and exploited." She can smile when she talks about it. The feeling didn't depress her while she was working and it doesn't depress her to remember it now. Margaret always felt free to quit a particularly unpleasant job. What she doesn't like about paid work she has always been able to laugh off:

"Want to hear about my first job? I sent away for seventeen tubes of Cloverine brand salve from the back of a comic book, so I could get a pony. I was about nine. It was the most humiliating experience . . . I think it conditioned my whole working life. Because I would go around the neighborhood with these ridiculous tubes of salve, for what? And people just really weren't interested. And the company came after me . . . It turned out that you had to sell like ten thousand tubes of the thing. So after I finished selling them to all the people in the neighborhood who took pity on me there was no one else to sell them to. So I was stuck with these boxes of Cloverine salve and the company out to get me . . . They didn't want those tubes back, they wanted the money . . . I think I learned very early that I did not like working for people.

"Now," she says, "I'm just a bum, a ne'er-do-well . . . When I started getting this inheritance money I thought, well, what am I going to do—go out and make money? I don't need money. Why should I go out and take a job away from someone who really needs it . . . I decided that I would do what I wanted to do, and that was to create a photographic documentation of

lesbians and I knew that no one was going to pay me to do that
. . . This is part of my life's work and I have to do it whether
anybody's gonna pay me for it or not . . . I had the resources, I
had the skills, no one was gonna pay me to do it, and I had the
time."

Margaret isn't even sure she wants to be paid for her photography. It feels terrible to her when people look at it and say,
"What's its worth? What's its salability?" . . . "It feels like prostitution." It is a feeling in which she can afford to indulge—
Margaret doesn't need to make money from her photographs;
and she admits it is a feeling that may only reflect her own
misgivings about their value. She is confused about her photography; she isn't sure what it's worth and how it serves:

"I feel different things about it at different times. I'm in love
with it. It's like a relationship. It's like a lover. Sometimes it's
good and sometimes it's bad. Sometimes it's totally sublime and
sometimes I hate it and want to throw it out the window. And I
feel like it's self-indulgent and who am I to be making these
precious little prints one after another, and who am I not to be
working in the factory with everybody else . . . who am I to be
privileged enough to do this work?

"If I really felt that my work served, then I would probably
feel okay about doing it. But it doesn't really serve because I
don't get it out . . . I don't take it around . . . I don't do it
because it's a drag . . . because it always comes back mangled
. . . I send them out in cardboard and I wrap them up nicely
and they always come back either dirty or bent up and I don't
feel like people take care of them well enough . . . And that's
part of it . . . So many times I've had my work either lost or
mangled in the process of going out and coming back, whether
they use it or not. When they use it, it's destroyed . . . And I
don't feel like there's a lot of respect for it. Putting something
out in the world where there's not a lot of respect for it anyway,
so it gets mushed up and I get angry at people who don't see it as
something of value, but then I don't see it as valuable either. It's
weird—this conversation is making me very very uncomfortable."

In order for her photographs to serve, she has to put them out
in the world and demand payment for them so that they'll be

recognized and valued; it is hard for her to do this because she isn't sure she values them herself. Just like the stereotypical volunteer, Margaret isn't sure she deserves to be paid for her work. She agrees she has backed herself into a corner—but doesn't stay there long. Sometimes, she adds, it seems that her relationship to photography is "just right . . . just the way it is now." Because the time she doesn't spend "getting it out" she spends on Yoga, meditation, hospital service, and peace work.

Peace work is easier for Margaret than any other kind of volunteering. It has none of the contradictions that go with working within an institution and it doesn't involve her in the questions of self-worth that go along with her photography. She likes to talk about her work in the peace movement.

"Probably the strongest act of service I ever did for a sustained time . . . was walk on the Peace Walk." This was a seven-hundred-mile walk that began in Montreal and ended in New York, in the nuclear freeze rally in Central Park in June 1982. "It was originated," Margaret tells me, "by an order of Buddhist monks from Japan whose total path is to walk for peace. That's all they ever do, walk for peace, and beat the prayer drum and chant—to bring peace to the land . . . We met with people all the way from Montreal to New York City, in small towns through New England, to raise consciousness about the special [U.N.] session on disarmament, the nuclear freeze and the effects of atomic war. We showed slides and talked about our experience and every night we had a potluck supper with a different community of people . . . I consider that to be work of service."

Service has become easier for Margaret lately because, she says, she is gaining a new "spiritual take" on it. She believes she is "on the planet to serve" and hopes she will one day be able to respond simply and directly to "whatever or whoever comes into [her] life," without worrying about all the possible repercussions of her actions. She should not have to seek out opportunities to serve; they will find her. It surprises me to hear Margaret echoing Ann Geller, who told me she found her work by simply keeping "her eyes open" to it: "I believed I would be guided," Ann recalled, "and when somebody said, why don't you come over and do this, I would say no if I had a really strong feeling to say no, but I would pretty well take that as a sign that that was . . . an open door, so I had to do it [and] I would."

Margaret is beginning to believe that she too will be guided down the path of service, so long as she remains receptive and committed to serve. She suspects this is the truth about service —and has been trying to accept it for about two years, since it was first revealed to her during a walk in a Polish forest.

"I had an experience in Poland when I was there that changed my whole attitude about service . . . I was walking in the forest with a Native American who was there. And we took this five-hour walk in the forest and we walked like snails. We walked very, very slowly. And at one point he took me and he put me up against a tree and he put my head against the tree very gently and he put my arms around the tree. And the tree started speaking to me."

I give up: "What did it say?"

"It said—'You don't have to worry about your path of service; it's not something for you to decide on.' 'Cause at the time I was going through this whole spiritual trip and I knew my life was of service. But how was I gonna serve? You know, I had to choose. I had to decide, what am I gonna do? How am I gonna do it? Meanwhile, I'd run off to Poland.

"And the tree said, 'You don't need to decide on your path of service. Just be like me. Become more like me. Cultivate tree-ness. Here I am: if someone needs shade, I'm here. If someone needs to build a house, here I am. If someone needs to build a fire, here I am.'

"So basically that let me off the hook in a big way . . . it really did; it let me off the hook in a very big way. And that's the way I've been ever since. I've been trying to cultivate tree-ness."

It is, she admits, laughing along, a great relief.

The Tradition

THE SURVIVORS:
FAMILY LIFE
AND A LIFE CAREER AS A VOLUNTEER

"It's so easy to look back and form judgments, but we
all work within our structure . . . Very few people
move beyond. Most of us are what we were brought up
to be, one way or another."

Dorothy Harnack, volunteer

It is difficult for many women of my generation to separate
the ideal of volunteering from the tradition—and to volunteer
without feeling co-opted or consumed by traditional roles that
have only recently begun to give way. It must have been nearly
impossible some thirty years ago, in the late 1940s and throughout the 1950s, when patterns for women were written in stone.
They would be full-time wives and mothers, and, if they insisted
on working outside the home, they might be volunteers. Our
stereotype of a volunteer—a housewife who dabbles in community work—is a legacy of the fifties. It is reflected in Mary Mc-
Carthy's wry description of the typical Vassar girls of 1951 who
"look forward to 'working within their community' for social
betterment while being married and having babies."*

It is, indeed, easy now to look back and judge these women
and to revel in our own liberation. But I suspect that the "typi-

* "The Vassar Girl," in Mary McCarthy, *On the Contrary: Articles of Belief,
1946–1951,* New York, 1962, p. 214.

cal girls" of my college class of 1971 who now enjoy paid professional careers would also have settled for babies and community work twenty years earlier. I don't think we were all braver—just luckier than our mothers—lucky enough to be raised during a decade of change and new choices for women.

In the 1950s, volunteering was the only respectable choice both for college girls and for women who had been welcomed into the paid work force a few years earlier, during the second World War, only to be shunted back into the home when the country returned to normalcy. Domesticity became a pervasive and dictatorial middle-class ideal, held in place by social pressures and economic inequities that denied women the career opportunities available to men. If they had the desire to break away and extricate themselves from the domestic order, they were denied the capacity. The thinking woman of the 1950s was much less likely to rebel against the conventions of her time than women are today. Instead, she did what she was supposed to do and worked within the confines of her culture.

Most of the women interviewed in this section on tradition were either college girls or young mothers in the late forties and early fifties. They made me understand the importance of volunteering at a time when paid work was not a respectable or even available option for middle-class women. Talking to them gave me a new perspective on the volunteer tradition, an appreciation of its usefulness to women who had so many fewer choices than I did. It does not seem to me that they were only exploited or oppressed or made powerless by that tradition. I see them as survivors, who used it and adapted, and somehow saved themselves by volunteering.

DOROTHY HARNACK

Talking about herself for two straight hours is a slightly illicit treat for Dorothy Harnack. She was brought up with the notion that "You don't tell people about yourself." It feels like "bragging"; it isn't polite or ladylike. I assure her that most of the people I know talk about themselves incessantly and, besides, I am here to listen. So, she lets herself go. "This is something I think everybody would love, chatting about what you've been doing. Who else would sit and listen to you for hours?"

Dorothy is fifty-five, with three grown children. She has had virtually no paid work experience; her husband has always supported the family in style; it never occurred to her to work for money, and she has been volunteering since the children were in grade school. She has worked with the PTA, served as president of her community arts league, and, for the past two years, has been organizing a nuclear freeze campaign in her town in suburban Connecticut. Dorothy feels she is "typical of a lot of people" and, like a lot of us, a product of her time.

Like many women, she began her volunteer career with the PTA. She didn't think of it as volunteering: "It was just part of being a parent." Dorothy wasn't looking for work; she had married young, without finishing college, and the responsibilities of marriage and motherhood were overwhelming at first: "I don't think I was prepared even to be married or to be a mother. Suddenly I had three children and didn't know how to wash or cook or do any of those things everyone should know before they're married."

Raising children became her primary activity and was always her first priority; there was not much time or energy left for anything else. "I felt it was important to be with children when they were little. Many times you're there and nothing is even happening, but you're there . . . And you may never know when you're there at an important time or not." She is not dogmatic about this now: "Who knows, maybe my children would have been better off if I weren't there all the time, you make mistakes as a parent." But she doubts it is possible to raise children and enjoy a career—not a job, she says, but a career. It is not just that children need "nurturing"; so does a career. "Everything has to be involved in it. It has to be your driving force. A career is almost like a growing, living thing. It needs all kinds of attention and care."

Dorothy went to drama school and trained for a career in the theater before she married. She decided not to pursue it because it would have taken over her life. "It was almost as if theater was a religion and you almost had to give your entire life to it. To be good at it would have meant total concentration and devotion. And I guess I thought if I was going to be in the theater business, I was going to be on Broadway or something . . . I couldn't be not very good and just kind of do amateur things."

She could, however, write and perform skits for the PTA: "That was different. That was fun." Dorothy gives me a copy of a play she wrote when her kids were young; it will tell me something about "what she was feeling" at the time. It is a 1950s domestic comedy about a harassed, slightly depressed housewife. She has no real work to do, only trivial household tasks, and she is too incompetent to perform them properly. She is "I Love Lucy" on a bad day. The climax of the play is a dream sequence in which the wife is a lawyer in her own defense, pleading her case before her husband, the judge. She wakes up to a happy ending; the family loves and appreciates her; she has only to stop feeling sorry for herself.

The early years of child-rearing were difficult. Dorothy enjoyed her children: "I found them interesting . . . it's exciting watching your child grow and change." But at the same time she went through a vague, inarticulate sort of depression: "I slept all the time. I escaped by taking naps and things . . . I wasn't good at what I was doing. Maybe it would have been better if I had an outside job." She still doesn't quite know what the trouble was; she has a hard time understanding it now because she didn't understand or even acknowledge it then: "My generation didn't look in. I talk to people twenty or thirty years younger and they're always talking about what's going on inside them. I don't think we did that, or I didn't. I just don't think I was aware. I think I was just living through the time . . . I reacted to things, but I don't think I was aware in a way."

She's not sure how or why the depression eventually eased, but as her children grew, Dorothy entered a livelier phase, volunteering for the arts league in her community. She began by taking courses and "ended up" as league president, in charge of administration, public relations, fund-raising—everything. "It was fun," until the league decided to build a new art gallery: "I became very worried. I thought, my Lord, how can . . .

this little organization build this big building . . . We'll be in debt for years. I thought, if I do this while I'm the president, I just can't walk away at the end of my term. I'll be baking oatmeal cookies to pay off the mortgage . . . I got so I couldn't sleep; I was a nervous wreck about that."

Fortunately the league found an old building and renovated it for a modest sum. Dorothy began sleeping again and became director of the new gallery. It was "exciting" and practically a full-time job. "I never clocked it, but I have a hunch I almost put in a full week." She supervised a staff of volunteers, arranged shows, handled promotional work and fund-raising.

What was it like for her to supervise people, I wonder. Did she feel like a boss? Did she like it?

She answers at first by telling me about the wonderful people who worked at the gallery and made the job so enjoyable for her. Being a "boss" wasn't the point, and she is not comfortable thinking of herself as one.

"My kids kidded me and said I got to be real bossy, and once in a while I'd say, 'My gallery,' and [my husband] would say, 'Dorothy, it's not your gallery.' " And, she agrees, it wasn't. "You're working on something together and that's, as far as I'm concerned, the main [thing] about volunteer work. It's not your gallery. Everybody's working together on it."

She also takes care to remind me that she was not selected as director of the gallery because of any special capabilities: "You're not there because they had to push away thousands of people eager to get the job. Many times no one else will do it . . . it's not because you're this fantastic, wonderful person. It's because very few people can give that time."

She did, however, enjoy the responsibilities of her job, and she grew in it. "You make decisions that you weren't used to [making] before and you're making decisions that are more or less important involving big amounts of money." For her, volunteering was the next best thing to a paid professional career; it was better than a nine-to-five job. "Volunteer work can be very exciting, and you have freedom that you don't have if you're a secretary and you go in from nine to five. And you can do things; you can try things . . . That's the fun of being an amateur. You go sailing off on things . . . Now I think I work as hard and have as much knowledge in a lot of areas as people who are getting paid."

Sometimes Dorothy thinks that younger women are rejecting volunteering with the same kind of knee jerk that characterized her generation's rejection of paid work. But this is easy for her to say, she adds. "I haven't suffered. My husband hasn't walked away and left me destitute and not . . . able to get a job at fifty-five." On the whole, she thinks feminism is a "good thing."

She thinks, in fact, that it may even play a role in the survival of the race, "if we survive." Dorothy has been deeply involved in the nuclear freeze movement, organizing her town and lobbying state and congressional representatives on the issue of disarmament. She hopes the feminist movement will bring women into the political structure and give them a voice in public policy; she hopes that "women will make a difference in the decision-making about peace."

Perhaps—she isn't sure about this: "Look at Margaret Thatcher, a great warrior." Dorothy wonders what women will be like when they begin to enjoy the opportunities and the power that has always belonged exclusively to men. But "there is a predominance of women in the peace movement," at least at the grass-roots level, and like social feminists of the last century, who believed that women were naturally more "virtuous" than men, Dorothy would like to believe they are naturally less "aggressive," more peace-loving, and more concerned about the future of their children.

She remembers thinking about disarmament for the first time in 1945: "I knew one thing for certain. I was never going to get married and have children if there was an atom bomb in this world." But she "put it out of [her] mind for about thirty years . . . I guess it took a Reagan or a Weinberger to shock us awake." For Dorothy, it also took her four-year-old granddaughter:

"When my granddaughter was getting ready to go to kindergarten . . . you think of all the things your own children did— getting them dressed up for Halloween, and the different parades you go to, the PTA, Valentine's Day. All those things that are just part of growing up and you suddenly think—they may never do that, that might not happen."

The only way she envisioned the arms race being stopped, she says, was by the emergence of an "overwhelming movement" against it that "everybody is involved in. So another friend and I decided we would meet once a week on Monday morning, and we started, just the two of us. We used to meet in my office and gradually more people joined us . . . One morning, no one could come, [and] I decided, well, I'd meet by myself."

Their primary activity at first was educating themselves about the arms race, defense capabilities, and weapons systems. Then they started writing letters to congressional representatives, state and local officials, and newspapers. They were written up in the local paper, attracted more members, and formed connections with similar groups in neighboring towns. Now there is a core group of fifty to sixty people who meet once a week at Dorothy's house. "I guess since it meets at my house and I started it, I'm sort of the chairman," she admits.

She doesn't think of this work as volunteering: "I just think of it as something I have to do . . . and that everybody else has to." Her one regret about it is that it is making her an "absentee grandmother." She is always busy, working with her group, writing letters to every member of Congress and "op-ed" pieces for newspapers in her town in Connecticut and her home state of Colorado. She can't estimate the time she spends on her work but feels it is never enough and worries about taking off on a two-week vacation she and her husband have planned: "You almost get so that you don't want to go on vacation because you're gonna be losing that time." This is the most impassioned and consuming work Dorothy has ever done, and, even though it can be "very depressing," there is also something invigorating about "being together with each other, working on something . . . Of course, this is entirely different than working on any other project . . . Most of us feel like we're working for our own survival."

SHIRLEY KRAMER

Shirley Kramer is used to being in charge. "What can I do for you," she asks, when we have finished exchanging hellos. She has been a professional, sometimes executive, volunteer for about thirty years, in the world of private, nonprofit service agencies, voluntary associations, and politics. She has sat on various community boards, including the library board and the Board of Education, and once ran, unsuccessfully, for the Connecticut state legislature. She served as president of her local chapter of the National Council of Jewish Women, chaired a statewide Council study on the juvenile court system, and now serves as a board member and staff volunteer for a nonprofit child welfare and justice coalition. Shirley has made a name for herself as a volunteer and has the manner of a professional career woman. She doesn't need to be coaxed into talking. I am here for an interview and she is ready for me—almost:

"Last week I was about to call and tell you, 'don't come' . . . I hit a low point. I was feeling unloved, unrespected. I'm sure people who have jobs do the same things. I'm sure people in marriages do the same thing. It was just one of those low points . . . It doesn't happen often, but periodically there's 'What the hell am I doing this for?' "

What triggered the low point this time was that the executive director of the juvenile justice coalition for which she volunteers moved in on one of her projects while she was on vacation. It was "probably appropriate," she admits; he is, after all, the executive director, and he probably would have done the same thing to a paid staff person. But a volunteer is on especially shaky ground when it comes to the territorial imperative in an office. She has no scope of employment, which makes it easy for her to do what she wants and hard to stake out a claim to her work. Shirley's relationship with her executive director is particularly "delicate" because, although she functions as an unpaid staffer, she is also a member of the board of directors. He is, in a sense, accountable to her for carrying out policies set by the board, but she is not supposed to interfere with the way he runs the office. "As a board member you don't do, the professionals do; you make policy, you don't run the show . . . I'm in the very anomalous position of not having a title, doing a lot of staff work and yet being on the board." It's just that board work is not enough for her, because "to me the satisfaction and the interest is in doing things, not just in shaping policy."

Shirley has a talent for generating ideas, but sometimes, at her low points, it is frustrating to watch other people run with them. She doesn't mind so much not being paid for her work, but she wants to maintain control of it and to get the credit for it that's due. Sometimes she feels "picked over." It is one of the trade-offs for the freedom and independence of volunteering, and most of the time it is enough to know that her ideas are of use. "If I'm feeling positive about myself, I can say with honesty that I've effected a lot of change. I've affected a lot of people's ideas and activities as well . . . That, and a whole lot of coffee, is basically my pay."

Shirley hasn't worked for money since the first of her four children was born, over thirty years ago. She married in 1943, soon after graduating from college, settled down in her husband's home town in Connecticut, and for two or three years worked in a local department store. "It was a job, not a career." She was in personnel, "doing training, teaching, writing the store newspaper, which was fine for several years." She quit to have children, "without thinking about it too much, that was probably more the pattern in those days." Her husband had a successful legal practice, she didn't need to earn money—"There was no financial need and, I guess, no ego need"—and she wanted to be there for her children.

But she also wanted to have work to do outside the home. "I don't play cards. I don't feel that comfortable in social groups of women . . . I like to have something to do." When her children were "very young," she started volunteering for the League of Women Voters, "which was my education in the community and in politics," and in the National Council of Jewish Women, because "they had a very active community service program." She was also "laboring in the vineyards" for her party, establishing herself politically. Volunteering has worked for Shirley; she had four children in about a ten-year period, became a recognized and respected executive organizational volunteer and community leader, and still managed to be home at three o'clock "ninety-nine days out of a hundred" while her kids were in elementary school.

Much of her volunteer work has focused on children; she has been an advocate for them, in education and in the criminal justice system. Her path into public life was a traditional and highly respectable one for a woman—but even it has gotten her into trouble at times. Her political career ended in the late sixties after one four-year term on the Board of Education, because of her support for a controversial school integration plan. "I had alienated enough people so that that was the end of that career." She was not reelected to the board, lost a campaign for a seat in the state legislature, and spent the next several years "moving through" a variety of volunteer jobs, as head of a school health council and president of a hospital auxiliary, "without any real heart in it." It was not until she took on the job of statewide chair for the survey of the juvenile courts for the Council of Jewish Women that she found work that satisfied and engaged her. "I learned an awful lot . . . we produced a report which . . . became part of a national report and which also found some interest in the state . . . That was just about the time (in the early seventies) of some changes in the juvenile justice system and I guess there were few Mrs. Citizens or Mr. Citizens who had an interest in or an understanding of the criminal justice system."

Her work on this survey was the beginning of a second career for Shirley in juvenile justice. She was appointed to a gubernatorial juvenile justice advisory board and was asked to serve on various public and private committees in the field. "People started calling me . . . the Boy Scouts, the YMCA, the Junior League, a couple of other groups that had started to get into this field . . . with a common interest in the status offender . . . the runaway truant and the so-called incorrigible kids who have been dealt with as delinquents even though they may not have done anything . . . You and I can run away but we can't be put in jail for it."

Several of these groups came together and formed a coalition which Shirley "helped start" and "informally chaired." They eventually incorporated into the "justice for children" project that now takes up most of her time. She sits on the project's board and works in the office, four to five days a week sometimes, putting out a legislative newsletter. It is "basically a summary of all the current legislation that affects children and families . . . juvenile justice, child abuse . . . youth employment, adoption, foster care . . . [and] some of the other family environment issues, like housing and income maintenance." The newsletter is essentially a one-woman operation; Shirley monitors the legislative sessions herself, gathers her own information, writes it up and gets it out to community leaders, paid social workers, and agency administrators in the field. Once in a while, she realizes that people get paid for this sort of work: "A couple of years ago, one of the women in a state department came into my office waving a little piece of paper . . . one of the state departments was looking for a person to do what I do, to be the legislative manager for the Office of Policy and Management, which is part of the Executive Department, and it was advertised at eighteen to twenty-two thousand. And she came in laughing—because, she said, 'You're giving away what you could be making money for.' " Shirley thinks about this "once in a while," but worries that if she left the Project, its newsletter "would go undone. It could not be taken on by the people there now . . . not that they wouldn't be able to do it, but there are just so many hours in the day and they're all filled."

The newsletter is important, she says, because it disseminates information to people in different disciplines in the field. She hopes that it will help "break down" the lines between various professionals and, in doing so, help promote "systems change." Shirley believes that she has an important contribution to make as a volunteer: she is more open-minded in her approach to problems; she has no professional prejudices.

"One of the things I have found is that social workers are educated as social workers, work as social workers, see things as social workers; psychologists are the same, teachers the same . . . I have nothing I'm selling, and I have no particular training, so that I can see the importance, the value of crossover and the problem with blinders." As a volunteer she believes she is freer to experiment: "I don't have a degree in whatever . . . so I can say and do outrageous things"; and she can afford to "push the system hard" without fear of being "pushed out."

Lately she has become interested in relatively new "child health" questions, "the correlation of children's behavior and nutrition"; it is an interest that grew out of her experiences with her own children:

"One of my kids is diabetic and when we learned about it I stopped being the usual lazy American mother and I stopped having Hi-C and Twinkies and all that stuff . . . Whether it was coincidence or whether it was maturing or whether it was a significant difference in eating habits, my youngest son, the next one down, suddenly stopped being a real hyper-super-charged-up kid and suddenly became a student." It would be a "whole 'nother career," but she would "love to investigate" the effect of "all the junk they're putting in our food on behavior." She talks to doctors about this, and they treat her like "a crazy nut lady." "Doctors don't know nutrition and nutritionists have no standing in the community." She doubts she can do much more than talk about the problem: "It's a whole 'nother field that requires a lifetime of study and . . . getting people to change." So, she tries to stir up young people: "I talk to kids going into medicine . . . maybe it's just that I'm non-directed or maybe I satisfy myself by saying that if I keep pointing out the possibilities, somebody will pick up on it."

One reason Shirley hesitates to begin a new career is that she is turning sixty and considering retiring. It is a difficult decision: her husband is ready to slow down and take off extended periods from work; but she is afraid of having nothing to do: "I say to myself, I've done quite a bit, maybe it's time for a change. On the other hand, I think . . . my mother's eighty-seven, given my mother's genes—twenty-seven years of what? I'm not looking just to fill my time . . . Not only have I amassed a great deal of information about my field now, I have an emotional commitment to what I'm doing . . . and I feel that I'm recognized . . . and that what I'm doing is valuable . . . I don't want to push a hospital cart around . . . Once in a while I wonder if I should take courses . . . I don't know if I could go back to a classroom and study and take exams and do papers. I don't know if I have the discipline."

Sometimes, Shirley thinks there is something "irresponsible" and undisciplined about volunteering: "In my more negative moments, my less self-assured moments, I sometimes wonder . . . if a lot of what I'm doing is avoiding accountability, responsibility . . . I'm not working for a paycheck . . . Whose measure of performance am I using, really—my own? I'm not taking an exam. I'm not in a hierarchy where I have to accede to other people's demands."

There has been a "good side" to this. "I can spit in anybody's eye. I'm not under control." She has her own work and doesn't have to worry about "other people doing or not doing . . . I'm only responsible for myself." She only wonders if she is responsible enough. There is something unsettling for her about not being graded. You have to always be on guard and challenging yourself:

"If I set my own goalposts in the game, then I can always win, and I've never put myself in the position where somebody else is measuring my goals . . . In a working situation you get promoted, you get a raise or you don't get a raise, you get a commendation or you don't get a commendation, you get to move to a better job . . ." These are all "measurements along the way of growth and achievement." How does she measure her own? "I have a coffeepot to thank me for being president . . . I have to say to myself . . . that my satisfaction is knowing that I helped change a law or that I have done things that have been of use to other people or that have made a difference and . . . that has to do the equal of my raise or promotion . . . I'm just wondering, if what I did were rotten, would somebody tell me not to come to work anymore?"

But it is hard for her to imagine how she could have pursued a paid career and given her children the care and attention they demanded and, she felt, deserved. She is concerned about the way young women "committed to careers will work out their lives to their own satisfaction" in their relationships with men and with their children. Her son's "girl friends" are all "very strong . . . feminist women," and she wonders about the forms their relationships will take. Her daughter is thirty years old, unmarried, and a writer in the public relations department of a New England university. She has "some very strong feelings about women's place and women's rights" and has had a harder time, in some ways, than her brothers. "She went through a great, deep, angry feminist period" and "whole bunches of twists and turns" about her work.

Volunteering was a major source of conflict between Shirley and her daughter for several years. "For a long time my volunteer work was an anathema to her. The usual thing—'You're taking somebody's place; you're being exploited, you're giving it away,' etc., etc., etc." Shirley "understands" her daughter's views, but she does not share them and still believes volunteering can be a good thing for some women. There is a group of young women in her community who do not work, "who are only shopping and playing tennis." They would be better off volunteering, at least. "There's a barrenness in their lives." Shirley is a "great believer" in having work to do. "The reason I'm as healthy as I am is that I have some place to go and something to do . . . I have things that I find very interesting and exciting . . . I've never suffered from an empty nest syndrome . . . I love it when my kids come visit. I love it when they leave."

BARBARA NOLAN

It took time for Barbara Nolan to get her children "out of the nest." She is in her early sixties now and has only recently gotten out the youngest. Barbara had four children in a fifteen-year period, with several miscarriages in between. For fifteen years, virtually all her time and energy were devoted to child-rearing, housekeeping, and helping out around the neighborhood. She has lived in the same town in Massachusetts for most of her married life and, like many women, has helped raise the "neighborhood kids" along with her own. She is eager to talk about volunteering; for better or worse it has been her way of life. Today she volunteers for the Audubon Society; she has chosen her work and she loves it; it has directed her in a life outside the home. But for many years volunteering was simply a part of being a woman at home with children; helping out was foisted on you, and it was not always easy:

"There's so much pressure on a woman . . . You were always required to give. A woman in the home is the giver. Anybody in the home . . . [And] if you raise children and are at home you become plugged in to using the time to help someone, and the easiest ones to help while you're watching your children are the people around your neighborhood. Or the church . . . It becomes a way of life and for my generation [it] was almost expected of you. [It was] the manner in which you utilized your talents."

Barbara accepts the choice she made for herself. She is both a lively and a thoughtful woman, so I believe her when she says she has not been unhappy in her marriage or with her family and that she was "not sorry not to work." They had very little money at first, but she never considered getting a paying job. "In those days, you didn't choose the same things," and besides, she simply didn't have time. It takes so much time and energy just to be around a two-year-old—"All the time." And she was doing all her own housework, even growing some of the family's food: "The women I knew, we did all our own work. Housework, cooking. We raised our own vegetables. I did all the canning. And all the laundry. So that everything was done at home. There was no money for anything else."

Money was a problem—not having enough of it and not having any of her own contributed to the "trapped feeling" that sometimes goes with being a housewife. She didn't have a car because she couldn't afford one; there was no getting away from the house, no "going off" in the car for a day and "getting a baby-sitter or something—that wasn't part of the picture . . . It's very difficult to go through the pressures and feelings of being a woman in the home and without money that she can control."

Talking about the difficult years at home doesn't depress Barbara or make her angry, and she does not suggest she should have done it any other way. That it was sometimes hard was simply a fact of her life—it was the way of things then—and when financial pressures on the family eased and the children "were busy with their own things," with her youngest in elementary school, Barbara "got out." "Once we got to the point where there was a little leeway in things . . . there was still a lot of pressure, but still I said, 'I've got to go out and do things. I've got to be alone. I've got to be able to be.' " Her husband supported her in this, she recalls gratefully. "At a time when he could have said, 'Well, you're supposed to be doing this [staying home],' he'd say, 'Can I help?' . . . He's perfectly willing to let me be myself." She didn't exactly ask his permission; she "insisted" on getting out of the house, but he "allowed" her to do it, she says—as if he were doing her a favor.

She did not go out and look for a paying job. Money was no longer a problem for them; she couldn't afford to be "frivolous," but they had enough; and she didn't need to be rich. What she needed was work of her own that had nothing to do with her family. Barbara began spending time at the local Audubon Sanctuary, taking courses, leading bird walks, meeting "a lot of nice people," and "being gradually drawn into Sanctuary work."

It was a natural, even inevitable choice for her. Barbara had spent much of her childhood on a farm in northern Maine and feels at home "outside . . . in the mountains and the lake country." She likes to just "wander" by herself, "with the things of nature around me, using my imagination." She began using it in her work at the Sanctuary, which evolved and became more specialized over the years. For the past fourteen years, she has been preparing and delivering her own lectures and slide shows for Audubon. She hopes they will help people "see . . . and really know . . . and treasure" their environment, so that they'll "want to save it."

"I've been accused of being a preacher . . . I can inspire people. I can stimulate people to be curious . . . to think beyond where they are . . . That's my gift." Barbara has always found it easy to "work with groups of people . . . to get up in front of groups of people and talk," and she often led programs and discussion groups at her church. She feels herself to be "full of ideas . . . nailing myself down is a really difficult thing . . . I nail myself down when I'm doing a new lecture, and that is

hard work." But she likes throwing out her ideas to people and
seeing "somebody grab one." She likes to talk to people who are
"searching."

Barbara sees herself as a sort of guide. She believes that she
has ESP—what she describes as "a sensitivity that gathers in
information that you're not consciously recording." It's like having "antennae," she says. Why or how it works is a bit of a
mystery, but she associates it with child-rearing: being at home
and caring for children nourishes a special kind of responsiveness and receptivity in women—or in men.

Her father had it. His antennae "went in all directions." He
was a Boston lawyer who raised four children by himself; his
wife died young, when Barbara was nine. He "devoted his
whole life" to his children and raised them "outdoors . . . with
a great deal of freedom." They spent vacation times together in
northern Maine, where Barbara was always doing something
"dangerous . . . like swimming a three-mile lake by myself"
and "Father" was "always up early in the morning, taking us on
hikes, even as little ones." He was "a very diverse person . . .
He knew plants and trees . . . He loved music. He loved literature . . . and the funny papers." He was not quite a superman;
there was a housekeeper to help out, but Barbara's father
shared in the household chores. He sewed: "if anything was
ripped, he'd sew it," and he was "a very good cook." There was
nothing feminine about domesticity: "never ever was [it] allo-
cated to the woman."

Barbara went to college, a small women's college in Massachusetts where she majored in math and took all the physics and
chemistry courses available. She then got a graduate degree in
engineering and went to work for Grummann Aircraft. It was
wartime, and there were engineering jobs open to women,
briefly. Barbara liked her work but only stayed with it for about
a year and a half. She was married, her husband was stationed in
Texas waiting to be shipped out to the Pacific, and she quit her
job to be with him. It is a decision she does not regret. "The
pressures of war were so different . . . A lot of people were
being killed . . . In those days, you didn't know whether you
were going to see somebody for three months and maybe never
again in their lives or whether . . . they were going to be

around for a couple of years . . . so there was a lot of pressure . . . You made what decision you thought was right."

Barbara liked engineering well enough, but she doesn't miss it: some of her engineering jobs were "a pain in the neck." She prefers the work she is doing today for Audubon, doesn't feel it is less "important" or satisfying because it is unpaid, and enjoys the freedom and flexibility of volunteering. Audubon has offered to pay her for her work—she not only delivers lectures for them but, for the past nine years, has been cataloguing their slide library. They offered her a full-time job several years ago, but she turned it down. "I said, 'Give me six weeks' vacation and a couple of weeks I can take on my own.' You know, nobody gets that when you work . . . I'm fortunate . . . we're comfortably off . . . I'm not looking to be rich. And I still do the vegetables . . . I still go up to Maine." There's a "comfortableness" to being a volunteer.

Volunteering has also given Barbara the opportunity to work for herself, according to her own inclinations, and to cultivate her talents. Her lectures are her own creations, and she has time to develop them. "I don't work fast . . . I think, I make notes— I have voluminous notes . . . I feel it takes me at least two and a half years to put together a new lecture." She has also become a photographer of the outdoors—"My camera is me talking"— and is beginning to write; she used to think of herself as a "mathematician, never able to write." But she has always written her lectures, and four years ago she put together a book of her photographs and writings. The book grew out of the lectures. "My lectures, I guess, are poems—tone poems."

Conservationists who have seen Barbara's book encourage her to find a publisher for it. It is a "new idea" for Barbara; she wrote without thoughts of publication. She likes her book: "I put it in a form that I thought was good," but she is not sure it is good enough or in the "right form" for a publisher. She is both modest about the book and content with it the way it is: "You know, I'm not afraid to have anybody tell me they don't like it. Maybe it's naïve. Maybe it's passé. Maybe it's elementary. That's all right. Because I wrote down what I wanted and what I felt at the time and it goes with the pictures."

Barbara knows what she has gotten out of her work and

doesn't defend volunteering to people who say, " 'You're still a volunteer' . . . It's as if, 'Oh, well, gee, you couldn't get a job; that's too bad.' " She doesn't explain or worry too much about what they think. "I wonder about recognition . . . Credit is a funny thing. I guess I don't trust it all that much. Cups and prizes, I mean. I see people who have worked so hard at just being whole or just learning some little thing they never learned before. You don't get credit for that."

Her mistrust of "credit" relates back, at least in part, to her experiences as a woman at home. Women often don't get credit for their work, and they can't afford to worry about it. It becomes a vicious cycle when you let it get to you. It undermines self-confidence and leads to "a feeling of being trapped":

"Women come out at the end saying . . . and I'm sure I've said it myself—you know, I've worked, raised kids, done all the housework, planned all the meals, not planned the money but presumably haven't wasted it all, and I can't do anything . . . So you go into volunteer work feeling that you really aren't worth anything financially. Now the world looks at you as dollars and cents. What can you do? I have no skill. My skill is having been able to cope with myself and my children. It's a human skill. And if I've coped with it at all I've done a whole lot of growing up that a whole lot of other people aren't doing."

It is, however, a frustrating process, because, Barbara says, you don't exercise enough control over the demands that come with having children and running a house. "I had no say over anything. You don't really control any situation. It's there and there are certain things that have to be done . . ." For the first time she suggests that, if something was gained in "human skills" from her years at home, something was also lost. She trails off when she talks about it; I think she has been circling it for years. "To throw somebody into a situation like that, from college, a good education, [with] a good mind—and you are submissive. You must be. You are submitting to—not the terror of children—my kids weren't a terror at all, but it is still a routine that is not yours. You have to do it . . . And you have to be loving and considerate and thoughtful . . . It is constant and it is demanding."

When Barbara went to work for Audubon as a lecturer, she

started using her own name, the one she was born with—Nolan is her name, not her husband's. She had to fight with Audubon to get them to use her name on their brochures, but it was worth it. The work she does is her own, not her husband's or her family's. She wanted it "identified directly" with her. It belongs to her—Barbara Nolan.

PIONEERS OF TRANSITION:
CHANGING THE RULES

I don't expect to find many married women, who do not work for money, working for free under their own names. Traditional volunteer jobs—in schools, churches, and community services —are housekeeping jobs. Women take them on precisely because they are married: they do not need to earn money, they have free time and a traditional obligation to use it to help their communities. Barbara Nolan volunteered for years for her church and community under her husband's name, because the work she was doing was only a part of being a woman at home. It didn't give her the emotional and intellectual independence from her family that she needed. It wasn't her own work; using her own name for it would not have helped.

The satisfaction and self-esteem that a woman derives from her volunteering may depend on whose work it is that she's doing. You can volunteer to do your own work—or to do someone else's, as someone's wife and mother. The difference is crucial to a homebound woman with children, like Barbara Nolan, who needs to work so that she can "be herself," or Dorothy Harnack, who was "never any good" at housework and never enjoyed it. Volunteering for the PTA because it was "part of being a parent" did not ease the depression that beset her during the early years of child-rearing or make her feel like anything but an incompetent housewife. Volunteering for a community arts league in an outside job that was not part of her job at home did.

The kind of volunteer work that does not simply relate back to a woman's role as wife and mother is also the only kind that develops professional skills and the professional style she may someday need to earn a living. Women who are used to being "nurturing people," whose volunteer work is only an "extension of their nurturing" never really grow up, suggests Beverly Selden, a former full-time volunteer for a parents' association, now the paid director of education for a national religious organization. Beverly "has problems with volunteerism" when she sees "individual women using it as a way to avoid coming to grips with life." A lot of women are "hiding" in volunteerism, she says, by "spending their time in jobs that are extensions of what they do all the time." Many of them are doing "some very good things," and they may be "happy and fulfilled" providing services and support for others; but they are getting "very little power" from their work and none of the skills that will enable them to take care of themselves if the time comes when they must.

"It's a tough world out there, in the working world. A lot of women my age, I'm fifty-two, we were not trained to go to work, we were trained to catch a good husband . . . The conditions of our marriages, in a sense, required dependency . . . Now most women unfortunately are not going to have the choice in the future . . . to work or not. More and more women are having to work either to supplement family income or because their husbands leave them or their husbands die . . . I'm not saying women should go to work . . . but use the volunteer experience to develop skills that you can attempt to translate."

Beverly spent fifteen years volunteering for the public school system. On one level she was, of course, working for her children, but in a professional, political capacity. She learned about the public educational system and the legislative process and acquired professional skills and confidence in a non-threatening environment: "I do a lot of speaking now . . . I will never forget the day I really messed up . . . I started a speech, knew it was going wrong, tried to adjust it, made it worse. It was a nightmare of a night . . . I was able by the next afternoon to tell people, 'Oh, I just really messed up.' I didn't have to go in and face my boss. There was not that kind of risk."

Volunteering was a kind of transition for Beverly. She was brought up one way, to be a dependent, domesticated, married woman, and changed midway through her life into a divorced (now remarried) paid professional. It was a slow and painful process; there is a line between a housewife and a professional woman that is difficult to cross and "a lot of friction" between the women on either side of it. "A lot of non-working women feel that working women look down on them, and I think that's true and that's one of the things we'll have to come to grips with over the years." When Beverly was volunteering, she always did "some kind of part-time work" just to bring in money, "even though we didn't need it. (I was married to a doctor) . . . I felt better that I could tell people I was doing something. I lived in a community with a lot of professional women. Betty Friedan was my next-door neighbor . . . I hated her. I thought she was terrible. I thought the book was nonsense and I realized later . . . it was just threatening . . . she was threatening everything I was brought up to be. ZZ1868.

"To change the rules is very hard," recalls Beverly. It was inevitable that the feminist movement would encounter considerable resistance from women like her who had devoted most of their adult lives to marriage and motherhood. If they had identified with the feminine mystique, they were bound to defend it, if only to defend the importance of what they had achieved at home. What they found threatening about feminism was that it challenged the traditional measures of women's worth, by which so many had agreed to measure themselves. Feminism introduced new goals and standards of achievement for middle-class women: success was no longer simply a matter of marrying well; women had to prove themselves in the paid professional world as well as at home and in their communities.

Those of us who were trained early on for professional life do not always appreciate just how hard it was for older women to accept the new rules and begin paid careers at forty-five or fifty, to support themselves after years of being supported by their husbands. It took courage and the willingness to challenge the

values and conventions that had shaped their lives. I imagine
that for many of them feminism was not so much a promise as a
kind of test.

What follows are interviews with three women who made the
change and entered the paid job market in mid-life, after the
onset of the feminist movement, after their children were
grown. Two of them entered it willingly, one because she had to
when something went wrong at home. All three had volunteered at demanding jobs that did not just duplicate their jobs at
home. They all had unpaid professional experience that prepared them for the "real world" of paid professional work.
Wives, mothers, and volunteers, now paid professionals—to me
they are women who changed the rules.

ZELDA GOLDSTEIN

Zelda Goldstein went to college when she was in her mid-
forties and the youngest of her three sons was entering high
school. She had spent the first twenty years of her marriage
raising kids, working part-time at a variety of clerical jobs, and
volunteering nearly full-time, primarily for a public school parents' association in New York City. She enjoyed her volunteering and believed it was important; as an advocate for the public
schools, she rose to leadership positions in her organization and
community. Still, the work came to a natural conclusion when
her sons were moving out of the system. She had always wanted
to go to college and, having gone, wanted to "do something"
with her degree. She wanted to get a "real" job, not just so that
she could "really earn money," but for the sake of the "standing" it would give her. She took volunteer work seriously, but
most of the "so-called real world people" didn't.

So, in her mid-forties, Zelda became a college-educated professional. She is now approaching sixty and, for the past fifteen
years, has been working for the New York City Board of Education. She is enthusiastic about her job: "I have a lot of responsibility, which I enjoy . . . I'm an officer of the Board. I supervise

a staff of about thirty people . . . I make a very good salary."
And she is enthusiastic about being interviewed: "I love talking
about myself."

Zelda was a highly visible and public volunteer. She has always been a "joiner," as well as a worker. It runs in the family.
"My mother always worked. She helped my father. They ran a
retail store and even though she always worked, she always
belonged to a couple of things. You had to belong to something
and you had to go to meetings. No matter how tired you were
when you got home at the end of the day, if it was your night for
a meeting, you went to it."

In her early married life, Zelda was active in a tenants' council in the Bronx. It was the late forties, and there was a severe
postwar housing shortage: "Tenants were in terrible straits . . .
and landlords were doing everything they could to make more
money." Women in the community took the lead in organizing
tenants' councils and handled most of the work. They knew
their neighbors, and it was their job to look out for their homes.
They called rent strikes, fought increases, and monitored housing violations. "Most of the basic work was done by women who,
theoretically, had the time."

Zelda's time was also filled by child-rearing and "all kinds of
part-time jobs." Working for money was something you did
along with volunteering. Her first job "goes back a very long
time" to when she was a sixteen-year-old, doubling as a waitress
and cashier in a coffee shop. She went on from there to become
one of the first women supermarket cashiers. "It was so unusual
that the union would not let me join because they didn't take
women in those days." They did as soon as the war started and
there was a sudden shortage of men to do the job: "They let the
women in and discovered they better make them join the union
. . . not keep us out." By then Zelda had left her job to marry
and raise children: Her husband hadn't wanted her to work. She
started again when he went into the service. She got a job as a
typist and worked full-time throughout the war, while her son
attended a nursery school for wives of servicemen. She continued working when her husband came home. "It was very hard
back then." Just making a living was a "terrible struggle." Her
husband was out of a job, it took time for him to find one and

time to accept the fact that his wife worked to support the family, that after three years of looking after herself and her son, she was no longer the "baby" he'd married:

"When he came home from the service, he found a totally new person from the one he left behind and we went through a rough period while we adjusted, so that he could get used to this new person . . . I remember him coming home, and Monday morning he said, 'What are you doing?' I said, 'I'm going to work.' He said, 'What do you mean you're going to work, I'm home.' So I said, 'What has that got to do with it?' 'But every other time when I came home, you didn't go to work.' I said, 'Sure, you came home for ten days. I would call up my job and say my husband is home on a ten-day leave and I would take a vacation. But you're home now. You're gonna be home. I have a job. They need me there.' He was absolutely unable to comprehend that. But he came to understand we needed the money and he was going to be home all the time now . . . so there was no need for me to give up my job. And he felt at that time that it was a threat to his manhood if he could not support me entirely. When we got married I had been working as a cashier and I stopped working because he was going to support me and I wouldn't have to do that anymore. And then I became pregnant after a few months and then he went off to the service. So he still thought he had to support me and that my going out and earning money was a threat. But after a while it was worse than a threat. It was a humiliation. Because I was earning money and he couldn't. He couldn't find work. It took him a long time. But he had to weather it because I could not turn myself back into what I was. I didn't like what I had been and I liked myself much better being independent and a true partner, and he just had to learn. I was going to be different."

Zelda kept on working when her husband found his work, and she kept on volunteering. Their struggles eased, they moved to a house in Queens, her sons started public school, and she became active in parents' groups, in her community and citywide. "You started out having little children and your oldest one in the second grade, so you spent a few hours here and there and on the telephone and you went to a couple of meetings and by the time all the children were in school . . . I had become involved in a citywide organization. I was president of one Parents' Association and I was delegate to the citywide group." Moving up within the organization was easy, even unavoidable for Zelda: she was recruited. People in volunteer leadership positions are "very astute": "If they see that you come and you open your mouth and have something intelligent to say, they immediately co-opt you into their organization, which was what happened to me." She became a board member citywide and chairperson of various committees, involved in investigating and reporting on conditions in the schools, lobbying for reforms and additional funds. She also did a "great deal" of public speaking, addressing parents in schools throughout the city. "I loved it, I was a born public speaker. I get up at the drop of a hat and speak in front of any number of people. I always enjoyed it."

Like the tenants' council, the parents' associations were primarily comprised of women, but it was sometimes hard to convince them to take on leadership roles in their own organization: "Some of the women felt they couldn't do as well if they didn't have men leading the group. We used to discuss that and say that we're just as capable. And the response would be 'We may be just as capable but does anyone listen to us because we're women.' In many schools they would elect a man to be president who would do absolutely nothing except . . . be the signature on the letter and sometimes they would actually get the man to lead the delegation to City Hall because they felt that a man would be listened to more." Zelda did not agree. "When it came to a PA . . . the women were so good, and women are accepted as leaders in PA's where they are not accepted as leaders in other things." It is hard for me to imagine someone not listening to Zelda and she agrees that, at least in a PA, women could always make themselves heard.

But it was hard work, and eventually she was putting in over forty volunteer hours a week—forty-seven, to be exact—including time spent in meetings and on the telephone at home. "Somebody did a study" and recorded her hours. They represented the major part, but not all, of her work week. She was still doing occasional clerical jobs on the side, to bring in extra money. Realizing how much time she was spending volunteer-

ing—and comparing the "high-level" work she was doing for
the PA to the "nothing office jobs" she did for money—convinced Zelda that it was time to go to college. With a college
degree she hoped to find a full-time paying job that would give
her the same "measure of satisfaction" that she derived from
volunteering. She was capable of being much more than a
clerk/typist.

"I felt if I can do all this and run my house and raise my
children, I really should be getting ready to go to work full-time
and earn money on a better level. And that was what really got
me to go to college . . . It was always in the back of my head.
But when I saw how many hours I was putting in (and I always
worked part-time) I said, 'I have to get into college so when I'm
finished with the PA . . . when my kids are out of school . . .
before I ever let myself get this busy in an organization I'm
going to get a college degree and go to work. It will be time to
get out there in the real work world.' "

Getting out there in her mid-forties was harder than she'd
expected. She had hoped to get away from the kind of work
she'd been doing as a volunteer: "I had a clear idea I didn't want
to have anything to do with schools and parents' associations."
But public education was, after all, her field, and it was only
through her volunteer work that Zelda was able to get a decent
job—with the Board of Education:

"When I tried getting a job in business, the first question I was
asked was 'What was your last job and what was your last salary?' And I said, 'It's not relevant.' I wouldn't tell them. I said
my last job was not a job and my last salary was not a salary. I
now have a degree and I have a lot of experience. I'm not a
twenty-year-old college graduate. I'm in my forties. I'm mature
and I have done a great many things. I ran a luncheon with
three thousand people and spoke before them with the mayor
sitting on one side of me and the state comptroller on the other.
When you do something like that, you have certain skills. You're
not going to tell them your last salary was at the minimum wage
doing some stupid typing. And I couldn't get anyplace. Agencies would say, 'Well, they always want to know what your last
job and what your last salary was. And if you're just a beginner
starting out with a college degree, then you start out as a begin-

ner.' 'But I'm not a beginner.' It was very difficult. I couldn't get past the low-level personnel person who knew one tenth of what I knew, except she knew she had to ask what your last job and what your last salary was and if you wouldn't tell her that, then you had to start out as an entry-level person. And I just wasn't gonna do it. I didn't go to college to start out as an entry-level person . . . So when I was offered a job at the Board of Education . . . I took it . . . and I've been here for fifteen years and I've worked my way up very nicely."

Zelda has thoroughly enjoyed her mid-life career change, but, in the beginning, it was hard on her husband. Being married to a college woman was something else he hadn't bargained for; it was confusing at first and a little threatening:

"My husband thought he was very cooperative. Every time I was getting ready for finals or writing term papers, he would always have very important household things or things connected with his business that I helped him with that had to be done the same time. It was very interesting timing. To this day he doesn't recall it or understand why I should have been conflicted. He was sure he wasn't doing it . . . He was very proud of me. He bragged to everybody he could about how I was going to college and I was doing so well."

His behavior was typical of a lot of husbands—and wives—of students in Zelda's adult education program: "I was going to school with other people my age . . . and everybody had similar kinds of problems. A lot of women ended up getting divorces, in school or right after school, and a lot of men came and complained to the dean that these courses were breaking up their families. And the dean's response was—'The family *was* broken up. It's just that your wife didn't know enough to leave or have the guts to leave. But now that she sees that she's going to be able to make a living, she's going in for a career, she's not so afraid. Can't blame it on us. It would have happened anyway' . . . As for the men that were in the program—some of them were there because their careers were ending, businesses going bad, and maybe [they] were training for careers they were not able to pursue when they were younger. Some of them were having trouble with their wives, because the wives were afraid this was going to mean that 'You're going to be a different person and discard me or you're not gonna find a job and we're gonna starve.' There were all kinds of problems."

Zelda and her husband worked it out. He had weathered a similar change once before when he came back from the war, and he had no choice but to weather it again. For Zelda and the women in her classes, college was "a completion of a woman's life that we did not have time to complete before, and if the husbands couldn't roll with it, then that was too bad because there was such a strong need.

"I was going to be different now and he could see that I was and I could see that I was. It was a deliberate change that I was making. I'd say, 'It doesn't mean that I'm leaving you behind. It's nothing. This is me. If we want to get along, we'll get along.' And now he is totally retired. He loves having me work and bring home lots of money. He thinks it is a great thing. He really enjoys it. So that he has grown a great deal too, with me. I was changing my life; he had to change his approaches to his life and he did it very well."

He may have to do it again. Zelda is thinking about going to law school. She wants a law degree so that when she retires from the Board of Education she can do "more interesting things as a volunteer." Maybe she'll be able to earn some money as a lawyer, "here and there," given the contacts she has made on her job at the Board. But Zelda knows she will probably never find another full-time paying job "as good" as the one she has now. Law is "a very crowded field," and she can't compete in it with twenty-five-year-olds. But in a few years she will be ready to retire from her job and, because she is a "long-range planner," Zelda is preparing for a third career as a volunteer. Law school will, at least, be interesting: "It will have been an intellectual experience that won't have hurt me one bit . . . I don't delude myself that they're waiting out there to hire me as a lawyer . . . I know that I'm not going to do it to have a better career, [but] to have a *different* career, as a salaried person or as a volunteer."

Paid work has been good for Zelda, and so has volunteering. Each has had its time and place: "When I was being a volunteer, I preferred being a volunteer. I did not feel that while my children were of a certain age I wanted to be committed to a job. Because if I had a job, I knew it would have to be a job where I would get responsibility. I would take it—and then you have an obligation. No matter how much I did at the Parents' Association, I always felt that being a volunteer I had no problem with going up and saying, 'I have a kid with fever and I'm not doing anything today.'

"I think it's good for people to do volunteer work. I think it's especially good for women . . . if they are not ready or able to go to work. I think it's good for them because it keeps them from forgetting that they have ability.

"When you start out in a marriage where you aren't expected to work or don't immediately have to have a full-time job for financial reasons and you have no career already . . . I didn't have any career. I had gone to high school . . . I didn't have any business skills, except typing . . . You don't have any skills, you don't know what you want to be. And then you get married and have children and you're there. But when you have the need to work, whether it's working for money . . . I think you're working because you need the satisfaction of knowing that you can do more. You need to do more. You're not getting enough satisfaction out of the household and the child-rearing. And you feel that there's a need for you in the community. There's a need for you someplace and you want to meet that need. And the need is your own need to be useful in the world. I think that really is what drives women into volunteer work, their own need."

PEARL LEHMAN

Volunteering was enough for Pearl Lehman for thirty years. She had worked her way up to national leadership positions in a major women's voluntary association. Her husband made a lot of money practicing law, there was no financial need for her to "go to work," and she simply never saw herself earning money, functioning "in the world of producing, in the commercial way."

Then the rules changed, overnight, eight years ago, and Pearl had to change with them to survive. Her husband was convicted of fee stealing in a highly publicized case. He was disgraced and disbarred and was suddenly unable to support the family in the lavish style to which they'd become accustomed. For Pearl it was a "bombshell" that blew apart her volunteer career along with everything else. She lost not only her financial security but her social and professional standing as well. Her husband brought his wife down with him. She had been in line for the national presidency of her organization and was passed over because of the notoriety surrounding his case. Pearl is still angry about this because it was done by a women's organization that was supposed "to fight for the rights of women . . . And they were saying to me after thirty years of work—and it was Pearl Lehman who did the work—they said to me I was really Mrs. Mark Lehman." (Perhaps there was some sort of perverse justice in this. She had shared in his wealth and the benefits of his name for thirty years; she would share in his downfall.) In her mid-fifties, Pearl was forced into the job market for the first time.

She had never held a paying job, never even written a résumé, and looking for work through employment agencies was a depressing process. They had no use for her volunteer experience; she was out of her element and quickly discouraged. "I found it too upsetting to say to myself, 'I really can't do anything.' " She stopped going to agencies, turned to contacts she had made while volunteering, and got an administrative job in a small New York museum. They were only looking for a part-time person when she interviewed for the job. Pearl wanted to work full-time, so she offered to do so at half-salary. After thirty years of volunteering, she had a few lessons to learn about the working world. "I said, 'Look, I don't care how much I get paid.' And I've regretted that ever since, because for the [last] seven years I've been bound with what I started with." But she likes her job; she has been promoted and her responsibilities have been expanded. She likes having her own salary and, for the first time, her own bank accounts. "It's given me a greater sense of independence." If she wants to buy something, she can say to her husband, "I'm going to pay for that; I don't care if you like it or not." Now, she says, "I have my own savings account. I have my own checking account. I have a different approach . . . and I feel more confident."

For most of her married life, Pearl spent her husband's money without knowing how it was made or managed: "I never wanted to have anything to do with any money decisions. I deferred everything [to him] . . . I never knew what stocks we owned. I never knew where his investment accounts were . . . Every so often I'd say to him, 'You know, I don't even know if you have any insurance . . . You're going on all these trips. I don't even know where there's a piece of paper. I don't know anything.' And he'd say to me, 'Why do you have to know? My secretary knows.' And I would resent it, but that's what I was told."

While she stayed away from financial decisions at home, she was immersed in them at work, as a volunteer. Pearl was national treasurer of her organization. People deferred to her there. She was an officer of the board and she had been trained as a lawyer.

She had never practiced, although she had graduated from law school and been admitted to the bar. She was engaged in her second year of school, married in her third: "It never entered my mind to work . . . I was never motivated to. I think I went to law school because it was keeping me in an atmosphere that I liked and I was doing something that I enjoyed and I had the luxury to be able to do it. And I don't think that I ever made a conscious decision that I never would work . . . but I never was tempted."

People think of her as a pioneer when they hear she went to law school in the 1940s. She wasn't one at all. "I didn't do it for the reasons that people think I did it. People say, 'My God, you were a path setter.' I never thought of myself as doing something . . . I really had no idea what I wanted to do when I got out of college in 1939. I knew what I didn't want to do. I didn't want to be a teacher . . . So the question was what do you do. And I was very fortunate because I came from a family able to continue to let me go to school, if that's what I wanted to do."

Her father was a lawyer and he encouraged her, up to a point: "He thought it was great . . . to go to law school, if that's what

I wanted to do, but he didn't think I should even apply to places like Harvard or Columbia, because why did I want to put that kind of energy and go into that kind of competition. I should go to a law school . . . I could handle very nicely . . . So I went to NYU . . . My father was just like all the others. Because really what you're supposed to do is to get married and you should have time so you can meet men. And in fact one of the reasons he thought it was great that I go into the academic world was that that's where you would meet people. So I was there for all the reasons that are not the ones you would think. [My father] was encouraging me to do these things for all the reasons that everybody else's parents were encouraging them not to."

She has always used her legal education as a volunteer, in organizational work. It shapes "the way you approach problems" and enhances your credibility: "It makes it easier to make your point when you're in the minority—you can set forth an argument in a lawyerly way and people remember you're a lawyer, so it helps." If you are going to volunteer within an organization, it is important to be one of the "tiny" number of women at the top, on the national level. Otherwise, "you don't really get the experience . . . never really get past the decision of whether it should be chicken salad or tuna fish." Pearl "put her mind to it," came up "right through the ranks," took her volunteering seriously and "treated it like a job." It gave her a profession. She had no need to practice law and good reason not to: she did not want to compete with her husband:

"I used to say one lawyer in the family is enough. And think how terrible it would be if I became more successful than he was. I could never handle that and I don't know who could . . . I know deep down that wasn't only humor." (Not that she ever could have been as good as he was, she assures me—he may have ended his career a convicted felon, but she will not presume to suggest she might have done better.) "I don't mean I really thought I was going to be more successful, that part was humor. The part that wasn't humor, I still do not think marriages necessarily work well, when women are working."

Pearl is hesitant about suggesting this. She knows it may not be an immutable fact of life; it is just that she can't help believing it—"I guess because of my background." And, she says, she has seen young marriages founder because of career conflicts, when a wife won't leave her job to follow her husband or when she surpasses him professionally. It may not be fair for a woman to have to defer to her husband she admits,—"I don't know how anybody determines who has more right as far as their capabilities . . ." But Pearl can't quite let go of the belief that it is somehow more fitting for a man to take the lead professionally, to get "first crack" at a career. It has always been an article of faith for her: "One plays up to a man and the man is the breadwinner in the family."

It was "very difficult" for Pearl to go to work when her husband's career had ended. He was home all the time, depressed, worrying about whether or not he'd end up in jail (he didn't), and she felt guilty about going off in the morning, leaving him behind.

"It was very upsetting for me to go . . . I did it because I had to. I had made a commitment." She kept on working and she handled it, apparently better than he did. "I got mad at him for making me feel guilty . . . I was very mad because he wasn't going out and doing anything . . . In those years when he was sitting home, I said to him, 'Well, okay, you can't go out and get a job,' 'cause he felt who would hire him if they didn't know if he was going to jail or not. But I would say, 'So go be a volunteer. It's the greatest thing in the world . . .' And he wouldn't do it."

Eventually he went into business, and Pearl went to work without feeling guilty. She never quite resolved the problem of working while her husband stayed home. It made her uncomfortable. She had never questioned the notion that a woman's work must always come second to her husband's.

Still, Pearl has changed her mind about a lot of things because of "what happened," and she suspects that she'd be making different choices for herself if she were starting out today. "I think now a woman would really have to analyze herself if she decided she wasn't going to do something. I think she'd have a terrible time justifying it in her own mind." Women were not so analytic in her time, she says. "I don't think we were conscious." Because of her background, she never considered going to work, never considered herself a professional. "I never had the self-image that would let me go out and be motivated to go to work. I think that women who really strive have a great self-image and I'm not sure I have that. That's where I was a product of my time."

It is clear that today she would, as she suggests, "handle it much differently." Pearl has always needed to work; she volunteered because, given her family life and the way she had been socialized, volunteering looked like her only option: "I couldn't stand being home seven days a week . . . I really don't like home life. I don't cook. I don't know how to wash a floor. I don't like little children. I would go out of my mind . . . Your mind will go stagnant if you stay at home . . . I wasn't going to work, so what do you do? You become a volunteer."

She was content to volunteer for thirty years and, looking back after all that has happened, she does not regret her choice. Although in recent years Pearl had begun to question the "truths" about men and women by which she was raised, they are deeply ingrained. She knows there may be other truths for other people, but she is "comfortable" with the notion that a man should come first, as head of the family, that he should make more money than his wife. At heart she is still a believer and accepts herself as a product of her time.

Perhaps she's made the best of it. Pearl's life was changed for her at fifty-six; she adjusted—and even changed a few of her ideas. Perhaps it is enough. If all that she was taught and has always honored about a woman's proper place was rotten and wrong, at this point in her life she would rather not know about it. Should a woman always defer to a man? She can only answer with stories about husbands who have "suffered" from their wives' "strong determination to get ahead." Maybe this isn't the way it ought to be, but it seems to Pearl to be the way it is. Must a woman sacrifice her work to a man at the altar? She is suspicious of her own instinct to say yes, and so avoids the question: "I don't think I can answer in theory, because, in theory, I don't think I would ever be serious enough or face the issue enough . . . I guess I just refuse to face it."

SYLVIA MALLOW

Women are still "confused" about their status and their roles, says Sylvia Mallow. "I think there's still a lot of conflict amongst women . . . about whether they plan to support themselves for the rest of their lives or whether they plan to be supported." Perhaps volunteering is bad for women who work for free because they can't imagine earning money. It has not been bad for Sylvia because, for some reason, she has always been able to imagine doing both.

She has enjoyed four careers in the past thirty-five years and raised three children. Now, in her early sixties, she is the full-time, paid director of a private, nonprofit youth service agency. Before that she was the full-time, paid director of her local Planned Parenthood chapter. Before that she was a full-time volunteer, in politics and the arts. Before that, she was a nurse:

"I went to college and I got out of college and decided I didn't know exactly what to do and some friend of mine said, 'why don't you go into nurse's training with me.' And because I was so stupid at that time, I went with my bachelor's degree into a hospital training program for another three years. I could have gone to med school or I could have gone to get a master's. But I didn't do any of those. I went to the hospital. So I was not really in the right niche."

Her sense of being misplaced professionally was heightened by the fact that nurses were so "labeled" by their work. You wore a white uniform and it typecast you as "a Nurse":

"Inside I always felt I was playing a little game: 'They think I'm a nurse, they think I know what to do if somebody falls on the ground, they think . . . and I know I'm just Sylvia.' When I was working in a hospital situation I knew I was capable of doing what I had to do . . . But it was riding in the subway and kind of assessing the way people would look at you and they would think things about you and gave you labels."

You also give yourself labels, based not so much on what you wear but on what you do. When she was a nurse, Sylvia thought of herself as a "science person": "My experience, my training, my work was all nursing and very scientifically oriented. I was married to an engineer and we had that kind of relationship where we were both science people"—until she left nursing, moved from New York to a house in Hartford, began having babies, and volunteering at a community arts center. Suddenly, Sylvia was someone "who was always into the arts . . . Volunteering changed my life very radically.

"Although I was an enthusiastic voyeur of the arts, it was peripheral . . . I never thought of that as my field. When I moved to Hartford I met a group of women who were also transplanted to this community, and many of them had very strong backgrounds in the arts. And they were part of a committee of a Jewish community center which was the arts committee, and because of my association with them, I became involved in that . . . It was a very special kind of experience, because the woman who had originated that committee was a very unusual artist and a marvelous teacher and started a school for the arts, and she brought in very exciting people to work in various kinds of art—painting, dance, music . . . and she was the chair of that committee, and it was an exposure to the kind of people I would never have met in my other kinds of work. And she really turned me on, and that work turned me on . . . I volunteered there for several years and eventually became chairperson of that committee.

"What we were trying to do was bring art things to this community, which was very barren at that time. There were no galleries, there had been a theater, this was like a Shubert tryout city, but that was it. And that was sort of dying out. So there was no theater and there was no dance; there was music . . . but very little other art, and this group tried to bring things so that they would fill the void in the community. And they did. At that time off-Broadway theater was just burgeoning (it was the early fifties) and it was not terribly expensive and we were able to bring in lots of things. We'd run a theater series and have art shows and organize all those things, really booking, but it was more than booking because there was production that had to be done to have these things on stage. So we were able to get fantastic kinds of things for this type of city in that era. Like bringing in Genet's *The Blacks* in the fifties, where they said 'fuck' on stage and half the theater walked out. But we were able to get Al Pacino when he was a youngster just out of drama school doing *The Indian Loves the Bronx* . . . We were able to get the Living Theater; you know what the Living Theater was like, filthy dirty people that came and did this fantastic theatrical thing. And we were able to develop an audience that would buy into it; it was the most exciting thing in the world."

It was exciting for her entire family:

"My husband was involved in the technical aspect . . . He would help us stage the show, he would hang the lights, do that sort of thing. He enjoyed being part of the theater 'in' crowd . . . Sometimes I sit in wonderment about three of our children who are all into the arts and realize it had to be that influence in there that was much stronger in their growing years than my whole academic training."

Perhaps it was because Sylvia felt more like herself volunteering for the arts than she ever had as a nurse and was more "turned on" by her work:

"I learned as chairperson that I was great speaking in front of large groups; that was a turn-on for me, that I could get up in front of large groups, in front of a television camera with not the least qualm, and I gave up the vanity—because everytime I saw myself I went, 'Oh God, that's horrible,' but I was able to get past that to realize that I could really be comfortable talking on my feet, you know, off the top, and it was a surprise, I didn't know that. I'd never had that experience before. It felt very nice having a title. It was the first time that I really felt I was my title."

Volunteering wasn't nearly as limited as nursing for Sylvia. You didn't wear a uniform, you didn't have a rigidly defined scope of employment, you could create your own job and even change your professional field. After twelve or thirteen years of volunteering for the arts committee, Sylvia began volunteering "in political things," in the early sixties:

"That was more in keeping with what my life had been like prior to that time. As a youngster in New York I was part of all kinds of protests . . . So I did have exposure to political activity

. . . I went to Hunter College, which was a very politically active school . . . I was with people who were much more into the radical movement than I was . . . I was always on the fringe . . . But I associated with them and I learned a lot about that, and I read, and that was something important to me. So that back here in Hartford becoming involved in political activity was much more something that you could have expected that I would do when I had the time to do it.

"I became involved with a group of people in West Hartford . . . and we initiated this program that's still going today . . . which bused kids from Hartford to the suburbs to a better school. It was fascinating to me because there again I was working with someone who was much more sophisticated than I in that whole movement. I mean I participated but I certainly didn't strategize, and I saw that whole process of being manipulated and how people could be moved into certain things, and the process of doing it fascinated me, and I loved it. And again by that time I already knew that I could speak easily, so I could go speak to groups and make statements, and that was easy and I enjoyed that very much and I worked with those people through the whole Eugene McCarthy period. I was the coordinator for the student volunteers."

At the same time, she was working part-time as a nurse at a local hospital. Nursing had not been the perfect profession but it was good enough to fall back on when her children were teenagers and she was ready to take on at least a part-time job. She took a refresher course offered by one of the hospitals in town and went to work as a part-time pediatrics staff nurse. This job led into a new field, family planning, and a new career:

"I was involved with many families where there were many children and where parents seemed to be having difficulties raising their children because they couldn't deal with their health care . . . Also at that time, one of my closest friends had gone into family planning work and sexuality and education, and that intrigued me and I was thinking, well, what am I gonna do next step when I really want to work full-time and in a more responsible position than a staff nurse, and I decided I would take some courses in sexuality and try and get a job teaching.

"I took those courses . . . and I started looking for work,

hopefully in a school system. And my daughter went through the paper one day and said, 'Look, they're looking for a director of Planned Parenthood,' and I knew people who were on the board so I called them up . . . and it seemed like my skills were just ideal for the job, so I walked in and got the job."

It was a major and very deliberate change for her:

"My big decision at that time, I remember deliberating about it, was whether I wanted to go back to work full-time or not. That seemed like making a very definite statement that I would no longer have the time to do any of the volunteer work that I had enjoyed. And I remember deliberating about that with my husband and he was very encouraging for me to do whatever I wanted to do. I could go either way as far as he was concerned . . . It was the first time in my life that I could sit back and see myself making a decision."

Volunteering had been more of a reflex: "I felt I didn't want to work when my children were young. I did enjoy being at home. I didn't feel the need for money . . . I also enjoyed being taken care of and not working, you know, that was nice. And I also enjoyed many of the housekeeping kinds of things that I really invested in a great deal—I loved entertaining, I loved cooking . . . I enjoyed those kinds of things. I always made a big fuss about some of the aspects of mothering, you know, the children's parties were very creative, with the hamburger train that runs [through] the kitchen, you know, all kinds of things that would come to me . . . So I did that . . . I don't know whether I actively considered my options. I don't think for most of my life I considered options. I assumed certain patterns because they were most common."

In some ways, going back to work full-time was following another pattern. It was 1969: "Times had changed and it became more common . . . You know, like a sheep, I always followed the general pattern . . . My children were older and seemed to need me less . . . I think I wanted extra money . . . I did want something more interesting, more of a feeling of responsibility, and that's why I went from part-time work to full-time work, 'cause there's no way of finding that kind of job satisfaction in part-time work in my field . . . I think maybe I also had had my fill . . . I'd gone through two different kinds of volunteer work and had achieved a degree of success. I had achieved the things I wanted to achieve." It was time to take her achievements and her skills and go to work for money.

The skills that made her the "ideal" choice for the job at Planned Parenthood included those she had developed volunteering. Sylvia was suited to the job, she says, not because of her "documented qualifications" ("I didn't have a master's degree at that time") but because of her "background." She knew how to stand up in front of a TV camera and talk; she knew how to lobby and work with community groups. She used these skills to redefine the job of director at Planned Parenthood and to expand the activities of her chapter:

"I saw my role as being an educational one, lobbying, educating the community, paving the way for education of kids and adults in sexuality . . . there was a lot of work to be done . . . It was a very small and loosely organized group at the time, the board was not that sophisticated, so that I had to take that responsibility, or maybe I wanted to, I'm not sure which . . . You know, I could have sat back and let them do medical things. It's interesting, but I moved away from that medical component myself.

"I loved it. I just loved it . . . I was a very important person. I was on television all the time. People came to my house and took pictures, you know. I could call up any television program and say I want to go on a talk show or I want to go on a hot line. And, you know, I was very public. And people would see me on the street and say, 'I saw you on television.' I'd walk into a store and everybody knew who I was . . . I think that my husband enjoyed the prestige. I made lots and lots of friends in very different kinds of circles, and he enjoyed that. In some circles, he was like Mr. Sylvia Mallow, but that didn't seem to bother him.

"The only part I didn't like was—if I could have been more fashionable . . . or been more beautiful in my perception, in what I looked like on those television programs or newspaper pictures. But I realized that I came across as being so comfortable that it really overcame some of that for me . . . It really looked as though I was having a good time. So I kind of forgot about that other stuff.

"It was not only that it was a paid job, it was the kind of paid job that it was that made me feel very significant. I liked it. I loved it." It was a little like being chair of the arts committee, only better, because it was paid and more prestigious. And, like a volunteer job, Sylvia's job at Planned Parenthood was one she had created for herself:

"I had really created it all. I had developed that position, I had been around. I had enough seniority. I had all that history in my head and I could deal with it all very casually and was comfortable in controversial subjects, about how I had to say things so that I never goofed or got into trouble . . . I felt very sure of my knowledge and very sure of my position."

Her experiences as a professional volunteer also gave Sylvia ideas about using volunteers at Planned Parenthood. One of her more notable achievements as director, she says, was to upgrade their status in the agency and put them to work:

"One of the things I felt very strongly about was that volunteers and paid staff were just staff . . . and that volunteers had to have training . . . and that they should be integrated into the program and that they had obligations and responsibilities. You couldn't do it on a casual basis. You really had to make a strong commitment. We had all kinds of guidelines for training and contracts that we initiated . . . We wanted a commitment of so many months. They had to find their own replacements . . . They had an obligation to take so much training . . . All kinds of things that sort of paralleled a contract for an employee . . . So the standards [for volunteers] were strict . . . we either rejected them or steered them into jobs where they would not be working at a level where they couldn't perform . . . and I think that also made jobs more important and it gave a lot of job satisfaction . . . Many of our volunteers went through our training and then went out and got the academic certification to do the things they had been doing, MSW, law school, counseling degrees . . . We did become a model in the state for the way you dealt with volunteers. In our agency, always, I talked about staff, paid and unpaid staff. We never talked about volunteers.

"Where people worked side by side and they were not supervising each other, I think there was excellent rapport between

the paid and unpaid staff. And a lot of consciousness raising
because some of the unpaid staff . . . had master's degrees in
something and they were working with people who had an
equivalency sometimes of a high school diploma. And, you
know, the ones who were on paid staff had more experience and
knew more about the clinics than the others. So that was a
wonderful relationship. And I think they learned from each
other."

Sylvia stayed at Planned Parenthood for about twelve years;
she left about two years ago. "When I left there, it was a surprise
to me, too. What happened was that I was thinking of different
moves that I might make and this again sort of fell into my lap."
"This" is her present job as paid director of a youth service
agency. "Somebody I knew was on the board and said to me,
'We don't have a director and we're interviewing . . .' So I
applied.

"This agency does various kinds of things, outreach, traditional counseling, groups, support groups; it has a runaway shelter for youth . . . volunteer training, peer education, job bank
. . . It has this 'Looking in Theater Company,' which is vi-
gnettes about youth concerns that I actually started at Planned
Parenthood and brought with me . . . with its funding." Sylvia
has a full-time paid staff of about fourteen people and, in any
given week, needs about twenty volunteers to staff the shelter
for runaways, which is open twenty-four hours a day—"They
come in for two-hour shifts, up to midnight."

She has some "conflicts" about using volunteers to do the
same jobs as paid staffers: "I understand that whole feminist
perspective that if you continue to give it away for nothing, you
don't get money for it . . . On the other hand, I'm not in
agreement that all the measure of our worth is money. And I
think that's the big conflict . . . that the measure of
somebody's worth is their income.

"I guess that's what I was trying to say in Planned Parenthood. I knew enough about nurses to know that people who had
lots of training were lacking in certain kinds of things that I
thought were important for working in that clinic, and they
could have gone through a whole nurse's training thing and
come out and be inappropriate for working there. Whereas

others who never had any nurse's training could work in the clinic very comfortably . . . And I feel the same way about this . . . There are some people who come out of that School for Social Work and who are horrible with people, and others who have been doing it all their lives without ever getting academic certification for it."

Sylvia is still leery of labels. She is a science person, an arts person, a volunteer, and a paid professional. Everything she has done in the past "adds up" and informs what she does in the present. When she turned sixty, she was still trying to figure out what to do next, when she "grows up." Not that she feels like a child, but that there is always time to change and try something new. It amuses her that others see her as an older, even elderly woman. She feels like she is "putting something over" on them:

"I'm aware that I'm working in a field where most of the people are half my age . . . I walk into a room and they think that I'm a middle-aged or senior citizen and they don't know that I'm not. Because inside me is one age, with all the experiences you add on to it. The perception of myself is not in terms of years. It's that kind of thing, you know, that when they look at you they think one thing, and you know inside that's so funny."

IN TRANSITION:
FROM VOLUNTEERING TO THE
PAID WORKPLACE

Changing the way others see them and the way they see themselves must have been especially hard for the next generation of women, those who came of age in the 1950s. They were defined exclusively by their sex, conditioned to conform to rigid sexual stereotypes, from the beginning. The sorrows and hardships of war notwithstanding, there were some advantages to being a young woman in the 1940s. Opportunities for women were expanded, briefly: Law schools suddenly had "plenty of room" for them, business and industry needed their services, and as long as their husbands were at war they could not be stigmatized for earning money. Zelda Goldstein probably had more freedom to grow up during the three years her husband spent in the service than she would have had as a young woman ten or fifteen years later. That a woman would want to work for money and deviate from the path of marriage and full-time motherhood, out of choice and not necessity, was practically unthinkable in the fifties. "Of course, some college women never marry," said one woman's writer, Marguerite Wykoff Zapolean, in 1956. "Many circumstances can interfere with marriage, notably wars, depression, and illnesses."†

I have always been grateful that I was born too late for the 1950s, just in time to pass through my teens in the sixties. I was ten years old in 1959; looking back, it seems like a narrow escape. The ideal middle-class woman starting out in the 1950s, with or without a college degree, was tracked directly into marriage; only an Act of God—war, depression, or illness— could derail her. She never had the chance to test herself out-side the home when she was young, except perhaps through volunteering: It wasn't the chance her husband had, to "build the kind of career that starts at twenty-one and is lifetime," but it released her from the deadening routine of domesticity. It gave her something else to do and something else to think about.

The next interviews are with two of these women. Now in their middle to late forties, they have each spent nearly twenty years caring for their families and volunteering; one has also worked at part-time paying jobs. With their children grown, both are now in the midst of a decision about what to do for themselves professionally, a decision neither had the opportunity to make as a college girl in the 1950s. For women of their class and generation, the transition from motherhood and volunteering to a full-time professional career seems to me to have a special poignancy.

† Marguerite Wykoff Zapolean, *The College Girl Looks Ahead*, New York, 1956, p. 14.

CHARLOTTE ANDREWS

"I married and came of age before the Women's Movement
. . . in the 1950s," says Charlotte Andrews. "Work yourself
back into that mind-set . . . the only acceptable option was to
marry, because a woman who did not was going to be regarded
as either a tramp or an old maid . . . The jobs that were open
to women in the fifties and the kind of work that you did if you
worked was not what you would have done had you gone to
professional school and been a lawyer or a doctor or a professional . . . When you say, did you miss work—most of what my
generation did in the way of working was not to be missed,
particularly."

Charlotte married relatively late for her generation, at
twenty-four, after college and one year of graduate school—she
has a master's in English—and after two years of work as an
editor for a university press. Now in her late forties, she has
three children, one in college, and a husband of twenty years
who has always supported the family by himself. He has been
practicing law, as a partner in a Connecticut law firm. She has
been raising their children, and volunteering for the PTA, the
League of Women Voters, and on the boards of various social
service and community agencies. She is a studious woman who
is also "always doing a lot of little stuff" of her own on the side,
like writing poetry or teaching herself New Testament Greek.
Charlotte knows that in another life she might have been a
college professor, a lawyer, or a minister—her ambition now is
to go to Yale Divinity School. She is acutely aware that hers, so
far, has been a "very conventional Second Sex life."

She has survived, and "somehow got past worrying about it or
feeling defeated by it or feeling sold or taken." There were
times when she felt frustrated and "unfulfilled . . . all that
stuff," particularly in her thirties, but looking back now, "somewhat dispassionately," she describes her life over the past
twenty years as an inevitable and not unhappy compromise.

Women were tracked into marriage by social pressures and the lack of professional opportunities; family life required certain sacrifices of them that Charlotte is not, on balance, sorry to have made. It seems to her that it could not have happened any other way:

"As a married woman of my generation you were absorbed into this other life, and I can say now that you've given up a lifetime in a sense . . . You gave up a career . . . the kind of career that starts at twenty-one and is lifetime . . . I did not have that, and I will never have it, and I gave it up and I regret it. But I'm glad as long as I had children that I did it that way . . . As I look back on it, I don't regret it for the children, as long as I had children. And I don't regret that I had children. It is an extremely interesting experience."

It was at least as interesting as the kinds of jobs that were open to her as a young woman in the late fifties. Charlotte had what was considered a "good job," as an editor, but it was not particularly satisfying: "It was not . . . what I would have done, myself, if I'd done something myself." She can't be sure today what she would have done or become—there was never the chance to find out—and, looking back, Charlotte can only see other people's "prescriptions" for her and social conventions she might have followed in choosing a profession.

When she was in college, her "perception" was that "if I had been a man, I would have gone to law school." It is "interesting," she adds, that "the first thing that happened to me was that I started going with someone in law school, to whom I'm married, and I quickly became aware that I would not have been suited [to law], that I would have had a lot of trouble with it." It is interesting to me that, at twenty-one, she imagined what she might have become had she only been a man, without feeling cheated or angry about her status as a woman. It wasn't like that then, she says; it didn't occur to you to get angry.

The other prescription—to be a college professor—was much closer to her heart and came from her mother, who had received a doctorate in English from Yale in the 1920s and headed the English department of a small midwestern college. She had been widowed young and raised two children, Charlotte and her sister, by herself, with the help of Charlotte's grandmother:

"Had I satisfied my mother's goals, she had two . . . she really did want us to marry . . . I think she wanted us protected and cared for . . . but if you could have done both, I think she would have had me repeat her career. I would have gotten a Ph.D. in English and I would have written books . . . I would have loved that . . . Nothing other than that would have satisfied my sense of what I was supposed to do . . . All the other stuff was little jobs . . . I had this crazy sense that I was the mother of young children and if I was to do anything it was to be a college professor."

The strongest prescription and the one that prevailed was to marry. Even Charlotte's mother did not believe it would be possible for her daughter to have the career she envisioned for her. "Her sense was that her generation had a great deal more freedom coming out of school in the 1920s than we did." Charlotte had the inclination and the credentials to pursue an academic career—she graduated *summa cum laude* from a Seven Sisters college—but the drive to do it was drummed out of her; it was never presented as a possibility. Even her women professors, of her mother's generation, "realized that what was true for them wasn't true for us . . . When I was coming out of college, the notion of a woman living either sexually independent and not married or having no sexual life was not tenable. And all of us knew that." Today, it still does not occur to Charlotte to suggest that she might have combined an academic career with marriage: as soon as you married you started having babies and stopped working, at least for money; the family came first.

So Charlotte married and had three children, but only after completing her master's and spending at least a few years in the work force. Having been raised by a single, widowed mother, she knew that you had to be prepared to look out for yourself. "I had that mother. It was very clear that it was not safe not to have an employment . . . that risk that you might have children and then have your husband die . . . It had happened to my mother and it was important to her that we have that master's before marriage . . . I definitely had that sense that I should be employable. But more because I might have to go to work if something happened to my husband than that I was independently going to develop my whole life or career."

Educated women of her generation were in a "bind . . . in a funny kind of box" when it came to even thinking about work. There was a vast difference between what you would have done if you'd been born a man and what was possible for you as a woman. You tended to identify with your husband: "One's sense of oneself, coming out of that educational process, is that one should have done what all our husbands did do . . . If you were gonna do it, that's what you should have done . . . Women my age . . . have this problem . . . their sense of what they should do is very grandiose in relation to what's realistic—if they were to work, what they should do is something comparable to what their husbands are doing . . . Not having that, almost anything else wasn't right either." In some ways, she says, this becomes another trap for women, a "psychological barrier" between them and the work force. The choices available to you seem so "menial." If you don't have to work, if there is nothing pushing you, like a divorce, you never get started, and never even try.

What you do, instead, is create "alternatives" for yourself within the limits of family life: You volunteer. Charlotte began when her children started nursery school, "doing the sorts of things that young mothers do." It was a reflex; she did it automatically: "I don't think I thought very much about it, except that it was very clear to me that I always wanted to get something out of it . . . And so I did all sorts of things that came my way because of the children's experience. Only I always did the part that had some intellectual content to it. So that, for instance, on a school PTA . . . I would be the liaison to the Board of Education, which means that I covered public meetings and I spoke on behalf of the PTA . . . And I joined the League of Women Voters and I did a lot of that kind of stuff because it was interesting . . . For a period of time a lot of things went together, the work that I did for the elementary school PTA and the League of Women Voters, and I was active in the Democratic Party—and all of that taught me about government in town, and a small amount of government on a state level, and about . . . the whole political process and how people function in it and what they look like when they're doing it. I learned an immense amount and it is something you never forget . . . Eventually I was willing to serve on boards—the one that I have [served on] recently is the board of a social service agency, and I was president of that . . . I learned a great many skills . . . The social service agency has to work with the town bureaucracy and the town council . . . I can go into one of those meetings where you're presenting your budget and it is very clear to me very quickly what is going on at that table . . . You've seen it once and you know what's going on. You never lose it."

Charlotte chose her work instinctively. "I didn't think it through, not the way someone today thinks through—how would volunteer work fit in with some career . . . It's interesting that I never was really willing to work on any kind of women's auxiliary and I was never willing to work in any kind of structure where there wasn't a power structure and you had the power. I can now look back and realize that I was never on the women's auxiliary board of a hospital or a church and I never did anything where it was in a kind of advisory committee . . . They don't really have any power." But she was not aware of making this distinction at the time or of the fact that she was acquiring skills. All that she was aware of doing was putting her children first, before her work. She needed the freedom of volunteering, she needed to be able to control her time: "You were making a value judgment, without any question, that I was conscious of. When my children were young, I absolutely put them first . . . I was just, in a sense, filling in time along with family life in a way that didn't seem to threaten that life."

Having made this decision and sacrificed a career to her children, watching them grow up and leave was hard. It wasn't fair. It was the only thing about married life that made her "really angry."

"It was an adjustment to have children and to give yourself to do that . . . Early child care is difficult and it has a lot of depression connected with it and you only understand it after it's over. I can't see that women have gotten a lot better at that—when I look at young mothers, it seems to me they make all the same mistakes we did, of basically not getting out enough . . .

There is just something that sucks you in . . . it's very absorbing and it finally takes all your energy . . . It's an adjustment while you're doing it . . . So you do it and then you have to undo it and both of them are painful . . . Seeing my children were gonna leave . . . I really got angry."

For a few years, in her thirties and early forties, the anger was directed at "that male world" that had relegated her to the home. She describes it now as a passing phase, as if the "male world" was only a convenient scapegoat for the problems of adulthood. "I went through a period of just not knowing how I was going to cope with where I was . . . I felt helpless." She feels now that she has "sorted out the issues clearly"—she has, at least, an idea about her future, and the anger has passed; it was "not realistic" to blame her problems on her sex: "No one has any real freedom. Every child is shaped unfairly by his parents . . . I think people in their forties do a lot of crying one way or another, I don't think it matters if they're men or women. I think it happens whichever path you take."

The men of her generation were just as "severely socialized, . . . as locked in" as the women. "If I look at my husband's life, he's had very little opportunity to develop himself as a person. And he won't if he's going to pay his bills for the next thirteen years. And I think that's true of most men who are working to . . . support family and children . . . A lot of men feel like drones . . . basically they feel that they are working like dogs to keep some lady dressed and happy . . . So if they feel that way and women feel the way women feel, then . . . what you're talking about is the whole shebang."

Lately Charlotte has been talking more to men, about their lives, about the kinds of things she has always talked about with women. For the first time in her life, she has a few of her own male friends; it is interesting. When you spend all your time volunteering and raising children, all your friends and colleagues are women. "It's not healthy. It's not whole." She enjoys listening to men for a change. "You get the other half of the whole picture."

In the best of all worlds, patterns for men and women would be fluid and flexible, and Charlotte would like to believe that "what we are moving towards is something that is a lot healthier

. . . Women will be earning and men will have the freedom to drop out sometime . . . and do genuine child care." But it does not seem likely. Charlotte's sympathy for men who "have been made to carry very heavy burdens," has not erased her mistrust of the ways in which they may abuse their power over women in the work force. She is afraid women have only made "token gains" that men "have the freedom to eliminate," and that they will be sorely tempted to do so as the economy worsens. She does not believe that women have very much power of their own; they owe their token gains to the "beneficence" of men, to a kind of charity. "As it gets uglier . . . men will be less kindly . . . The women's movement is something men could turn around very easily." Charlotte has not been "defeated" by her "Second Sex life," and she is no longer angry about it; she is merely resigned.

Child-rearing also seems to her like an insurmountable obstacle to the professional advancement of women. Men who succeed in the professions and in corporate America, like the young lawyers in her husband's firm, work excruciatingly long days, six or seven days a week, she says. And "as long as there are men who will do that, as long as there are men who will live that way, women will be in a subservient category in the working world, until women are willing to say, 'We will not have children.' " Perhaps she cannot imagine women combining this kind of career commitment with children because she is convinced that it is crucial for a child to have one non-working parent, and, in her world, that parent has always been the woman. Charlotte has given up a lot for her children; she has to believe it was for the best and does not think in terms of full-time child care or day care as an equal alternative to full-time motherhood. It also does not occur to her that "career women" seeking equality with men in the work force can take time out to have their children later, once they have established themselves professionally—but she welcomes the suggestion. There is an advantage to having children late: "You will not have a mid-life crisis when you have teen-agers in the house. That is what is happening in this old traditional pattern . . . everyone in the house is crying . . . everyone is in tears at the same moment. It's very very funny. It makes for very funny behavior."

It would be good, she agrees, "to see a little bit of everything," but in the meantime she has stopped crying; she is as content as she believes anyone has a right or opportunity to be, and she does not envy her husband's financial responsibilities or powers. Charlotte has missed having a lifetime career, because she would have liked to have made a full-time, lifetime commitment to work, not because she has missed being paid. She has always had her own reasons for volunteering, found her own rewards in it, and has never felt exploited. And, she has always believed in her ability to support herself if something ever happened to her husband. "I have no doubt in my mind that I would manage fine if Bill died tomorrow . . . Because that's what I saw. I did not see women not managing without men." The point of going to divinity school is not to increase her earning power; given her educational background and volunteer experience, Charlotte is confident that she doesn't need another degree to find a job. "I could teach in a secondary school right now. I could teach English . . . I could get a job as executive director of some agency." Divinity school is something Charlotte wants for herself, instinctively. It feels like what "she would have gravitated to" on her own, twenty years ago, "if society hadn't had a whole set of prescriptions for me." She wants to do pastoral counseling and "actual ministry work" and will do it for free, if she must, if she can "really" do it: "It is the most closed world for women . . . the last bastion . . . Money is not a big issue . . . As long as I am getting to do what I want to do and if I'm doing it with a skill base, I would be content to volunteer for the rest of my life."

Charlotte thinks her plan must "really sound bizarre" to me. It is off-track—"experimental"—and there is "no apparent reason" for her to want this. It is not yet clear to her "what it will come to," how it will work out: "I may just go back to teach in high school or I may end up trying to write for the local newspaper. But I think if I do, I will do it with more conviction, somehow. I just have to experiment a little bit with this . . . I need this for myself."

NANCY ROLLINS

For the past twenty years Nancy Rollins has been raising five children and building a professional life for herself from "bits and pieces" of paid work and volunteering, in nursing, community services, and, recently, as president of an alcohol and drug awareness group for parents of teen-agers. She started a nursing career in her early twenties, set it aside to marry, and, since then, has not had the time or energy left over from family life for a full-time career commitment. She has always looked for flexibility and independence in her work, and control over its demands on her time. "I try and burn the candle at both ends, play it both ways. I guess that's why volunteering suits a need for me." Like Charlotte Andrews, Nancy, at forty-five, misses the person she might have become had she pursued a career in nursing twenty-five years ago; volunteering has helped compensate for that loss in a way that her family never could. She has "enjoyed" her children and "receives a lot from them," but has always needed to work outside the home "to find something out about myself."

"You go from . . . school to getting married and having a family . . . like we did in the fifties . . . and you don't have that opportunity to get out and explore what it is you really can do and what your strengths are . . . Then that part of you lies dormant for a great number of years . . . There are potentials and resources in myself that I haven't developed over the years that are beginning to surface through volunteer work."

At first, volunteering was primarily a way to meet other mothers of young children. Shortly after she married and began having babies, Nancy joined a women's club in suburban New Jersey. It was "service-oriented"—she was involved in establishing a tape lending library at a school for the blind—but the social connections it gave her were at least as important as the work. Without them, the early years of child rearing would have been lonelier and much more difficult:

"I found other women who were in the same situation. There was a lot of camaraderie and support. We were all home . . . As difficult as it was, there was a lot of good and a lot of growth and a lot of security in those years, and a lot of support from other women my age. And that's something that's very precious to me. I treasure that memory."

The women's club was enough for Nancy until her children "began to get older": "At some point" along the way, she began to need "something a little more than volunteering . . . I felt I needed to go back into nursing." The family moved to Connecticut and, instead of joining another club, Nancy looked for a nursing job—part-time; her children were still "really very demanding." She needed "banker's hours" and, having been "out for so long," she needed to be retrained. Job prospects were "a little depressing . . . I went back to hospitals and I really couldn't sell myself on the terms I wanted to work . . . I tried to volunteer as a nurse in the hospital and there was no such animal as a volunteer nurse. There were too many liabilities.

"I wound up working in a nursing home . . . It's a little bit easier to move into nursing through a nursing home . . . It's not a high level of crisis-oriented nursing care . . . They welcomed me with open arms . . . they took my life experiences as worthwhile . . . I went into a paying job and worked at that for four years . . . part-time."

Working part-time was frustrating. "There were many things that needed to be done and you cannot have that effective an input two or three days a week." Nancy wanted to organize the nurses "to talk about the issues that were troubling them"—job-related issues and problems in patient care. "I even approached my paying job as a volunteer effort . . . I saw a need to develop a nursing association there—a place where the nurses could come and talk about the issues, so a couple of us got together and we developed a professional nurses' group. We'd meet once a month and we'd raise issues and we'd discuss them and try to problem-solve. And I think that was fairly effective."

But even a part-time job put some strain on Nancy's family life and left her feeling "torn" between conflicting obligations. Her children ranged from elementary school to high school age; the youngest, a girl, was in the second grade and "didn't really like it very much" when her mother went to work. "That gave me a lot of guilt. I had a lot of trouble with that. But I just felt this need . . . It was my turn." She depended on her oldest daughter, in her early teens, to "cover the house at times," and it was hard on her too: "I think maybe there were times that she needed to talk and I wasn't here, and I have trouble with that." Her two sons, both in high school, didn't mind their mother's absence, nor, it seems, were they asked to "cover" for her. "On the whole," none of the kids were "scarred" by the experience. It probably made a deeper and more lasting impression on their mother:

"I can really sympathize with women who struggle with that guilt of having to be out there and working and wondering what's going on and how to juggle it. I think it's a tremendously difficult thing to do . . . People who are successful at it have a very high energy level and not everybody has that . . . I have a lot of respect for women who are out there and seem to be doing both very well. Maybe that's because I feel I couldn't do it."

Nancy is hard on herself for not doing everything. Her best friend is a nurse, with "a very respectable administrative job" in a California hospital and five children of her own:

"We raised our kids together . . . and somehow I think of her as a role model . . . She went into nursing full-time, got a degree, and is now vice-president of the hospital in charge of nursing services. I just have tremendous respect for her because she's doing everything so well . . . As far as I can see, her kids are solid. She's very happy with what she's doing and she wouldn't want to do it any other way. It was always very important for her to be in nursing. It was never that important for me, I guess. It was more important to be at home, to have the flexibility of shifting from one thing to another."

"I just did not feel that I could handle what I wanted to at home and on the job. I just didn't have the energy, the dedication, the drive, or whatever it took, or wasn't motivated . . . I have always been frustrated about going back to school—feeling that I should have and never did."

After four years at the nursing home, Nancy wanted to get out of nursing care and into an administrative job, but she would have had to go back to school to do it. She had to decide: "Should I go back to school and track into nursing? And when I looked at it, it was so terribly expensive . . . and I was at this point trying to put my own kids through college . . . It became very expensive . . . to go back for your bachelor's, and then you really have to go on for your master's. You must go on to the next level. And I just had so many other interests. I wasn't sure I wanted to put all that time and money into it."

So she retired from nursing, once again. "I did enjoy it for about four years and then I decided I needed to make another change." She came home: "Fortunately I had the luxury to make that decision. Not everybody can do that." She became involved in the PTA, "being a little restless at home and trying to figure out what would be fulfilling." Her kids were in junior high and high school and beginning to get involved in "beer drinking and keg parties and Senioritis and the whole bit . . . We were worried about the drinking." Other mothers in the PTA had similar worries, and they decided to put together an "awareness" program for parents on teen-age drinking: "There was a need and there was a concern and there was an anxiety on the part of mothers that I was associating with." Nancy was program chair; "starting out from nowhere" and working mostly by herself, she organized a panel of "people in the field" to discuss alcohol and drug abuse and ways in which parents can prevent and treat it.

"It was about three months of planning, but it was worth it because it was very well received—it was much appreciated." There were follow-up meetings with people who said they were "willing to become involved"; they "wound up" with a core group of about eight women that Nancy organized into a nonprofit parents' awareness organization; of all the concerned parents "willing to become involved," it was mothers, not fathers, who took the lead and "wound up" doing the work:

"It was the women who came forward and said, I will be your secretary, I will be your treasurer . . . Most of these women were working . . . one was a nurse friend of mine. Two other women who had supported me from the beginning had gone through difficult times with their own children . . . they were the backbone for me . . . and gave me direction and helped me understand what the problems and the needs were."

Nancy gave them organizational direction; she gave them a structure. "I brought to them a little bit of leadership and organizational skills that they were looking for. We worked well together." They have been together for about three years, working with schools, police, and social service agencies in the community, developing training programs for teachers and support groups for parents. Nancy puts in about twenty to thirty hours a week as president of the organization. She has been lucky with her children, feels "successful as a parent," and takes pleasure in her family. She wants to somehow "give back a little bit" of this to others:

"There's a lot of pain in families . . . When you're dealing with disruptive behavior as a result of drug abuse or alcohol abuse, you're dealing with a lot of violence and terrible relationships—a real breakdown in love and family relationships, and there's a lot of power play that goes on, and it's just very destructive. The ultimate is to put the child out, and that's a very difficult thing to do and it's not always the best answer because they get in more trouble when they're out many times . . . But the parent is so unbelievably frustrated, the parents are caught up in it emotionally. They need . . . to disengage . . . to be a little more objective and a little more effective . . . they need help."

Not being paid cash for this work has never been a "problem" for Nancy. She is "paid in other ways . . . There's a growth I see in myself—that is payment for my efforts. There's a connection with other people I find rewarding, and a sense of accomplishment. All those things take the place of monetary reward."

But talking about this makes her a little uneasy; she does not want to sound too holy: "I can afford to have that attitude. I don't like to abuse it. I don't really like to talk about it very much because I think that some people get defensive, or they'll get bitter, or they'll get resentful . . . So many people are struggling today to make ends meet. I just think it's hard in so many areas—I would just like to contribute something and not worry about how much money I'm gonna get paid for it."

Not that she feels she shouldn't work for money for fear of

"taking somebody else's job," and she would not want to volunteer as a nurse, although she once offered to do so in order to be retrained. It is important for her to be paid for her work as a nurse and to be paid well. It would have been "demoralizing to work in the nursing profession as a volunteer . . . Because I don't think you're really accepted in the mainstream . . . When I was working as a nurse and getting paid, I felt good about that. In fact, I also felt very strongly that nurses were underpaid. I wanted to be part of that organization to uplift the nursing profession. I think they deserve and need more recognition and need more unity, so in that context I would be fighting for more pay . . . I enjoyed being paid and I felt that I was underpaid. But I don't resent the volunteer work that I do."

She is in a productive and satisfying phase of volunteering now and expects it to continue for another two or three years. By then she will be ready for a change, again, and there should be someone in her organization to take her place. She would like to move on, leaving something behind, "something in place for someone to continue."

"Where I move on . . . I really don't know—once the kids get off . . . I guess I expect my interests to develop as I move along because that seems to be the way my life has gone. I usually get involved in something that's pertinent to whatever it is that's happening in my life at the time. When I had teenagers, I got into this . . . Now when they're off, maybe I'll get into a grandma group or something."

With "the kids off," she'll have more time to work. Maybe she'll get a paying job, maybe she'll volunteer in a new field— the local cable TV station has jobs for volunteers, and she would like to learn "media skills." Maybe she'll go back to school. Nancy is still bothered by what she considers her failure to go back and establish herself as a nurse and still wants to somehow make up for what she didn't do at twenty-five:

"I think I'm disappointed in not having had the opportunity of reaching my potential in nursing before I got married and had my children. I think that's basically something I look back on and might have wanted to have changed. And I have been trying to change it for twenty-five years, and I have never really been successful at it . . . I feel that I should have done it twenty years ago . . . But there are so many people who do it, now, and I don't have the motivation to get back and do it and I guess I struggle with that a little. It must be my disappointment in myself."

She does "receive a lot of satisfaction" from her volunteering, but "it's not the same." She has "a lot of confidence" in her capabilities; the problem is not a low self-image:

"I'm even surprised that I'm revealing this to you because I'm not really dissatisfied with myself. I think what I'm dissatisfied with is the fact that I didn't do what I felt I should've done between twenty and twenty-five. I'm not unhappy with the rest of my life; it's just that part of my life that I somehow feel strongly about . . . I'd feel more complete if I'd completed something I felt I should have done at that age. Maybe I feel it would help me now. I don't know. I am a little confused as to why I feel like that. You know I'm satisfied with the ability I have. I get a lot of satisfaction from what I'm able to give. I'm satisfied with the return I get from people. I don't know whether any of this makes any sense to you."

Still, while women in her generation "struggle with career goals and how to get back to work at forty," Nancy thinks "there's a greater problem for the young girls coming up now," the "career-oriented" women in their twenties and thirties. "They reach all their potential, get all their education, postpone their family. The terrible crisis they face at thirty-two—or whenever it is they decide to have their family and give it all up —must be just as painful." She assumes it must be "given up." She has never been able to figure out a way to do both. How are women in my generation managing, she asks. What is it like for them? What will it be like for her daughter, who is training for a career in computer science and expects to raise a family? Nancy hopes she can be everything—"wife, mother, and career person."

"We talk about it because I'm really very curious about how she feels. And I tell her how I feel and what went on in the fifties, and what we did and how comfortable I was with it, and that there are certain realities in the eighties and that she's gonna have to be a little better prepared than I was. I was lucky I wasn't widowed or divorced or something and needed to go out and support myself. That is a reality that [she's] gonna have to prepare for; it would be stupid not to."

"Basically, she wants to get married and have children . . . At one point I was very concerned about that, I was concerned that she would almost want to get married and not reach some of her potential. But now she wants to postpone that a little bit and go out and work . . . I think she wants to have a career in terms of being able to support herself and fulfilling herself and knowing that she can do something and grounding herself in some profession . . . Kids change very quickly and that's good, that means growth . . . At one point I thought she'd be coming home after college for a year or so, which I said they could all do for a year and then . . . they don't get thrown out but I would encourage them to get an apartment . . . Now she's looking to go where a job is . . . Her motivation is to get in her own apartment and have enough money . . . She wants the independence. She really wants the independence to control her own life. I don't think she has felt in control of her own life yet. I think she feels dependent on her family and her father . . . And she really wants to get out."

She knows it will be easier for her sons: "I often think how easy it is for a man to be on track . . . with the whole support system they have around them. And it's one of the things I try and convey to the girls, at least my college student, and that's why I feel it's so important that she feel comfortable and secure . . . because she's . . . gonna have to have the flexibility and . . . provide the balance in the family to make it all work. I don't think the male population is ready to accept creating that balance. I don't think they understand what that balance is. I kid my boys about it.

"I feel so strongly about this because I've been such a strong support system for my own husband. And my own particular generation of friends that started out—we've all had husbands that have gone on to create very satisfying careers for themselves. But I'm not sure that would've happened as it did without the kind of support they got. And I don't mean somebody being a corporate wife . . . [but] just allowing them to do what was important for them to accomplish what they needed to accomplish . . . running the house and putting clean socks in the drawer. They never have to worry about what am I gonna eat for breakfast and who's gonna press my pants.

"I would not encourage my daughters to go the route I did. I don't think it would be economically feasible. It's a very different world and I think they have to be just a little better prepared for it. I'd really like to see my girls reach their potential, whatever it is, however long it takes them."

THE NEW GENERATION:
VOLUNTEERING BY CHOICE

Not many daughters are being trained for full-time volunteering anymore. They are expected to go to work for money, at least for a while, and always to have something to fall back on. It is primarily a matter of necessity—they have to be "better prepared" than their mothers were—but it is also a matter of pride.

The decision to volunteer to the exclusion of paid work is an especially difficult one for middle- and upper-class women of my generation, the first to come of age along with the contemporary women's movement. We started out career-bound, in college, with a mission—to break into the male professional world, en masse, for what felt like the first time. Fifteen years ago feminism was a relatively new phenomenon, and the new ideal it posited for women was just beginning to gain acceptance. To us, the volunteer tradition represented an old ideal that had held women back and kept them at home: it was an obstacle to our professional success. If we had a party line, it was, in general, opposed to volunteer work, just as the party line of the past opposed paid work for women.

This attitude has had an inevitable effect on the volunteers among us and generated mutual distrust and disrespect between those of us who work for money and those who don't. In interviewing volunteers, I encountered more initial resistance and defensiveness from women my own age than from older or younger ones. As an unmarried "professional" woman, I was expected to "look down" on them and their volunteering—as if the different choices we'd made between professional and family life put us in not just different but opposing camps. What they seemed to expect from me was peer group disapproval, because it is often what they get from peers who are feminists and paid professionals.

Volunteering makes you a "second-class citizen," says thirty-four-year-old Laurie Marcus. You need an excuse for doing it; volunteering is not considered work. A woman like Laurie is not taken seriously by paid working women her own age, who look at her in wonderment and ask, "What do you do with yourself all day?"

It is a question she is bound to ask herself. Because of the pressure to pursue a paid career, the educated, leisure-class, thirty- or thirty-five-year-old woman of today following a traditional pattern of marriage, motherhood, and volunteering is likely to have made a much more deliberate decision to volunteer than her counterpart of twenty or thirty years ago. "My generation didn't look in," says fifty-five-year-old Dorothy Harnack. Women who grew up in an age of consciousness raising do. And they have to "look in" on the decision to volunteer precisely because volunteering is no longer a reflex for women.

The next three women interviewed, all volunteers in their early to middle thirties, have not fulfilled the ideal for our generation. They are constantly asked to explain themselves and their volunteering; it is not what they were supposed to do. We imagine all volunteers to be over forty-five or fifty at least; how does one in her thirties imagine herself?

LAURIE MARCUS

Six years ago Laurie Marcus was teaching in an elementary school in California, supporting her family. At twenty-eight, she had a two-year-old son and a husband in graduate school, and had been teaching full-time for seven years. She stopped when her daughter was born—"A sick baby [who] required a considerable amount of attention." Laurie came home, and her husband went out looking for a job. He found one teaching math in an Eastern university, left school, and finished his Ph.D. "through the mail." The family resettled in a Massachusetts suburb, and for the past six years Laurie has been looking after her children and volunteering—first as a board member and teacher at a co-op nursery school, later in the local elementary school, as chair of the town historical commission, at her church, and for the League of Women Voters. Someday she may go back to work for money; now she needs the flexibility of volunteering and time for her children, particularly her six-year-old daughter, who is fighting off a childhood cancer. But she also needs work that is "totally" her own, that has "nothing to do with being a wife and mother," and she enjoys the "give and take" of volunteering, in simple jobs like helping out with day care at her church, exchanging services for services or simply appreciation, instead of cash:

"If you're paid to do something, you're required to do it. I'm giving of myself . . . some people value that . . . Somehow if you take care of someone's child for them so they can go off and listen to the church service . . . and you give that child some affection and love, there is gratitude there . . . They appreciate that you've given that and you benefit from that appreciation as well . . . If I were paid to baby-sit, I would be the baby-sitter. I feel I could go to those same people when I need help. It's a family substitute in some sense. We have had occasion over the last few years when we've had to ask numerous people for help. You have a lot of needs when you have a very sick child, and, in a way, [volunteering] is an opportunity to pay that back. I also don't think it's possible in the modern world to pay everyone for everything they do."

Still, Laurie is surprised that someone wants to interview her for a book about volunteering. She doesn't think of herself as a volunteer: it is a name for housewives from another generation. She considers herself a working woman and has chosen her volunteer jobs carefully, in accord with her professional interests and goals as well as her personal needs and those of her family. Working at the co-op nursery school, her first experience volunteering, was a way for Laurie to meet other young mothers in the community when she moved in, and it was good for the children. Her historical commission work reflects an interest in history and preservation and should, she hopes, enable her to get a paying job in the field without going back for an advanced degree. Teaching Sunday school keeps her skills "in tone" in case she decides to go back to teaching, and she enjoys being part of the Church community. It is a Unitarian church and, she says, attracts a "talk-oriented group of people . . . you discuss ideas . . . and talk about world events . . . For someone who is at home with small children a lot, it's a very good place to be." Her work in the public school, serving on curriculum committees and sometimes helping out in the classroom, is for her children, but she also believes that, as a teacher, she has "something to offer" other parents. Working for the League of Women Voters is simply interesting, and she has always been active politically.

Laurie thinks her work is good for her and the community: It is satisfying and, she says, socially responsible: "I can't think of anything I've volunteered for that I don't consider [has] something in it for myself. My time is valuable and I want to be sure it's placed in something growth-producing, helpful, and productive . . . I consider myself to be leaving something better off than if I had never touched it . . . I don't replace anyone who's ever been paid for doing what I do, I know that. It would matter to me. I'm the one who won't cross the picket line at the grocery store . . . I don't do scab labor . . . Jobs are immensely scarce and people are fighting to find anything they can do to make ends meet . . . I do not have to go to work right now . . . I volunteer for things I know will not be done by anyone except volunteers . . . I still have the enjoyment of being heavily involved . . . The only thing I don't have is the paycheck."

It is maddening to Laurie to be "looked down on" by paid professional women because she volunteers. She lives in a community of well-educated, professional people, where volunteering is low-status work, particularly among the women. It is only "one step above stay[ing] home." Even the women she meets at

the League of Women Voters, most of whom have outside paying jobs, have an "attitude" toward Laurie's volunteering:

"The people I come into contact with there are very interested in the kinds of jobs they do that are recompensed. There's
a lot of lawyers, a lot of teachers who are working, doctors, a lot
of people who in real terms are recognized by society—as having very high-powered jobs, and they know it. And they are
justifiably proud of it because most of them have scrounged like
hell to get where they are and frequently with great odds
against them."

They don't consider Laurie a professional and have little respect for her work: "They don't necessarily come out and say it;
They will say things like, 'Well, you're not working . . .' [or]
'Oh, you do volunteer work.'" Laurie feels stigmatized and is
angry about being judged and always put on the defensive by
other women: "People [I know] who are in my situation who
aren't working . . . generally have a lot of good reasons why
they aren't working. I try to spend very little time justifying
why I'm not, because I frankly consider it to be my business."

She would, however, like to talk about her work with friends,
and the ones who have paid professional jobs have the same
attitude toward volunteering:

"The town government, which is heavily male-dominated,
gives out more strokes for volunteering than most of my women
friends give me for the work I do. And you would sort of expect
. . . that [friends] would stroke each other . . . People who I
value highly will tell me, 'You sure spend a lot of time on junk'—
Junk! When they don't even really know [what] I do . . . even
though I would like to explain." Sometimes, some "historical
buff" will want to hear about her work for the historical commission, but her own friends rarely do. Even her sister, a successful and well-paid actress, "wouldn't dream" of asking Laurie about her work. "She considers me to be a housewife, home
taking care of the kids. And is not really interested in what I do
beyond that . . . It does become kind of painful, hurtful."

Most of the support Laurie gets for volunteering comes from
her husband and children. What they think is important to her,
and she likes to believe she is giving her daughter a positive
image of women, as versatile and productive people:

"My husband and kids think what I do is really good. My son, at age eight, thinks it's absolutely wonderful that his mother is the chair of a commission. He brags about it to everyone. He thinks for his mother to be in charge of something is a real measure of something valuable. I've thought about this a lot because I have a little girl who is very bright and fantastic and I have high aspirations for her to be able to try and do whatever she would like . . . I want to be sure that when she looks at me, she sees someone who is also productive."

There is no doubt in Laurie's mind that she is just as productive volunteering as she would be in a paying job. "I'm teaching my children valuable skills, providing something for the world, and keeping my mind going . . . People continually change and grow and the only way to keep that going is to keep yourself stimulated one way or another, whether you're paid for it or you volunteer." This is a "major push" for Laurie to keep on volunteering. She has seen too many women "withdraw into their homes." She saw it happen to her mother:

"My mother did no volunteer work. She was a homemaker, always home when I got home from school, very steady in that respect. When the children left home she really had nothing left to do. She had four kids; we've all been gone from home over fifteen years. She really has nothing to do. I think it was very hard for her when everyone left. I believe it was also mixed with some relief. But I think my mother at this point . . . is unable to change her life . . . She is not a happy person in . . . a productive or particularly interested life . . . I think it comes from being confined in your house. My mother, for example, will not drive a car anymore, although she drove when I was a child. She simply decided one day that she couldn't leave the house to drive the car anymore . . . It's very secure to be at home all the time. I think there are women . . . so secure in their homes they can't leave."

Laurie considers herself a feminist and sees volunteering as a way of connecting to the outside world, instead of hiding from it, while her children are young and need her. She is not afraid to leave the house and go to work, she knows she can support herself, and doesn't feel she is living off her husband:

"For the first eight years of my marriage we had a reverse

situation. He stayed home as a graduate student; he wasn't getting paid for it, and I was employed. And he never felt it was my money; he always felt it was our money . . . At this point . . . I don't consider it his money, I consider it our money."

Her husband also volunteers, in a local high school computer program and on a computer science committee of their children's elementary school. When they were in the co-op nursery, he took days off from work to share "parent helping" responsibilities there with Laurie. They have tried not to sexualize paid work and volunteering, not to fall prey to the belief that "your worth is less because you're not employed for money."

It was easier at Berkeley, Laurie says, than it is in a community of educated, Eastern professionals. At Berkeley, "People really didn't care too much what you did." Now she is constantly reproached for volunteering; social pressures to get a job are strong, and she may soon succumb:

"A point comes where one is no longer quite satisfied with doing everything they do and not getting paid for it . . . In a society that values the dollar as much as this one does, there is not a tremendous, high regard for people who don't get paid for what they do."

In the meantime, she does what she can to make people recognize her work: "I do tell people that I do work . . . If you walk up to someone and . . . say, 'Well, I'm volunteering . . . ,' that's going to put them off fast . . . When I talk about the commission, I always introduce myself as a member of the commission or . . . as chair of the commission and proceed to discuss the work we do . . . what it is we accomplish."

It is still hard to get past the question of money: "Even with that . . . people will say, 'Is this a volunteer group? Are you paid?' It's important for them to know that, and that has always struck me as very funny. And then once they know that, they have you categorized . . . it gets infuriating at times . . . You have a lot of self-confidence and understanding about what you're doing and why . . . but it is hard to resist this bombardment of other people not recognizing it—from the outside.

"If you say, I'm a lawyer, or I'm a social worker, or I'm a teacher, people say, 'Oh, what an interesting life . . .' I would

like to be able to say to people that I'm a very busy person—I
work for the historical commission, I work for the church, I do
these things—and have someone say (and some people do),
'What an interesting life.'"

MICKEY LOGAN

Mickey Logan began her volunteer career about three years
ago, hoping "to follow my own interests . . . to center myself
and find out what it is that I want." At thirty-two, she had been a
high school teacher for ten years and had just given birth to her
second child. She was ready for a career change, wanted to
spend time with her children, and decided to give herself five
years out of the paid work force. First, she signed up for a music
course: "I love to sing. I always had star fantasies." But she was
soon immersed in a demanding, full-time volunteer job as
chairperson of the local co-op nursery school that one of her
children attends, in suburban Boston. It was an opportunity "to
do something administrative in education . . . It was nice to
be working behind the scenes and being the teacher advocate
rather than the teacher . . . I felt it was a nice move for me. I
saw it as a place to experiment with something."

It was also a challenge. Being asked to chair the school board
was "surprising, flattering," and "very scary . . . I really didn't
know anything about running the school. I had mixed feelings
about taking it. But I also didn't know anyone else who could do
it any better.

"The first year it just took all my time. Every day, something.
Every day—and nights. I mean, there were meetings that went
four hours in the afternoon. That's how I met this woman who
baby-sits for me. She's on the board. And I said, 'Joan, I can't
cope, you know. I've got to have some help.' And she started
taking Lisa. And, oh it's so much time."

And so much stress. Mickey's first job as chairperson was to
fire a controversial teacher, who was also school director. "I had
a lot of people who wanted her out and a lot of people who

adored her." Mickey wanted her out; she thought she was "a flake" and disagreed strongly with her educational philosophy and its effect on the children: "She kept saying, 'The children are happy.' And I was saying, 'The children are not happy.' So we had to fire her. And here I am the new board chairperson. I'd never done anything like this in my life. I really didn't have a board behind me because I was just beginning . . . I had it all by myself.

"Well, we have this procedure called teacher review, and when I took the job I knew I had something to do in this area. I didn't know we were going to have to not renew a contract. It wasn't a firing; it was a not renewing. So we formed a teacher review committee and we reviewed [her] . . . and decided not to renew . . . And, you know, it was awful. I mean, we said to her, 'We really do not want you to come back.' And she really fought mean . . . And so I spent from February to June dealing with that . . . It was just chaos.

"I didn't sleep at night. I'd never been so upset about anything in my life . . . Saying, you're only doing this out of the goodness of your heart. And this is when I started running. I was running five miles a day, just because of anxiety. It was so awful. And I vacillated . . . I would think, Oh my God, how can I do this. I mean, fire somebody? Couldn't I have given her one more year? Couldn't I have told her what she needed to do and given her a chance? But I really felt that, you know, by that time I had gathered up some support and I had people behind me, and I just stuck with them . . . I was feeling strong and I was doing the right thing and I needed to learn to do this."

The firing took up her first six months on the job; the next six were just as busy. Mickey had to hire two new teachers and do a "total house cleaning" of the school:

"Hiring a new teacher . . . that took a month of afternoons and evenings. We interviewed twenty-five people. And, you know, two-hour interviews. And just an incredible amount of time. And then in the summer the school was a wreck because these teachers didn't care about the beauty of the place. There were never any bulletin boards or anything. And it was a mess. So we completely took everything out, cleaned, organized, threw away, painted that whole school."

Mickey's teaching experience was invaluable that first year; it gave her confidence and credibility: "I felt my education background, my expertise, the fact that I was a person of, an expert in the field, really came to bear. I mean I did represent somebody who knew what they were doing. And I did, I think, inspire confidence in people. And even though there were people who were very angry with me—you know, they were parents, and they want to think they are sending their child to a good school. They wouldn't have chosen that school if they didn't think so. And it was an insult to them that I fired that teacher. And I kind of understood and accepted that. I decided if I was going to take it, I was going to take it. And I took the bull by the horns and I did it. And we hired two outstanding teachers . . . I did do that. As professionally as I knew how."

Sometimes Mickey thought, "You know this should be paid; this should not be required of somebody. But then, the nursery school was begun with the idea of being of service to women. And, at that time, the women didn't work. And they still don't. Most of our parents in our nursery school don't work. Because it's hard to work and do a cooperative. I mean, a cooperative nursery school requires a lot of your time . . . And so, because of that commitment to non-working mothers, we feel we need to keep the tuition low . . . I mean, I've sent my child there, and I would have had to pay more money. And I see all we do there to keep the budget reasonable . . . And I just couldn't bring that up . . . I could not even bring it up; I couldn't do that.

"I guess . . . I really feel the board chairmanship and even the registrar position should be paid. I really do feel that way. But this school is thirty-five years old. . . . We had a reunion last year of all the board people and chair people. And I just would feel so bad if I were to start accepting money, knowing that they had put in the same blood and guts for all those years for nothing. It would just really look bad to me . . . Everybody has been willing to do it for the sake of the school and the sake of the community, and the tuition being low, and to be able to give money to the teachers who don't make much, and to start taking money for myself, it would just be very hard. I would feel selfish and I would feel embarrassed."

She was, after all, getting something for herself out of the job. In some ways, "it was giving to me as much as I was giving. Because I was in there growing. And I saw it as a very real potential for a job shift. If I wanted to do something administrative in education now, I think it would be an incredible piece of experience. And that was something I considered."

She was also becoming a respected, even renowned person in her community:

"I was a professional person for ten years. I never got my name in the newspaper for one thing. And since I've been working as a volunteer my name has been in the newspaper several times. I've gotten a lot of recognition for it. And I like that. And people really look to me now as the person who did pull a very sad, sinking ship together in a very short period of time. I mean, now we have waiting lists of people dying to get in. And we had visitors from Japan the other day, and a call from England. I mean—it's incredible. And I certainly don't take all the credit for it, but I was taking a lot of the [blame] when it was going so badly. And so, I have to say, I participated in it. The recognition is nice—and I do see it as short-term."

Mickey plans on going back into the paid professional job market within the next few years:

"For me, volunteering isn't forever . . . I don't think I'd be happy with this forever. I think I'd get bored . . . And I'm very competitive . . . I'm very competitive with my husband . . . And he has a very lofty career [as a psychologist] and is well respected, and I feel second-class." It is also very important "to be able to support myself.

"I saw my father die at a young age, and my mother's whole support system was just wiped. And she had money, she worked, and she hated it. She was one who wanted to be at home and she would have been a good person to be at home because she's a very organized housekeeper and loves doing that and thinks that's very satisfying. She's a teacher of young children, so she was great with little kids at home. But she had to work."

She had to work not just for the money but "for something to do . . . Because I got married, my brother went to school, and she was really alone. And it did get her through . . . But I just watched that and I thought, I could never allow myself to put all my eggs in one basket like this."

Volunteer work does not, of course, satisfy Mickey's need to be self-supporting, but it does give her something to do and makes her part of a community. She grew up in the South, in North Carolina, and had no personal connections in the Boston area when she moved there with her husband. She has made them since, by volunteering:

"That's part of the high of finding all this community stuff; it's real important for me to have that. Because I'm alone here. I mean my sense of not having a family, so that's another big part of it. And I want to keep that."

She had it as a child, growing up in a church community, playing the organ for her local church as a teen-ager: "I was so proud to be able to do it . . . At church where I grew up, nothing was paid . . . And my parents, you know, they were poor and they contributed so much . . . At church, you give everything you have."

Mickey's father was an active volunteer:

"He was very much a community person. Saw the needs of the community and what needed to be. He was raised on a farm, a poor kid, and was one of those people who pulled himself up by his bootstraps. And he had a very literal idea of what it took to do that. And so he wanted to provide that opportunity for other people. And he worked with a lot of farmers. To provide knowledge for them. He was an agricultural teacher and ultimately administrator. But he not only taught in the school, he saw himself as a consultant to the parents who were the farmers—for teaching them about the latest things in agricultural research, soil testing, how to borrow money, how to get money for your farm, how to invest, how to run your business better. Just everything. And in terms of the students, he believed it was really important to be able to speak before a group in a way that was acceptable, and project it, and he thought that was a really important skill to develop. So he did a lot of public speaking, contests and things with boys . . . from the back hills. So he really did a lot.

"And he was gone every night. I mean, Jack gets mad at me now because I'm so involved in things and so much. And I remember my mother being furious with my father that he was gone all the time. I just kept thinking, 'But Mom, he really believes in it—stop it—he's really doing things that are important to people.' And I look back and think, 'Gee, I wish he'd been at home.' And I really understand my mother's point of view now, but, at the time, I understood my father."

Now, Mickey has "mixed feelings" about volunteering—"Just seeing my father die is enough to know that I can't depend on Jack for support. It doesn't feel good to me." But she knows, too, that paid work is not always "very satisfying" personally. Her last job as a teacher left her feeling "angry" and "resentful."

"A job takes so much of your energy and time . . . I was so angry that I spent this big chunk of time at school . . . I really felt required to be there, that I owed it to them, [and] after all that I owed it, there was nothing left for me." She does not now resent the time spent volunteering because she was "growing" as a volunteer; in her teaching job there were no "career measures of growth." She worries sometimes about returning to another paying job like it: "It's scary to think about trucking back to work because I remember how stressful and difficult that was. But I think that was partly because of the demands of the job and I wasn't that happy in it. I think if I were, it would be different. Because I've certainly worked hard with this nursery school."

Mickey isn't sure what her next career move will be. She does not want to return to teaching; she would like, at least, to "shift to another area" of education, like administration. In the meantime, she is giving herself a little more time to decide; her five years are not up yet, and she can afford to make use of them: The family can manage on her husband's income. Although she feels it's "just not right" for him to have to work so hard—"He just keeps working harder and harder and harder to make more and more and more"—she supported them while he was in graduate school, and now it is her turn:

"I'm committed to work and also committed to finding work that fits me. And sometimes I feel that's an impossibility. I'm really struggling with it right now, but I feel I'm on to something and I do have time to search for the Holy Grail. And I keep thinking other people have found it. And I will too."

BETH HALLER

More than anything, Beth Haller has always wanted a family. "I'm cut a little bit from the old mold," she explains. Since I called, she has been thinking about why she volunteers and how to account for her contentment living a very traditional married life. She knows it is not typical of her generation. "I graduated from college in 1970 and that was a period, I think, of change. All of a sudden, in a matter of two or three years, no longer did people—girls, women—think of going to college, walking out, and walking down the aisle and getting married. All of a sudden they were going to college and gearing toward a career, toward doing something . . . But I had invested a lot already in my family . . . I came from an interesting family in that we were very spread out . . . I have a brother who's fifteen years younger than I am . . . I decided early on that it was really a wonderful thing, and if I could do that and do it well . . . that I was not going to pressure myself into thinking that I had to have a career besides that, and, for me, it's worked out. I'm married, I have two children, a really wonderful family situation, and I'm fulfilled doing that, to an extent. Where I have needs that aren't met, I meet those through volunteering."

Beth never really "sat down" and decided to volunteer, "but it happened." She married—her husband is a lawyer who earns enough to support the family—they moved into a house, she started having babies and "looking into" other things to do. She turned first to the League of Women Voters "because that's basically a group of bright women who are interested in what's happening today and will . . . get into meaty topics and good conversations." For five years now she has been serving on the board of her local chapter and putting out their monthly newsletter.

Once she joined the League, her volunteer activities expanded rapidly. Her son, now nine years old, started elementary school, and Beth began working for the PTA, helping out in the classroom, and writing a newsletter for the school principal. She also volunteers at a community center for teen-agers, as a board member, staff assistant, and the writer of yet another newsletter. "You start with one organization and then someone else picks up on what you're doing there . . . It goes on and on and on, and all of a sudden you find that what was one small job has now become two or three and your phone is still ringing . . . I'm getting to the point where I have to say no a little bit." Her five-year-old daughter, Janie, is only in school until eleven-thirty in the morning: "It's not as if I have time coming out of my ears."

Beth doesn't want a full-time work commitment now. Her life, even her work, is centered on the children:

"My first priority in volunteering is at the school. There is nothing more important to me than being visible there and letting people know there that I'm interested and that I care and that I'm around. So this year, I'm co-president of the PTA, which is going to be very time-consuming . . . Even more than that, I like to go in the second or third day of school and sit down with the teacher and say, 'I'd love to get into the class-room and work with these kids if there's anything that I can do.' When Peter was in the second grade, we'd sit in the hall, trying to encourage the children to read more, asking them to do independent reading. They'd come out in the hall and report on whatever books they'd read for the week. It was really very exciting for them and I enjoyed that. Last year I went in once a week on Wednesdays. Peter's teacher had some special project and she basically needed baby-sitting for an hour on Wednesday afternoon . . . Janie and I would both go in and do that . . . The kids have benefited from that immensely. I know every-body from Peter's class . . . Janie was like the mascot of his class . . . last Christmas, for their school play, she was invited to be in it. That's very rewarding, that's rewarding to me to have that happen. That's why I don't need the thank-you, maybe, or the money . . . I get the benefits from that sort of thing all the time, more so really from the school commitment because I can see it through the kids."

There are other benefits for Beth from volunteering that

have nothing to do with her children. It has given her professional skills and confidence that she may someday transfer to a
paying job. She is becoming "more assertive," beginning to
participate more in board meetings and, for the first time, she is
able to stand up in front of a group of people—and speak.

"The thought of getting up and speaking publicly was something that I would have run from three years ago . . . I would
have avoided the job like the plague, would have done anything, would have paid anyone to do it for me. Last year I had to
speak in front of the Board of Education . . . and now it's easy
. . . it's very easy for me to get up and do that. And I attribute
that to my volunteering. It's done a lot for me."

Perhaps the most important thing it has done for her professionally is to give her confidence in her ability as a writer; Beth
would never have accepted a paying job writing newsletters
five years ago; she has always been too afraid of deadlines:

"I was an English major; I really enjoyed writing . . . the
one thing that discouraged me about writing when I graduated
from college was a terrible problem with deadlines . . . and I
thought I could never get a job or do something that had to do
with writing. Well, that's what I'm doing now. I have structured
it now so that I've gotten very good at deadlines, because I had
to. That doesn't frighten me anymore." She knows there are
people who are paid to write newsletters; a friend who works in
a large insurance company says Beth can "come over" and
write an in-house newsletter for them, as soon as she is ready for
a job. "I feel now that I could, if I wanted to. Right now I just
don't want to."

Perhaps it would be different, she says, if she'd ever had a job
that "excited" her and made her "anxious to get back." When
Beth graduated from college, she worked as a waitress to earn
enough money to go to Europe for a few months. When she
returned she worked as a docket clerk in a government office
for a year while her husband finished law school. "And I took a
fast typing course, thinking I might need it for a job . . . I
thought I'd better get something under my belt, so I could go
out and find something if I had to . . . I was an English major
and [that] was a ticket to nowhere unless you're going to go on
to graduate school." Beth never considered graduate school;

she never considered a professional career. She was "geared" toward having children. Otherwise, she thinks she would "have probably gone to law school." But this is only a suspicion. "It never really crossed my mind and it hasn't really since."

She is still not interested in a career, not yet; as long as her family can survive on one income, she will stay home with the kids, while they're young, and volunteer. She and her husband made a "commitment" to each other, "to try and stay a one-income crowd, as long as we could afford to." He even worries now about the time she spends volunteering:

"My husband and I talk about it once in a while . . . if meetings come . . . this week I'm out Tuesday, Wednesday, Thursday night . . . I hate that. I just hate to do that . . . Greg says, 'Don't feel that you have to give, give, give.' And I always accept it all; if I say I'm going to do something, it's my responsibility to do it. He says, 'But it's volunteering—you can say no. If it gets to be too much, you have to back off . . .' And we got into a discussion about how I do it because I enjoy doing it and I don't really want to say no."

What "frustrates" her husband is that Beth is working so hard for free. They decided to stay a "one-income crowd" so that Beth could "be there" for the children; if she is going to put in a full work week, she might as well be paid for her work: "He likes to think of the time I spend in terms of dollars and cents . . . He's understanding about it. He supports all that I do. He's cautious about watching it and wanting me to watch it . . . [My] time commitment now is equal to, if not surpassing, the time commitment I would have in a nine-to-five job . . . and that's the point at which you think, maybe I have something here . . . I have a lot of friends who sat down and tabulated the amount of hours per week spent in volunteering and they march right out the door and get a job."

Right now, Beth doesn't even want to think about going to work. She doesn't want to be tempted: "In a sense, I feel fortunate that I've never had a job I really liked." If she had, it would be hard for her to continue volunteering. Her life is simple and unconflicted now, and she wants it to stay that way:

"I'm basically at peace with my life right now. I have two terrific little kids. I thoroughly enjoy them. They fulfill a big part of me . . . I'm a little nervous about when both children start school full-time. I don't know whether then I'll be sitting here and saying I'm fulfilled doing what I'm doing. I think I probably will. There's a part of me that's wondering. That's a question mark . . . But it's important for me . . . to be here at three o'clock in the afternoon . . . I don't let myself daydream too much."

If she does, if you poke her a little, she thinks about "trying to do something related to writing or editing . . . Maybe I'd go off to the library somewhere and write a book." If she had a daydream, it would be about writing, "maybe short stories." Beth wrote fiction in college and would like now to write a story about an elderly man she visits once a week with her children:

"When we first moved here, we lived in a two-family home . . . Beneath us lived an elderly couple . . . The woman died, and he was left by himself and was very much alone and had never done anything by himself, so I sent him a note right after . . . and told him that we would be over every Monday afternoon with some macaroni and cheese at three-thirty, and if he was there, fine, and if he wasn't there, that was fine too. I just wanted him to know that we cared about him. Well, it's been three and a half years now. Every Monday afternoon we go over there, and it's been just wonderful for the kids . . . letting the kids get that wealth of what an eighty-year-old man has to offer has been just magnificent . . . To see this nine-year-old child sitting down for two hours playing games, talking, and bringing all his football and baseball cards, spreading them out, and Lou sitting there telling him about guys from thirty or forty years ago . . . My husband is always saying I should write a short story or write something about Lou."

Beth is hesitant about trying to write a story. It is easier for her to talk about her visits with Lou and her ideas of doing more volunteer work with the elderly than it is to talk about writing. Volunteering is safer. The prospect of writing makes her nervous. It isn't child- or community-centered work. It would be too much her own; it would somehow disrupt their life as a family:

"Everything right now . . . everything is fitting together very nicely and I don't want to decide that I'm going to start writing and decide that I'm going to have [to] sit in a library or somewhere for four hours a day to do that. I don't want to do that now . . ."

She knows she will have to make a change, when the kids grow up, and just thinking about it now is too unsettling for her: "I'm not the sort of person who can sit around . . . I'm not a sitter. So I know there will come a time when I probably want to do something more than I'm doing right now . . . Half of me is excited about that and the other half is a little leery, a little nervous . . . wanting to think about it, but not wanting it to interfere at this point."

Beth hopes she will never want to "give up" on volunteering entirely, "because there's such an incredible need." But she is nervous about maintaining her commitment; she has seen too many women "burn out," knows it may happen to her, and sometimes, even now, resents the fact that "the nitty-gritty work of volunteer groups is almost always done by women."

As one of the few "non-working" board members at the community center, Beth "gets the calls" during the day to stop in and help out with staff jobs. Sometimes, it seems fair enough: "I can stop in; I'm there . . . I knew what I was getting into." But sometimes she resents it: "I find it very frustrating to sit on a board . . . carrying the load for everybody else who's sitting there once a month and meeting . . . Because maybe there are times when I'm real busy and I think, gee, I'd like to just go to a meeting and have somebody report to me what's going on for that month."

It bothers her, too, that the board is run by a man who gets credit for work that is primarily done by women. There ought to be "a woman at the top getting credit for it." Two years ago there was a woman president of the board, and that was a "totally different ball game . . . She probably spent three or four hours a day at the center on a volunteer basis . . . She just gave . . . She just really committed a year to that. And I guess what struck me last year was how different it was having a man, because you never see him, you never hear from him, but everything still goes on, and it's the women doing it."

Beth "recognizes" this but doubts that it will ever change, and it is "not really an issue" for her: "That's probably a fault of mine, to accept that—but I do." Whether or not people ought to be paid for social services, whether or not women ought to be fighting their way into the "corporate structure," Beth believes that, for now, her role is to volunteer.

"I can see the sides to it . . . I just can't get beyond the fact that we need volunteers. If I've got the time, I'm gonna do it. If somebody else can't, somebody else can't." She is "just as pleased as the next person" when another woman goes out and "lands a terrific job and ends up high up in the power structure, but it's not for everybody." Neither, she says, is volunteering:

"I'm not saying that anybody else could do what I'm doing and survive and be happy . . . part of that is because I haven't done other things . . . I haven't exposed myself to other environments . . . And I'm not saying that's good; I'm just saying that's the facts of the way it is right now."

THE CASUALTIES:
STAYING THE SAME, INSTEAD OF CHANGING

The tendency to say, "This is not forever—only the way it is for now," the willingness to change and to question traditional roles prescribed for them as women, distinguish for me all the volunteers heard from so far. Although they are women who have not rebelled but, instead, followed traditional paths of marriage and motherhood, they have not followed them blindly. Most of them understand as well if not better than I the drawbacks of volunteering and can discuss, without defensiveness, the limitations of their roles. They are not dogmatic about the virtues of volunteering and so do not see it as the answer or as a mandate for women. The tradition has worked for them because they have been capable of entertaining doubts about it.

Their open-mindedness is the difference between women who have benefited and grown from volunteering and those for whom it has only been an exercise in femininity. Not every woman is capable of entertaining doubts about her proper place. Some refuse to question the socio-sexual order, and their stories are the ones that illustrate what's wrong with volunteering. They are familiar stories that have shaped our stereotypes of volunteers, and I do not intend to repeat them all or give them equal time. But no discussion of the volunteer tradition would be complete without at least acknowledging them and what they reveal about the usefulness of volunteering as a way of staying the same instead of changing.

Because it is so supportive of traditional family life, volunteering won't compel a woman to examine her choices or her roles at home and in the workplace. If she wants to hide out in femininity, it will let her. For some women, especially twenty or thirty years ago, volunteering, as an alternative to paid work, was a way of avoiding troubles with domesticity that had not yet been legitimized by the women's movement and given a name. It was there as a refuge, if one was needed, an excuse for not "really working," a defense against their own dissatisfactions, a quest for social status parading as the fulfillment of a social responsibility. This, too, is part of the legacy of volunteering:

"I remember my mother going to her meetings, and she would put on her lovely suit and hat and high heels and trip off to the luncheons . . . She was involved with the Florence Crittenton Homes . . . She went to teas; she went to luncheons . . . And I thought it was the most ridiculous thing that I had ever seen in my life. And then she would come home with these lurid tales of poor, pregnant girls—not a tinge of sympathy . . . there was no real concern being generated, certainly not by my mother."

This was the tradition inherited by Pamela Carter, and it "turned her off" to volunteering for many years. Now, at forty-one, with two small children, she has become a community volunteer, after several years of working for money before she started her family. She expects volunteering to help her back into the job market when the kids are grown, enjoys her work, with the PTA and a community arts center, and believes it is good for her children and the community. Pamela is careful to delineate her reasons for volunteering and to differentiate her work from her mother's luncheon meetings and teas. For her mother, volunteering to help "poor, pregnant girls" was "voyeuristic [and] purely social . . . it pegged your status. I think that's why she did it."

Martha Standish, at sixty-five, has been volunteering at a natural history museum for about twenty years, since her kids were in their teens, because she was interested in birding and natural history—and had nothing else to do. "It was either that or staying home and doing housework . . . or doing something along the social line . . . bridge clubs, that sort of thing." She never considered a paid professional career because she doesn't believe women belong in the professions. She thinks the women's movement is ridiculous: "This organization for women, they sort of get carried away . . . because they're trying to say that women are equal to men. And they're not equal . . . I don't think they're equal to men in any way. Mentally or physically. Physically, it's different, no argument there. Nor are they equal to men mentally . . . To say that they're equal to men and can carry on jobs that men have always done . . . I think there certainly is a place in society for the women to work . . . there's all sorts of jobs for women that are good . . . They make good teachers. They make good secretaries."

Martha worked as a secretary for seven years before she married, and had no desire to go back to an office. She didn't need the money and thinks "it is a little bit silly" for a woman to get a paying job if her husband can support her. Not being paid had no effect on Martha's self-esteem, she says, adding, "Of course, I don't know what people said behind my back."

Her volunteer work was actually quite important to the museum, and she served as an unpaid, acting curator for several years; but Martha acts as if nothing she (or any other woman) does is important and merits discussion. Volunteering is "mostly routine idiot work . . . I don't see how you're going to write a book about this." She is completely dismissive of any attempts by women to discuss their role in society—"Women's rights, women's organizations . . . I don't agree with any of it"—or even to talk about their work. Martha presents her work at the museum as just a way of filling time that was a little more interesting than playing bridge. She knew her place, and volunteering helped her keep it.

Life was probably easier before the women's movement for women like Martha, who were not willing or able to admit that something was wrong. Feminists were snakes in the garden. Lyn Hirst, thirty-four years old and the mother of three, seems sorry to have missed out on the fifties, when all a woman had to do was volunteer and perform "good works." Now, thanks to the women's movement, she is supposed "to be independent . . . to take care of herself," and, somehow, it doesn't seem fair. After thirteen years of child-rearing, Lyn feels compelled to go to work at her first paying job. She is ready to volunteer; it would be "selfish" not to, now that her children are less demanding of her time—she has, after all, an "obligation" to the community. But it is clear that she is unhappy and a little angry at the prospect of going to work for money. It is not what she imagined for herself—the traditional family life associated with volunteering. She has been cheated out of her expectations:

"They don't talk about family anymore in terms of man, woman, two children. Back in the fifties, you were in your shirtwaist, your husband came home at six-thirty, dry martinis, two neatly dressed children . . . I grew up in a very traditional family . . . I grew up thinking that's what life was." Now, she can't "imagine" being a "housewife" and volunteering: "Given the framework of social assumptions for us today, that just doesn't compute." Lyn is trying to adjust, because she must—the family needs a second income, and with all her children in school she has no excuse, in the 1980s, for not earning one. But she is frightened by her new responsibilities: "It [was] very comforting to think life could be wildly traditional. But it's not like that now . . . The world is bigger, and it's scarier."

The "Other" Tradition:
Combining Volunteering and Paid Work

"I've always done three types of work, I guess . . . the paid work, whatever the paid work was; family—I have raised two daughters by myself, for eight to nine years I was alone with them; and the community stuff . . . I don't consider that volunteer; I sort of consider it my obligation."

Roseann Navarro, volunteer

The stereotypical volunteer is a married woman who never works for money. Her first allegiance is to her family; her husband pays the bills while she looks after the children and the home and spends her free time helping out in the community. She is a woman who can't take care of herself, for whom volunteering represents the safety and security of home and family, across a line from paid work, which represents the big and scary world.

There is some truth to most stereotypes, and, perhaps, this is the kind of volunteer Lyn Hirst might have become, if she hadn't been born too late. For her, volunteering would have been nothing more than a safe and respectable adjunct to family life. But Lyn is not typical of the traditional family women for whom volunteering is also a job that fulfills a profound need for work outside the home, and the volunteer world for which she yearns is hardly the world of self-supporting, paid working women who also work for free.

There is another tradition—of women who volunteer alongside of full-time, paying jobs and professional careers. Not generally associated with "volunteering," they are likely to be called, and to call themselves, civic leaders, organizers, and activists. It is fair to call them volunteers, but the fact that they also work full-time for money does indeed distinguish them from women who only work for free. They don't have to wonder if they are capable of supporting themselves or worry about hiding out at home or in their communities. Volunteering is easier for women who earn their own livings; it is not a source of conflict for them—a symbol of dependency.

The next section of interviews explores this other tradition with six women—paid professionals and volunteers. They volunteer for the pleasure of it—because paid work is not always fulfilling and isn't everything—and because they must—out of a sense of personal, social, or political obligation. For those who have been lucky enough to find salaried jobs in their fields, it is hard to distinguish between the work they do for money and for free. Their jobs don't end at five or six o'clock, and they use professional skills and contacts volunteering; it is an extension of their professional lives. For others, volunteering and paid work are unrelated: one pays the rent, the other provides the kind of satisfaction that only comes from doing freely chosen work, in pursuit of an ideal or in service to a chosen community. And sometimes volunteering is simply a way of getting what you want. "How else would you get things done if you weren't involved?"

ROSEANN NAVARRO

Roseann Navarro has been working to support herself since she was in her teens and volunteering since she was nine. Today, in her early thirties, after several years of struggle, Roseann is director of a community health center in Hartford, Connecticut, a community volunteer on the side, and a recently remarried, former single mother of two teen-age girls. She is also a part-time law student, intent on succeeding in the professional world so that she can "get involved on a much higher level . . . to advocate for change"—at the salary she deserves. But she is equally intent on always being a volunteer. If someone wants to "buy her skills," she expects to be paid well for them, but if the community needs her, she feels an obligation to respond for free: you don't charge a neighbor for a favor. She sees herself as a "community participant": "The kind of work we see people doing in our community, we do not think of as volunteer. We just think that's part of what they do, part of living on that block." Still, Roseann doesn't mind being called a volunteer. She is proud of her commitment to "helping out": it is, she says, part of her upbringing and her culture:

"Since I was a child . . . I always did what was considered volunteer work . . . helping out neighbors and doing services for neighbors . . . I was raised in New York City . . . in a Puerto Rican neighborhood in which . . . very few people knew English, especially the older people . . . so when people had to go to hospitals or any of the institutions, I would be dragged along as an interpreter . . . I was young, about nine years old when I started interpreting . . . And I did it quite a bit . . . And I got to be real good so that everybody wanted me to go with them to the welfare department, to the health department, to the school, wherever it was. And that was to me the beginning of what I would consider volunteerism."

It was time-consuming but worth her while. She was providing an essential service—people "could not communicate" without her—and acquiring new skills. "I learned a lot through it . . . especially verbal skills in both languages, which was an asset then and is an asset now. Because I didn't have the opportunity to learn Spanish when I was a child. They did not teach it in school; you weren't allowed to speak it in school . . . Having to interpret, I had to go back and forth in both languages and . . . it really improved and helped me to maintain my Spanish." It also "started" her in health and hospital work. Most of the interpreting was "hospital-related . . . most of it was [in] either an emergency room or a clinic . . . The hospitals didn't have bilingual people."

Roseann got her first full-time paid job, as a hospital interpreter, when she was eighteen. She'd married and had her first child at seventeen, her second a year later, and moved with her husband from New York to Hartford, where she started working in an emergency room:

"I didn't like the job . . . felt very much oppressed, first time in my life I felt oppressed . . . I was the only paraprofessional in the unit . . . everybody else was a professional—a social worker, a doctor—something like that. And I felt I was treated very differently from everybody else. I got the shittiest job. I got demands put on me that nobody else had. I could not take breaks like everybody else . . . had to follow certain policies that I felt nobody else had to follow, and basically it was because they were professionals and I wasn't."

She turned to a "Manpower center," a federally funded job training program, which eventually led her to paid professional jobs as a community worker and organizer; but it was a slow, arduous "step by step" process. She had dropped out of high school, had to get an equivalency diploma, and took college courses "on the side" for years, in order to get her B.A. In the beginning, Roseann was simply not marketable; even the people in the Manpower training program had little to offer:

"They had a skill center . . . they would do an assessment on you and then . . . decide what they would do with you, based on your skills . . . They would give you a stipend, less than what I was making at the hospital, but I figured this was an opportunity. They did the assessment . . . and all that, and they said, 'Well we have this problem. We have nothing to offer you because you're way above any of our participants.' They didn't offer me very much . . . My counselor offered me a maintenance job . . . and I said, 'If I needed a cleaning job, I sure wouldn't need you to get it. I can get that on my own very well. That's not what I'm interested in.' They said, 'Well, you know you're choosy and you can't be choosy.' And I said, 'Well, I *can* be choosy and I *will* be choosy.' "

Her first opportunity to do some "professional" work was teaching a math class at the Manpower center, as a volunteer. She liked the work but knew she was being "exploited"; someone with teaching credentials would have been paid for the job. All she had were skills:

"I had very good math skills, and their math teacher quit on them . . . and one of my counselors said, 'Teach this class until we can get a teacher and in the meantime we'll try to get you a job.' They were paying me as a participant, but I was actually teaching . . . I wasn't getting paid as a teacher . . . I loved it. It was a lot of fun. The students were all adults, most of them over forty, and I enjoyed working with them . . . So the work didn't bother me. What bothered me was the fact that I wasn't getting paid as a teacher."

It also bothered the director of the center, who "blew up" when he found out what she was doing and hired her as a Manpower community worker. "This was similar to a social worker, but they called them field workers. I think they wanted to pay them less, that's why they did that . . . It was minimum wage, that's what you got paid at that time, and that was about $2.50. It was a horrible situation, but . . . that's what started me off in the community . . . I always saw things as another step . . . I always had a sense of moving along."

Her job as a field worker meant working with community groups. Roseann became involved in a number of organizations in the black and Puerto Rican communities, and the lines between volunteering and paid work blurred. Her jobs as a volunteer and as a Manpower employee differed in scope, but they were both centered in the community.

"On my paid job I was basically helping families get services . . . helping people get jobs . . . health services, fighting with teachers, because they suspended somebody's kid, translating materials, translating, interpreting, helping people get food . . . If their welfare check was cut off I was calling the social worker and yelling and screaming and being an advocate for people, individual families.

"In my community work, it was not on an individual basis, it was on a community basis. The things I worked on were activities to [have an] impact on a larger group of people . . . If I worked on housing, it was housing for the neighborhood, not getting an apartment for an individual person. If I worked on education, it was trying to deal with the educational system and how it relates to Hispanic or black children . . . on a community-wide basis. My community work was broader [in] scope."

Roseann enjoyed the work she was doing for Manpower but wanted to be paid more for it. By now she was in her early twenties, in the middle of a divorce, and the single parent of two little girls. She would not have accepted money for her own community work, but would have welcomed a raise on the job and felt she deserved one:

"I don't think I've ever felt I should be paid for the things I've done in the community. I've always felt I should be doing something. I feel everybody should be doing . . . This is your community, you should be giving something back to it, instead of bitching all the time—'There isn't this, there isn't that . . .' I used to do things for people and they would want to pay me, and I would say no, because I knew they didn't have the money . . . It wasn't that I wanted to get paid for that work. It was just that I needed a better income at the [paid] work I was doing . . . In the beginning, I had other little jobs I had to do because the money wasn't enough to support my family. I was alone."

She was "very resentful," and now that Roseann is an administrator herself, making a "good salary" as director of her own agency, she still resents the fact that her field workers are paid so little: "Every job I had in the community always required extra time that you never got paid for. And the first few jobs were very hard because you got paid nothing and you had to do fifty or sixty hours a week of work. Well, that's a lot of work . . . And they didn't care if you had to do it on weekends, evenings, if it affected your family. You got absolutely no compensation, no reward for what you were doing except for the fact that you were doing something for the community . . . Should I be paid less because I happen to like what I'm doing? Why should I be paid less than a social worker, because that social worker has a degree and I don't? Maybe I'm even a little more successful than that social worker because I come from the community. I know the problems. I know the resources. So maybe I can move a little faster . . . Community organizers get paid nothing. And they do very important work, but they're not recognized."

Roseann is willing to use her professional skills volunteering, helping out in the community; it is just that she doesn't want to be underpaid at her job. She is very clear about this: "If you're gonna buy my skills, then you're gonna buy my skills. It's either I give them to you for nothing, and that's fine, or we negotiate a price for them. I feel very strongly about that." This is a "value" she has tried to impart to her daughters, now twelve and four-teen.

"They've done favors for neighbors . . . and the neighbors want to pay them. I've always told them, you don't accept payment for a favor. A favor is a favor. A job is a job. If someone hires you for a job, then that's negotiated up front. But if you do a favor, you don't accept money."

One favor that Roseann has done throughout the years is to provide informal counseling for women and families in her community. She is well known as a "community participant" who knows her way through the social service system, so she is always "getting calls" from people for help:

"I get calls at home, someone says, 'Are you Roseann Navarro; somebody told me to call you. I have this problem . . . Could you help me?' It could be anything . . . and then you end up working with these families for whatever time period . . . eve-nings, weekends . . . And I've done a lot of that. I still do a lot of that . . . I've done a lot of counseling with women . . . around issues of separation and divorce, [or] women who want to work and don't want to be home anymore . . . and are having problems with their spouses because their spouse doesn't want them to go for education or doesn't want them to take on that job and feels threatened by her. I've done a lot of counseling around that, and that's been on a more personal basis . . . I get counseling and I give counseling."

This is not "volunteering," she says: it is simply fulfilling an obligation, but Roseann also gets "a lot of satisfaction out of working with someone and being able to help them"; and it is a relief from her paying job: "I'm an administrator here. I hate being an administrator . . . I spend my time on budgets and fiscal matters, supervisory stuff. I hate it. That's not what I like to do best. I like working with people and I also want to change the system, and I find that working with families I have contact with the institutions and I can do my little advocacy and do my little pressuring at different levels at different points. It has worked on some level . . . I don't think I've created any big changes in any institution, but it gives me that opportunity . . . Most of us have no choice, we've got to do it. We've got to do these things."

It is not just the women in the community who "do," Roseann says at first. The men also "help out"; they're "gentlemen"— like her husband, she says, who is "always helping somebody . . . There was a housing crisis and he brought home four women and twelve kids . . . 'They were on the streets, they had no place to live,' he said. 'What was I supposed to do?' " But, while "the men participate just as actively as the women . . . our leadership among our women is a better leadership . . . Every time I've been involved in an activity and there have been men and women involved . . . the men seem to get hung up on fighting about politics . . . about who should be the leader . . . The women end up doing the work; they do it very well."

Roseann is not resentful about this and does not want to criticize the men in the community or separate their interests from the interests of women:

"For us the struggle is not just for our women; it's also for our men, and we try to be very sensitive to their issues. We're very concerned about the men in our community. Unemployment is very high for them . . . alcoholism is very high among our men, and drug use."

The women will "get down" on the men on one issue—wife abuse; but it has been a struggle and a long time coming:

"We're beginning to say, wait a minute, we can't tolerate this nonsense anymore. That's not an easy issue for us. It's a hard one, but we're trying to get our men to join us to say, we can't tolerate this nonsense. Because there's a lot of wife abuse in our community . . . very hidden, kept in the family. Women in those situations, we get to know about it. We try to help them out of that situation. One time you wouldn't touch it. You'd say, it's none of my business. Now we're saying it *is* our business."

This is the way her community survives, she says. They help each other out and make the community business their own. It is something she does for herself as a member of a community and something the community has a right to ask of her. "It is my duty as a resident to participate in those activities that affect my people and my community . . . Someone should be making those demands on me."

The work her community demands, in addition to her paid

work, is also a demand on her family. Roseann's daughters have benefited from her volunteering—it has taught them about doing favors—but they have also paid a price for it, and so has she. When her children were young, she was alone, working full-time to support them and volunteering, and it was hard to find time to be with them:

"It was very tough . . . I would take my daughters with me to meetings and activities. And I had three roommates and they helped me out quite a bit. I would always make sure I was home between five and seven; by seven o'clock they were in bed. So between five and seven I would feed them and spend some time with them and make sure they were in bed before I would go out. My meetings were usually at seven-thirty in the evening. It was very tough, and I think they've paid a price and I've paid a price for it. My daughters are very aggressive, very assertive; and it's good and it's bad. They're twelve and fourteen, but they really aren't; they're a lot older, and yet they're not . . . They're very independent, both of them. They don't need very much, and that hurts me now. I wish they needed me more. And they don't . . . and it's been the way we lived for the last ten years. They've grown up kind of on their own. They've learned to take care of themselves. They've been doing their own cleaning, their laundry, everything, for a long, long time. It's good, but there are some negatives to that too . . . We've paid a price for it . . . But I don't think I would change it. I don't think I would do it any other way . . . I'm glad they are able to take care of themselves . . . This life is hard, so you've got to learn to be hard."

ELLIE PETERSON

A typical day for Ellie Peterson runs from about eight-thirty in the morning to ten at night. She works an eight-hour day as a hospital administrator, in charge of ambulatory and emergency room services, and spends most of her evenings at meetings. Ellie serves on the boards of about twenty community groups, involved in a variety of development and service projects, and she is active in her political party. All her work, paid and unpaid, is centered in the community. She has three priorities of her own as a volunteer: "youth, employment, and economic development."

She never "set out" to volunteer: "I never said, I have free time, I think I'll give it to the community . . . It never happened that way . . . It's just there was a need. Somebody [was] needed to organize and talk about youth employment, as an example. I was one of those. It was my interest, youth employment. It kind of evolved. Then you wind up on several boards . . . It's kind of a middle-class thing—volunteerism—that's why it's our obligation to do it. It's very difficult to talk about a general housing problem when you don't have an apartment."

Her community work began about twenty-five years ago, in the most ordinary way—with PTA volunteering when her children were young. Ellie had worked for money as a teen-ager and continued working after her marriage, but her husband insisted she quit her job when their first child was born; they had four sons, and she stayed out of the paid work force for about ten years. At first she resented staying home—"I missed working"—but now believes it was "for the best"; her children turned out to be "dynamite human beings," and working with the PTA started her off professionally. "I was president of the PTA, and we did some very dynamic things in that school; we were one of the strongest PTA's in the city . . . My volunteerism kind of exploded from there." She became politically active, eventually serving a term on the City Council, and began volunteering in "areas of special concern," working with youth in her community. When her youngest son was six years old, Ellie embarked on a paid career in community services, working with anti-poverty and youth employment programs throughout the 1960s, until she assumed her present job in 1969, administering hospital services to the community.

Volunteering and paid work have always been closely related for Ellie. She does not volunteer "haphazardly"—"My volunteerism is geared around what I do professionally"—and she approaches her job at the hospital as both a paid professional and a volunteer: "If I belong to a block association, I'm on that

association as a representative of the hospital . . . I become
the link between the hospital and that organization . . . that
way they don't have to look for who they want to speak to in this
institution . . . I become the community's link to the institution."

This does not mean that she would work for the hospital for
free or for less than what she deserves. Working for the community is different—"Most community groups don't have the
money to pay anyone, anyway"—and Ellie draws lines between
the kind of work that ought to be done by volunteers and the
kind that ought to be salaried. She does not use volunteers on
her staff at the hospital:

"I had one volunteer. She begged me to [let her] volunteer
for a position that I had vacant in the emergency room. But I
told her I couldn't let her do that for long 'cause the hospital
would take that position away from me, and that's a job loss for
the community . . . I know the politics in this institution, if
they find I could staff that emergency room . . . I said to her,
once we get the job filled and you want to come back as a
volunteer, fine."

Ellie had never encountered this problem herself, in her own
career as a volunteer, because she has never volunteered for a
service job in an institution; she does, however, do some individual service work, providing informal career counseling to
teen-agers. This is, perhaps, the one volunteer job that is not
"geared around" her professional career. It is more of a personal priority:

"I share my information . . . I've done that mostly with
teen-agers . . . 'cause that's my priority—teen-agers and
whatever I can do to assist teen-agers in their career development, and just developing as human beings . . . It's a thing
with me. Because I feel it's an obligation . . . I'm speaking
primarily about black teen-agers . . . Black professionals, re-
gardless of what their area of expertise is, have an obligation to
share information, to be of assistance, to any young black teen-
ager who is struggling, who can't get the information at home—
we should be the next resource. So . . . whenever they call me
and say, 'I just need to talk to you about where I am,' I sit down
and talk to them, and I don't have to know them. All they have

to do is just say, 'Joe Blow told me to call you, that you'd talk to me . . .' I'm known in the community . . . I've been here all my life . . . so a lot of people know me from way back."

Because of her work with teen-agers, Ellie was asked to join the board of her local YMCA and, eight years ago, became the first black and the first woman to sit on the board:

"It was an experience . . . My reason for being on that board was to be an advocate for teen-agers, and for inner city teen-agers. That's why I consented to serve . . . Things I would bring up, the men would say I was emotional, you know, the whole thing. 'Oh God, Ellie, your information is good but you're too emotional,' and all that kind of crap, you know. And I would tell them, 'Maybe you need to become more emotional about it and then I wouldn't have to be.'"

It wasn't that bad, she says laughing, because she had been through this sort of thing before, during her term on the City Council in the mid-seventies: "If I spoke on the floor around an issue, then I would be told that I was emotional . . . But I would always have my facts along with my emotionalism, I would have my facts together. I would have done my research on whatever it was I was talking about and trying to get support for . . . I've gone through that whole thing about being emotional and all that, 'cause I'm a very vocal female. And I don't mind being called emotional. And I don't think that's a slap in the face. It's gotten me this far in forty-seven years, being emotional . . . You know, it has."

Ellie believes that most of the work of voluntary associations is done by women, which is also just fine, she says. She doesn't resent the fact that men don't do their share: "I think we do a better job anyway, we have a tendency to hang in longer than the men . . . they don't have the stick-to-itiveness for the nitty-gritty stuff . . . If it doesn't happen right away for most men, they're gone—on to something else . . . they don't hang in there. It's the women. It's the women."

Still, Ellie doesn't think of herself as a volunteer—"I know that's exactly what I do, I just never think of it. It's just my community work." And she does not expect this work to go on forever. She has invested enough in volunteering over the past twenty years and is considering at least a semiretirement:

"When I get to the point where I'm burned out with volunteerism, I'm gone . . . I'm going on fifty years old. I don't plan to spend my golden years going to community meetings. I'm gonna have fun . . . I'm forty-seven now; I'm giving myself till fifty. When I turn fifty, good-bye community. I've done it since 1962. My Lord, if I haven't had any influence in the changes in the community, and I've been involved since 1962, I never will. So I'm not gonna hang in there till I'm sixty-five. I'm not saying I'll give up all of them. I might have one or two special interest groups. I'll always be involved politically. 'Cause I love it. I really do."

She doesn't worry about her organizations getting on without her. Ellie has always tried to "pull other people" into whatever she was doing as a volunteer, to "share" her information and her power. She has no desire to be indispensable:

"I lend to the organization, but if I felt that the organization depended on me I wouldn't be involved in it. 'Cause that's very, very wrong. Because whatever the work is of that organization, if that work does not go on when one person is gone, then you're doing a disservice . . . 'Cause you can drop dead and what happens in an organization? Nobody should be irreplaceable . . . I don't want to be indispensable, 'cause if anything happens to me then the whole shebang falls apart."

It is one thing to be a "honcho" on the job, but volunteering is something you do in concert with the people in your community. "Even if it's something that I initiated, and there's quite a few things that I belong to that I organized, my first responsibility was to get other folks involved . . . I would hurry up to move toward getting other folks involved . . . so that they would know as much of what was going on in that organization as I did. And that's what volunteerism should be about."

There is nothing exploitative about this kind of work; it is not about making money, and Ellie gets a "personal satisfaction" from volunteering that "keeps her going":

"It's not for nothing . . . I do get something from it . . . It has a lot to do with how my four sons grew up . . . with some of the morals I've instilled in my children . . . And I have people walk up to me—young people who I had talked to maybe ten years ago and steered them in a particular direction and never

realized it—come up to me ten years later and say, 'You know
. . . you were the one who got me into this area here. You're
the reason I am where I am now.' And I can't describe what that
feeling is . . . So if I'm helping one person in my lifetime, I
think I've done something . . . And I think that becomes part
of your legacy . . . To me it is. Because we all have a reason for
being here, not just to exist in between the birth and the death
—you know, that there's something we're supposed to leave
here. And this is the only way I could feel [there was] to leave it.
I don't have any money to give anybody."

She might, of course, if she weren't volunteering: "I know it.
But it wouldn't be the same. It wouldn't be the same."

KATHRYN PARSONS

Kathryn Parsons has a passion for political work; at seventy-
two, she has devoted over half her life to it, serving as a state
legislator, as an administrator in various federal and state agencies, and as a volunteer. She is "almost feverish" about the need
for volunteers to participate in politics. "Getting people to do
stuff," she says, is the only way to save the political process from
media consultants and professional organizers. Kathryn served
fifteen years in the Massachusetts legislature, has an old-fashioned faith in the possibilities of representative government,
and ran her campaigns the old-fashioned way, talking to people
in her district and ringing doorbells.

"To me a person who goes through this kind of process goes
into the legislature, let us say, not a prey to special interests.
When you're elected, you're supposed to be a representative in
some way or another, certainly if you're in the legislature. If you
see this as something that emanates . . . from the people that
you're going to represent, it seems to me one of the tests as to
whether you've got it or not is to . . . get together in one-on-
one groups a lot of the kind of people you think you're going to
represent. And you start talking about whatever it is this district
needs . . . and begin getting feedback and begin getting peo-

ple involved in [determining] what they want to be represented as. You can do the same thing by ringing on doorbells . . . I just cannot imagine running for anything without getting a reasonably good committee of different kinds of people together to sit down and yak and tell each other, No, they don't want that, you're crazy—you know, all that stuff, and having all the dissent and the fun of building something up, and having come out of that with some sense of what the needs are, who really cares about it . . .

"If you've talked to this many people, rung this many doorbells, had other people out working for you, giving you some feedback from time to time, you know what people are really interested in . . . I was not in a position to be snowed by a good sales talk . . . I didn't know what all of them wanted, but I knew what a lot of them wanted and I at least had some to attest to that.

"If you sit up there and are skillfully portrayed as Mr. Wonderful or Mrs. Caring, or whatever you like, and go through all this crap, and then you walk in and you think, boy, you *are* a Mr. Wonderful, and clearly you *must* be Mrs. Caring . . . you divorce yourself from what you're doing . . . and you don't go in there and represent."

Kathryn began her political career in the 1940s, after the war, when she moved to Massachusetts, with her husband and started working for the League of Women Voters. She became president of her local chapter, served on the statewide board, and, in 1952, at forty-three, decided it was time to run for the state legislature:

"With a great deal of hard work and a little bit of luck, I made it." She served two years, was defeated in her campaign for a second term—"With a fair amount of hard work and not as much luck"—and was reelected in 1957. She gave up her seat in the legislature in 1970, ran an unsuccessful campaign for statewide office, and then "did a couple of things," paid and unpaid: "I was on the Advisory Board of Public Welfare; then . . . the Parole Board . . . and worked half-time in the Republican floor leader's office for free. In 1971, the governor appointed me to the cabinet . . . I was Secretary of Manpower [until the mid-seventies] . . . Then I started to do some other things and

[was] asked if I was interested in being a part-time professor [at the University of Massachusetts] in the new school of management, which I did for a year, and toward the end of that year the regional director of HEW was appointed to a new job and I was invited to be regional director."

HEW was "fun," but her tenure there was brief; it ended with the Ford presidency in 1976. She went back to the University of Massachusetts for two and a half years, resigned because of curriculum changes, and for the past two years has been involved in "a variety of things," paid and unpaid, as a board member of several profit-making and voluntary, nonprofit organizations. She also has continued doing "a lot of political stuff, working for candidates and so forth."

The fact that so much of her work is now unpaid is, for Kathryn, only incidental. Her husband is also retired and involved in a number of volunteer activities, but they have all they need for themselves, and haven't any children: "Money doesn't really make much of a difference . . . I like to have the feeling that I'm doing something that I want to do, and if you're getting paid for it, well—peachy . . . It isn't that I've been rich, you understand, but it's the feeling of doing something that you think is worth doing . . . If somebody said, what are you doing now, I wouldn't say, I'm a volunteer . . . that's not a description of what you do, that's a description of how you . . . or somebody else values what you do."

Kathryn did not start out with this commitment to volunteering and "doing something that you wanted to do that needed to be done." It wasn't a family tradition; she bumped into it in her thirties, after a relatively brief career as a secretary, when she went to work for the American Friends Service Committee.

"My mother taught until her late thirties, when she was married, and then she went back to teaching when my younger sister was about twelve years old . . . She did some things, but teaching was more her life and her mission . . . She really wasn't much of a community worker; neither was my father . . . I grew up in Swarthmore, Pennsylvania, went to Swarthmore College, graduated in 1930 with honors in economics. At that point, not having enough money to go to law school, or anything else, I took a quick secretarial course . . . I took a job as secretary and assistant to the comptroller at Swarthmore, where a few years later my husband came to teach psychology. In 1940, when the draft had gone through, my husband was still teaching at Swarthmore. He was asked . . . if he'd take a year's leave and run a Friends camp for conscientious objectors, which we did . . . went to California, opened the first men's camp on the West Coast and worked there for a year. Came back to Philadelphia, and I went into the Friends Service Committee and continued to work in the CO section for the duration, plus six months.

"I'd like to tell you about the Friends Service Committee because that is a very interesting world of the volunteer, or at least it was then . . . It had a philosophy that said that everyone [who] worked for the Service Committee was a volunteer. What they did was interview you to work there, they asked how much money you needed in order to work there. I said that I could work for carfare and a couple of lunches . . . So I worked all through the war as a volunteer on that basis . . . side by side with people who were getting paid full-time. Other people that worked for the Service Committee full-time didn't get any money at all; they had enough money, and they contributed to it.

"It was a wonderful introduction to the feeling of being a volunteer, because everyone in the Service Committee was a volunteer. There was not a hierarchy of jobs which were for the staff as opposed to those [for] volunteers . . . You did a job and you were a volunteer, and you got paid enough to make it possible for you to work there, or nothing."

Kathryn has never worked at a job and "needed to get paid like other people needed to get paid and was getting paid less than other people," and she "probably wouldn't stand for a job like that." But she believes that if everyone is paid fairly and equally, everyone should be encouraged to approach their work with the commitment of a volunteer, particularly in the public sector:

"I have the feeling that the somewhat old-fashioned, conventional view of incentives, extra vacation, extra pay, punishments, that kind of reward system . . . It isn't as effective as people think it is . . . And therefore you have to be thinking about other ways that you can get people involved in their jobs, get them to share in their jobs, and get people to sense what it's all about, and do it not because you tell them to, but because they have joined in whatever their organization is doing and this is their hunk of it, and they essentially feel responsibility to it, commitment to it . . . That's the kind of volunteer commitment to a paid job, which I think is terribly essential in the public sector."

Perhaps this is easy for Kathryn to say; she has held high-level positions in the bureaucracy, of responsibility and authority. It is a lot to ask of someone in a boring public sector job. But Kathryn's ideal—the ideal of an "enlightened" manager—is that by convincing people they are contributing a piece of the puzzle (and she believes they are) you will make their jobs less boring; they will feel better about their work—and get it done: "You just can't fall back on, 'Where does it say I have to . . . Where does it say I can . . .' You like to get everybody you can . . . going ahead and doing something because the job needs it and nobody is standing in their way."

This is why volunteers are so important in the political process, she adds. Volunteers, voters, who are brought into a campaign, not just to lick envelopes but to contribute to the formulation of policy, are not apathetic and, in an ideal world, can hold the people they elect to account:

"The political system is really out of hand as far as money is concerned . . . I don't think it works . . . It has a lot to do—I think it's a vicious circle—with the apathy that people feel toward politicians, toward political campaigns . . . Two things happen. A lot of volunteers think, Why in the world should I be working my tail off if this guy is pulling down all this dough? And also, the guy that's pulling all the dough says, I've got this in my hot little hands and I'm not going to allow you amateurs bumping into it . . . He's making money out of it; he wants to keep his act going . . . You've got two know-nothings throwing dollars at each other . . . the one with the best adman or the one with the most dollars may make it . . . You're not getting representation out of that."

Money doesn't get the job done; it doesn't make people care about their work. Kathryn's own motivation to perform is based on a "social obligation" connected to her ideal of a "democratic form of government." For some people, the motivation is more "personal," a need to "do something for somebody else." Money is only a way of getting people to go to work when they have no reason of their own for being there; it doesn't make a boring job interesting or make their work worthwhile:

"I think that money is a substitute; it's necessary, absolutely necessary; but essentially, beyond the point where it's necessary, it becomes a substitute for a lot of the things that you don't get if you're in a different kind of structure, or if you don't have the feeling that it's yours, or you don't have the feeling that what you're doing is an important part of something and that people you're working with recognize that. All those other things are way ahead if all you have when you come home at night is the feeling, Well, today, by God, I racked up another hundred and thirty dollars, it's pretty boring . . . It isn't the money, it's the fact that what you're doing is worth . . . something."

ALICE WILLIAMS

"Just say I'm a busybody," says Alice Williams. "It's the busybodies who do the things, you know . . . Because you see a need and you want it done . . . And they say, put your efforts where your mouth is."

Alice has been volunteering for nearly sixty years; she was "initiated very early," at ten, when her mother sent her around the neighborhood to collect gifts from local merchants for the church bazaar. She was "a little afraid to go into the stores at first, and the first day didn't do so well," but since then, she has become an active—and, I'm sure, assertive—volunteer for her family, church, and political party. Today she is president of a local commercial development corporation in her neighborhood in Queens, New York; ten years ago, she became the first woman president of their civic association. She has always been active in church, doing the committee work of men and the daily work of women, and with the NAACP. She worked with a tenants' council when she lived in an apartment, with the PTA when her daughter was young, and has been working full-time for money since she was in her teens. For the past thirty years, Alice has been working for the city of New York; having started out as a clerk, she now has an administrative job in a city agency. It is a "good job," and she is comfortable in it, but it doesn't affect her need to volunteer "to get things done."

Sometimes it is simply a matter of standing up for yourself and your family. When she was a tenant, Alice was a tenant activist, because "you have to have a good place to live." In the forties, when her daughter was a baby, she lived in a building that had "no decent place to leave the baby carriages"—just a dirty, unattended basement. "And I was very concerned about . . . cats sleeping in the carriage . . . infantile paralysis was a thing we dreaded . . . and I heard on the radio that the fleas carried the germs. I wrote a letter to the mayor and I told him about the basement and the conditions it was in and I didn't want to leave my baby carriage there. I didn't want my baby to become ill. In nothing flat he had an inspector up there, demanded that the basement be whitewashed and cleaned up . . . They had to build a room . . . with a lock for the baby carriages . . . That was the beginning, because I found the mayor always responded . . . I always got a response from Mayor LaGuardia. He was fantastic . . . And if there was any problem, I wrote a letter to the mayor . . . The landlord said to me, 'You are a troublemaker.' "

As soon as her family moved to a house in Queens, in the early fifties, Alice started making trouble in the local civic association, which had always been run by men, who "tried to ignore the fact that women were part and parcel of the tomorrow of this country.

"In the very beginning, when I joined the civic association almost thirty years ago . . . women attended, [but] since it was so predominantly male, they were afraid to step in . . . They ignored you if you raised your hand . . . They met in the schoolhouse. One night I took a seat in the very first row knowing they could easily say they couldn't see me in the back. I went to the front, I raised my hand, they looked over my head.

So the next meeting I went back to the same seat and when the call for volunteers came . . . I didn't raise my hand, I stood up and stepped into the aisle of the auditorium and I said to myself, I dare you to go past me. So the president said, 'Yes, can I help you?' I said, I'm volunteering for service in the civic association. He began hemming and hawing; he didn't know what to do. They'd never had a woman before. And the others said, 'Oh, let her be. Take her on; you don't have to give her an assignment.' So I became a volunteer for the civic association, and as luck would have it, the next weekend the recording secretary wasn't there and they didn't have anybody to take the minutes. So someone said, 'Well, what about that volunteer?' So they said, 'Can you take minutes?' I said, 'I'll try.' I went home and typed them and sent them to the president for review. He was absolutely flabbergasted. He said, 'They're accurate . . . You didn't miss the motions . . .' They made such a big issue—'Can you take the minutes? You think you could do that?' So I said, 'I'll try' . . . accepting whatever it was that he gave me to prove that it could be done . . . And then there's absolute amazement— 'Well, you recorded the motions!'

"So I filled the next position as secretary and went on to treasurer and vice-chairperson and vice-president . . . until finally I became president of the civic association . . . The men had all served for so many years, so it was imbedded in them, no woman could do what they had done. Proved to them very easily that it could be done."

Other women followed Alice into the association and, as usual, she says, proved themselves to be better volunteers than the men. "I don't say men don't do, but women do more, without all the fanfare . . . without the whole business . . . they are the ones who move everything . . . [The men] get so formal and hem and haw, women just go ahead and do."

She would like to see women given credit for the work that they do: "They laud the men for moving a piece of paper. You could move roomfuls, [and] they say, 'Oh, you got it done.' " But she also believes that when you volunteer, doing the work is what matters most. On a paid job, you fight for job titles and salaries; as a volunteer, you *do*. "Even if it is menial, it has a place and [is] a part of something else, and therefore whatever you're doing with that little part is important, because it fits in like a jigsaw puzzle to something else, and when the puzzle is all completed, do you know which piece was the most important?"

This becomes especially clear in a time of crisis, Alice suggests. During the civil rights marches led by Martin Luther King in the early sixties, she helped organize a food drive for people marching from Selma to Memphis who had been "cut off from food . . . the towns would not let trucks deliver food to them and the stores ran out after a while." With the help of the teamsters and community volunteers, they collected food for the marchers and got it out:

"The unions brought the trucks to us and they camouflaged the trucks with old clothing flapping out the back doors, and food in the center of the trucks . . . so they could move into the South, with rags and stuff flapping out the back of the truck and get the food down to the people . . . That was such a satisfying thing to do . . . the ministers really went at it, getting the food together, getting it packed. Men came in the nighttime, volunteers . . . Everybody gave a little something to help load the truck, get it out . . . No matter how tired these fellows were, they came in, and we said, 'Who are you?' And they said, 'It doesn't matter who I am; I came to help my brother.' And they packed those boxes and brought bits of string. You know, we had more knots in the string around it than anything else."

Money has nothing to do with this kind of work, and Alice has never accepted gratuities or even expenses for any of her volunteering: "I never accept them because then I have the feeling that I really *have to* do a thing . . . And I want always to do it because I *want* to do it. So I do it on my own." Taking money would "take away that feeling."

This feeling does not lead her into taking paid jobs away from anyone else, she adds. There are simply certain services that people in a community have to provide for each other if their community is to survive and prosper. Alice has always worked for money and always volunteered and sees no conflict between her paid and unpaid activities, even as a former trade unionist. She became involved in the union movement in the thirties, when she went to work as a milliner after graduating from high school, and, as a city employee, she is still a union member today. "I know what you should fight for and I also know where you must give . . . You cannot just sit back and wait for everything to be done by a paid person . . . How would you get things done that are so beneficial to so many people?" You try to get whatever public services you can, and you contribute what you can, working with the people in your community. For Alice, volunteering is very clear and simple:

"When I first moved to this area, I noticed that the women met in the middle of the street . . . There were a lot of widows; we were the only couple . . . They met in the middle of the street, every day around two o'clock, there was this gathering. I looked out the window and I watched. They met and they talked. They greeted one another. Everybody had a rake, and when their little greeting and their little talking was over they raked in the middle of the street, back on both sides, back to the curb, on both sides. The entire street was cleaned.

"We had a Department of Sanitation, they didn't wait for that. They went out every day and cleaned the entire street. They never interfered with the Department of Sanitation . . . They weren't doing a good job, anyway . . . They cleaned the street that they lived on so it would be clean . . . And it was a pleasure to come home to that street where the leaves had fallen, they picked them up . . . They came in friendship to the middle of the street, to talk and greet one another and then they'd move back, each one working to make that street perfect . . . They were volunteers . . . You can start by meeting in the middle of the street . . . Those women were all widows and they weren't alone. This was their way of meeting and talking and then they did their little thing . . . and they waved and went into their homes. They talked and they laughed . . . it was friendship . . . raking and going back."

DENISE BAINES

Before she will consent to be interviewed, Denise Baines wants to be sure I'm a feminist, with a feminist perspective on volunteering. She would not want to help me glorify a tradition of service that "exploits" women and reinforces their economic powerlessness; volunteering stands for everything that is wrong with the status of women: "As women we serve our husbands, serve our children, serve our community, and that clearly is part of the whole economic system, that puts us in the position of thinking that our time and energy should be for the service of everyone else [for] no remuneration . . . That's the part that angers me about volunteerism . . . It directly contradicts everything I believe in . . . It so much reflects what our culture does to women."

Denise, at forty-one, is the single divorced parent of three teen-agers, a social worker, and an "activist." She has a paid job teaching in a New England school of social work, coordinating a special project on domestic violence, and she has worked for free for about fifteen years "around issues" of family planning and reproductive rights. All her work, paid and unpaid, focuses on protecting women and securing their rights; almost all of it is devoted to "policy issues" and "systems change."

As a paid professional, Denise prefers administrative and policy work and believes that social service work "tends to be a sort of band-aiding approach that blames the victim; it's the sort of analysis that sometimes can say, 'This is your problem, let me help you.'" As a volunteer, she refers back to the 1971 resolution adopted by the National Organization for Women opposing social service volunteering. Denise will only volunteer "to be an activist to challenge the system," not to deliver individual services—except, perhaps, to other women.

"I've worked with a lot of battered women in my most recent job and I see a lot of direct service volunteering that women have done in just providing shelter for battered women . . .

Rape crisis centers, battered women's shelters, they couldn't survive without volunteer work . . . A lot of services that are clearly identified as women's services are never . . . fully supported at the level they should be . . . And I think that's where women as feminists come in and say, we have a commitment to other women."

We do not, it seems have a similar commitment to servicing the poor, the sick, or the elderly—people with more traditional service needs that are also not being met by government. Should a woman volunteer to help out at the nursing home down the block instead of a rape crisis center? "If we get into providing that direct service . . . we undermine the ability to challenge—it's collusion in a certain sense . . . When it comes to direct service, I say that's the responsibility of government."

Whether or not volunteering to provide services to battered women is equally collusive is unclear. Perhaps it doesn't matter. Denise has made a personal commitment to a community of women that is at least as important as her political theories: "It's like having an . . . ideal that you're working toward and yet acknowledging the existing circumstances of our lives as women and the need to provide some of that direct service work if it's gonna happen at all." When women are the ones at stake, Denise will compromise her theory and try to "go both ways." She feels "connected" to other women, and so is willing to help them on the way to social change. Apparently this is the only connection her politics will allow her to feel.

That we live in a sexist culture is the first fact of life for Denise, who was nearly one of its victims. She grew up without the women's movement, in the 1950s, with traditional expectations, entered into a traditional marriage as soon as she graduated from college, and had three children by the time she was twenty-eight. This does not now feel like a life that was freely chosen, but one that was foisted on her by the culture, and she is grateful to the women's movement for showing her the way out of it: "I look at myself and my own evolution . . . clearly the influence of the women's movement is so powerful because I started out in very traditional ways, which a number of middle-class women have . . . My choices, my view of seeing choices, was so limited by the expectations and the roles that the culture had given me . . . Beginning to challenge and look at that, I've made a lot of changes in my life." She was not happy in her marriage—"It was not terrible; it just was not enough"—and it was over in about ten years. Denise went back to school to get her master's in social work and got a job administering a family planning program. In her previous life, she had been a volunteer for Planned Parenthood.

She became involved with Planned Parenthood in her mid-twenties, in her own childbearing years. She was living in Florida with her husband—he was in the service and they'd "moved around a lot"—and she was looking for something to do that "fit in" with her liberal arts background in sociology and psychology. Someone referred her to Planned Parenthood, and "It sort of fit, coming out of sociology, coming out of psychology, being a woman, being a mother . . . the population control issue at the time, in the sixties . . . It was an organization that I'd heard about that made sense."

Her work on reproductive rights intensified in the 1970s, after Denise moved north, divorced her husband, went back to school, and became a feminist. She helped organize a statewide chapter of the National Abortion Rights Action League—"I spent about nine years establishing and building an organization, particularly as threats began to increase around denying reproductive rights"—and she began working with the National Women's Political Caucus. This was a "liberal feminist" phase, which lasted through most of her thirties and left her somewhat disenchanted:

"I did lobbying for women's issues for about eight years . . . I still know that system well enough that I will be involved and do some small pieces, but I have a lot of frustration and anger about how reform[ist] that whole strategy is and after a while . . . you sort of burn out . . . Obviously it's really important to do, but personally I don't want to go back up to that legislature constantly. Because I have a different vision of how much impact the work I'm doing will really have. I'm much more cynical about it now . . . so I can't go back with the same kind of energy."

Now she is interested in working at the community level with "coalitions" of women, with minorities and the poor, and in the courts. She has "moved away" from NARAL and "electoral politics" and is working on reproductive issues with a "grass-roots" group of low-income women: "Right now it's very much a class issue since only poor women still have limitations and restrictions on access to abortion . . . We've been working on a lawsuit to provide state funding for Medicaid abortions, and I really worked hard and was one of the main organizers . . . Because when you analyze the abortion issue, we haven't won in state legislatures or in Congress, we've won through the courts . . . Another volunteer activity that I've been doing recently is working with community television. I've been putting a lot of energy into that as a way for people in the community to be able to control community awareness and education through television and the media. It's been an interesting combination, because I still bring in my feminist views and issues into a broader community group to make sure that gets part of broader community programming."

It is clear that Denise has gone through a progression as a volunteer—from concerned housewife to liberal feminist to a slightly disillusioned "grass-roots activist." I suggest to her, tentatively, that volunteering has helped shape her politically, that it has been as powerful and positive an influence on her "evolution" as the women's movement; volunteering for Planned Parenthood was the beginning of her professional career. It is hard for Denise to agree that there can be anything good about traditional volunteering: "If I had a different awareness and consciousness starting out as a young woman now, there's no way I would . . . set up my life to be in that role, as strictly a professional volunteer." The fact that she may have grown in that role and advanced herself professionally doesn't save it: "Men never have to do that to move up in society." And, even though much of her previous volunteer work may have been "fairly similar" to the work she does now—Denise has never been a traditional service worker—it is hard for her to take pride in her early efforts as a volunteer or to praise them:

"I was doing a lot of what I believe in now, but I was doing it almost by chance, not with any awareness that I have now of how I would focus my work. The fact that I was working around . . . abortion rights and family planning would fit a lot of my

concerns as a feminist, but back then I didn't have an understanding or an analysis. I just felt that I should be contributing."

Looking back, Denise feels that the simple desire to contribute is a "trap" for a woman; it means always playing a servile,
nurturing role and always being dependent on men. "I believe
that everyone should be working and everyone should be paid
for their work, because I think we all need that common sense
of economic equality to really have rights in the system. I think
as long as there's a free labor force and it's based on gender, it's
always going to feed into the oppression of women." Volunteering gives a woman freedom and flexibility in her work and
makes it easier to be a mother—but at the price of economic
power and professional success. What's needed is not a return to
the volunteer work ethic but "support" for women with children who work for money. Child-rearing should not deprive a
woman of a paid, professional career. Denise's children were
five, seven, and ten when she went to work full-time; raising
them herself was an ordeal:

"Arranging transportation, child care—that's an overwhelming task. And it's exhausting, but there are a lot of us out there
who do it. It's hard work. I always say you can't appreciate it
unless you've done it . . . It's really hard to share what it
means to be a mother in this culture—where there is not . . .
support around child care, around so many aspects of your life—
particularly since so many women do end up raising children
alone. It's a very hard job. I've often said, of all the things that
almost define who I am, I think being a mother is one of the
most powerful. . . . My life and how I arrange it and what I do
daily is really determined by the fact that I'm a mother.

"A lot of women . . . I know that have not had children
[and] that are now in their thirties are really struggling with the
question, do they want to have children or not, and will ask me
. . . Classically there really was no choice, there was an expectation. I certainly love my children and that's been an important part of my life, but I also realize it wasn't the same choice
that women have now."

CARLA RAYMOND

When Carla Raymond was seven years old, she went on her first march on Washington. "It was 1955 and it was a march to urge the Congress to implement the school desegregation decision quickly . . . I remember going on a bus with a group from my church with a lunch box and marching on the White House lawn . . . I do remember being kind of in awe of Washington and the White House and the Capitol. I also remember very clearly what I had been told then about desegregated schools and the Supreme Court decision—that it would mean something very real in my life. That I would have a chance to go to a better school. That all that had to happen was that we had to convince Congress to do something quickly. So one thing, I'm sure, stuck with me . . . I remember having a sense of things being doable, that I could make a difference somewhere. If you thought things out clearly and had a definite plan, people could act on that and something would happen."

Today, nearly thirty years later, Carla is the full-time, paid director of education programs for a national civil rights organization, the divorced, single parent of a thirteen-year-old girl, and still a volunteer—for the same "hokey" reason: "It keeps me from feeling powerless." Much of her work has been political; she has been a movement activist—for civil rights, black nationalism, and, lately, women's rights. But she prefers doing individual service work, on her own, providing informal educational or career counseling. Carla's paid work involves her in the administration of after-school, scholarship, and college placement programs. She has a good deal of "information" to share, she is known in her community, and people call on her for advice. She finds some "emotional fulfillment" in giving it, particularly to other women:

"I feel a very strong personal motivation to do things of service to women . . . In the last few years, there has been more of an emphasis on women; prior to that it was the black community. The concentration on women just comes out of my own personal need to do that . . . Information that I have and skills that I have I will share with other women on a one-to-one basis . . . I do a lot informally with women . . . People have called me about going to school, helping to fill out financial aid forms for their kids . . . People have called me with résumés . . . I have counseled women who want to leave their husbands. I have taken women into my home who are making that transition.

"I feel very good when I get someone into school or someone gets a job or irons out a situation in work or their personal life with the help of information I've given them . . . To help them talk that through, figure out what's going on beneath the surface and how they could better handle it . . . even to the extent of role-playing, and I've done that with people. And it does help me, because nine times out of ten, I'm giving people advice that I don't follow."

It gives her a feeling of accomplishment that she doesn't get from her job or from her political volunteering: "You can see things happen . . . Because there are things that I can accomplish that I might not do in the regular course of my job, the paid work . . . I have a stronger feeling of things being doable in the service context than I do in the political context. If for no other reason than that the political context requires a lot of other people for a solid accomplishment. The service context does not. In the service context, I can accomplish something. Something can happen from just one-on-one imparting of information, and I can assist someone . . . and see something happen. Political activity requires the involvement and cooperation of a whole lot of other people, and the more people required, the more unpredictable everything is."

Carla was mixing political and service work when she was in high school, joining marches and sit-ins for civil rights, working with her church, and teaching in a tutorial program to help young kids "get some information . . . that would put them a little ahead of the game." The fact that the educational system itself was unfair and needed changing did not make it wrong to give a handful of kids the "knowledge" they would need to beat it, "to be on an equal par with someone else." Carla had been through the system herself; when she became involved in the tutorial program, she was a senior at a highly competitive, predominantly white high school, having transferred from all-black grammar and junior high schools, and had a "strong personal sense of how unequal education was, in this city and the country.

"And I felt very strongly the need to do something to equalize the situation a little more for black kids. Now it could be argued that the way to really do that is to improve the schools in the black community, or integrate the schools, or whatever, and that's important, that's clearly a priority. But what I felt then was that that would take years to do. And somebody ought to work on that, and I would go on later in my life to work on that, but in the meantime, if there were twenty-five kids right here [and] I could do something to change the situation for them immediately, that that was important to do, and that that would have a multiplying effect. Sending those twenty-five kids back out in the world informed and better educated and ready would be very important. There'd at least be twenty-five that were better off."

The fact that she was not getting paid for this work was incidental, and there has never been any conflict for Carla between her goals as a political activist, service worker, and paid professional. She has always had her own reasons for volunteering and has always used her volunteer experiences "to create a job or fill out my résumé." She suspects women don't "do enough" of this. "Women certainly appear to do more volunteer work than men [but] . . . we probably don't get as much mileage out of it as a man would for doing a third as much work." Carla learned early on how to use her volunteering and how to get a job:

"One of the first jobs I had was at the Harlem YMCA where I had done some volunteer work for a tutoring project after school, and when they needed to hire counselors for day camp I got one of those jobs immediately, because I had been working on a volunteer basis at the Y."

Then, when she was thirteen, she got a part-time job that lasted through junior high and high school and turned into a full-time job when she finished; she was a researcher for a federally funded project "studying" youth in the Harlem community:

"I'd go by that office all the time and say, 'I know everything, just ask me what you want to know,' and made a pest of myself in this office. I'd say, 'You want to interview people about housing. I can introduce you to people who've organized rent strikes. What else do you want to know? I'll tell you who the real leaders are around.' And I went to that office regularly doing that kind of thing and eventually they hired me. And not only me. They decided they ought to hire a bunch of kids to work in that project to add another dimension to that research."

Carla has always been able to manage for herself despite all her volunteering, and she is impatient with the prohibitions on traditional community service work that came out of the women's movement ten years ago; she attributes them, in part, to the insensitivity of white feminists to the needs of the black community:

"It is fine for white women in NOW to say that kind of stuff, but the black community has survived in that way. The role of the black church and informal networks for information . . . has been very important in this community . . . The numbers of black kids who are informally adopted by friends and distant relatives within the black community is tremendous, and the moves to formalize that have not always been successful. People are not always willing to go down to the adoption agency and do all the papers, open their families up to scrutiny and investigation to do a formal adoption, but they will just take in the kid next door . . . I can't think of a single black family that I know where that has not happened on one side or the other . . . You know, when mother felt the streets here were developing too strong a pull on this kid, send him to Virginia to live with Aunt May."

Carla "grew up in this way"; her family was "very active" in church and community work, and as a child she was participating in block parties and cake sales, as well as church-sponsored bus rides "to demonstrate about one thing or other." She worries now that what was true for her has not been true for her thirteen-year-old daughter:

"Somehow, there was something negative that happened to

the spirit . . . I grew up with that sense of personal responsibility and obligation, and maybe women get a whole lot more of that dumped on them than men do, but I don't find that all wrong. I have a concern that my daughter doesn't seem to be growing up with that. It's a real concern for me. I think it will mean something very different about how she relates to people. What she feels responsible for doing for other people. What she feels would be available to her from other people and the links she feels to other folks . . . She's really just interested in hanging out with her friends and having a good time. I'm concerned that she seems to have no political consciousness. None. I did at thirteen . . . I think she'll have something very different from what I had, and I'm very concerned about it because I think it will be negative."

Something has been lost—"the linkages that people in the community feel to one another"—both the impulse to do service and a collective political consciousness. Carla doesn't separate "volunteering" from "activism"; one informs and shapes the other. Every march and every demonstration is a social service to "make things happen" for your neighbors. And every favor, every deed that links you to them is political.

The Coming Generation:
College Women on Volunteering

"I was brought up with the absolute assumption that I was gonna have to support myself economically. There's absolutely no question of having someone support me while I do volunteer work. That's not an option. That's not ever been anything I would consider. When I think of volunteers, I think of people who have a certain amount of extra time and want to give it to their communities in a positive way. And I have always supported that."

Sara Kane, volunteer

Today's young women are supposed to be dressed for success. What was prescribed for them, in popular magazines from *Cosmopolitan* to *Savvy* to *Ms.*, was not community service or even political activism, but the acquisition of power. Power—"from bedroom to boardroom"—was the buzzword of the seventies. The newest ideal woman goes to business, law, or maybe medical school, runs with the big boys on the fast track, and makes a lot of money. By the time she has children, as she must in order to have it all, she has established herself professionally. She may take a year off or even two to have a baby, but if she works part-time while her child is young, preschool, she works for money. The ideal young woman today has "choices" and can "juggle" them in a variety of respectable career/family combinations that rarely include volunteering. At work, she is always a paid professional. Whatever else she may be, wife or mother, she is not a volunteer.

This is the ideal, the new prescription, and it reflects, in part, the enormous expansion of career opportunities for middle- and upper-class women of the first post-feminist generation. "Women represent one-fourth to one half of the students at most graduate and professional schools," according to Diana Zuckerman, Director of the "Seven College Study" of life and career goals of students at the Seven Sister colleges. A preliminary, 1981 comparative survey of Radcliffe women and Harvard men in the classes of 1981 and 1984 revealed "striking similarities" in the professional expectations of male and female students. Law, medicine, business and journalism were their favored professions: "traditional women's careers," teaching and social work were chosen by less than 5 percent of the women in the survey sample, the vast majority of whom expect to combine career and family life. Of the students surveyed in both classes, 95 percent "would like to marry. Most would like to have children." Of the women in the class of 1984, 84 percent (compared to 92 percent of the men) "hoped to have children," as did 92 percent of the women in the class of 1981 (and 86 percent of the men); 97 percent of the women (and 98 percent of the men) want to work full- or part-time while their children are in elementary school. Volunteering was apparently not considered a work option for women during those years, nor was it projected as a "priority" fifteen or twenty years after graduation. The most dramatic finding of this preliminary Radcliffe/Harvard survey is that there is no "meaningful" difference between the career and life goals of male and female students. They both expect to marry and have children and to succeed in "prestigious" paid careers.‡

Still, I found at least a few future professionals in college today who are also volunteers. Nine of them are portrayed in this final section of interviews. All but one are members of a Smith College service organization who met with me as a group to discuss their career plans and their volunteering. To some extent they fit Diana Zuckerman's profile and my own image of today's college women; but one thing about them surprised me —how clear and simple it is for them to volunteer.

‡ Diana Zuckerman, "Career and Life Goals of Freshmen and Seniors," *Radcliffe Quarterly*, September 1982, pp. 17–19.

Although these women, because they volunteer, do not see themselves as wholly typical of their generation, their approach to volunteering has been shaped by the now typical expectation that they will be independent and self-supporting—even if they marry, which most of them expect to do. They assume that they can and will care for themselves. They seem to have been untouched by the earlier feminist controversy over volunteering. Several were even unaware of it and looked at me blankly when I mentioned that ten years ago feminists were, in general, opposed to volunteering because it was associated with dependence and domesticity. For these young women, volunteering is simply something "extra": it supplements instead of substituting for a paying job. The new woman doesn't have to defend herself against volunteering because it is no longer an exclusive career alternative for her. It isn't keeping her out of the professional world and doesn't touch off fears about having to depend on a husband. It needn't conflict with her image of herself as a feminist.

When I returned to Smith for an afternoon to conduct my interview I had to remind myself not to think of the students as girls. They refer to teen-agers as "adolescent women." (It is clear that, at thirty-three, I am already an older one.) But in 1967, when I started college, there were quite a few girls on campus. As eighteen- and nineteen-year-olds, a lot of us then felt rather girlish at heart. Even a few years later, in our early twenties, we didn't know quite what to call ourselves: women still sounded too grand. Now it seems we must have been the last generation of girls to graduate from college. Today there are only women, preparing to "exercise their options."

SARA KANE

Sara Kane grew up with the women's movement. At twenty-two, she is a "second-generation feminist" who was raised with the notion that women are independent people who take care of themselves, just like men. She has always known she would support herself; getting married and depending on a husband for her keep has never been an option or a goal. "I was a tomboy . . . and was brought up to be very independent, and I was also brought up with my Mom's consciousness raising group meeting in the living room when I was very young . . . So I was really raised to be a feminist . . . I started marching in the third grade . . . I come from a family that believes in political work."

Her family is hardly typical: both her parents are Harvard professors. Sara agrees that she was brought up "outside the system," in an idealistic academic environment in which good work was not necessarily salaried: it was work that served a political ideal—"A society in which people are not given or denied fundamental necessities of life [because] of race, sex, class, or sexual preference." Sara was brought up to be a volunteer, to do social change or service work for free, to try and redress systematic and individual inequities. "My proving ground is not an economic proving ground. It is a political proving ground." She thinks of herself as an idealist, an activist, and a volunteer—"absolutely."

For the past year she has been volunteering in a women's prison in Massachusetts, while she finished her senior year of college:

"I work for a program called Aid to Incarcerated Women . . . its fundamental purpose is to provide transportation for children to visit their mothers who are in prison . . . to maintain that bond between the mother and her child while she is in prison . . . So one of the primary things is transportation, but all kinds of things come up for women doing longer sentences . . . things come up involving the children, things come up with welfare, things come up with housing, things come up with the Department of Social Services . . . In my work I have done intervention between a woman and her landlord because she was being evicted . . . I have done a fair amount of welfare advocacy . . . We've done everything from helping people do shopping who don't have cars . . . It really depends on what you set as your own personal limitations; the needs are just endless."

This is important work, whether or not it is paid, she says, and doing it is part of being a feminist:

"I feel like one of the most profound things that have come with the women's movement and one of the most profound benefits of feminism is a sense of community and taking care of each other. Not necessarily in a stereotypical nurturing kind of way, but looking out for each other. And I feel like what I'm doing is looking out for a lot of women who need help right now. [I can't] say that I believe in sisterhood and I belong to a community of women but [that] only those who don't need help can belong to that community . . . I get a lot back from these women, I'm learning a lot. I'm learning a lot about bonding between women in a different kind of context . . . I feel a deep commitment to the women in the prison at this point. I've gotten very close to several women there."

This is individual service work that Sara considers a personal and political priority. She has made her own commitment to serving a community of women and believes that "real good social service work . . . that's not being done elsewhere . . . is a real way to effect very important social change." It is also sometimes more satisfying than working at the policy level for systems change:

"You can look around and see definite needs. One of the reasons that I really find this work rewarding is that I can look at those women and I can tell exactly what their needs are—not all of them, but some of them—and I can fill those needs. And there are very few opportunities given us . . . to concretely do something positive for the world, to have a real sense of accomplishment. I think all of us have a hard time finding places where we can really feel like we have an influence, we make a difference, like we're important. And to me, the volunteer work I've done has been the most significant of that kind of work. I get a lot of self-esteem from knowing that I'm doing really effective and important and necessary work, and whether or not I'm getting paid for it doesn't matter."

It is not that she volunteers indiscriminately: "I would not do volunteer work for any kind of agency that could afford to pay me and wasn't . . . And I doubt that I would do any volunteer work that didn't seem to be fulfilling a real important political need in my life." And she would not take on a volunteer job for which she was not properly trained, in a program that was not properly organized:

"When I was in high school, I worked for a tutoring program . . . It was . . . young white girls going into the projects in Cambridge and working with kids who had learning problems. Their problems were that there were no really good textbooks, and no good teachers and no good schools, so they weren't learning to read or do math. So I went in and I tutored in reading and math in the projects, lasted a very short time because it just didn't work . . . I had a little girl assigned to me, she walked in and said, 'I didn't know my volunteer was going to be white . . .' Her immediate reaction was horror. There was no reason for her to learn to read. She was not interested in learning to read. Her mother was very interested . . . but she just didn't feel like that was an important thing in her life, to learn to read at that point. She was in the third grade . . . She just didn't concentrate and didn't try and do it . . . We got to be friends, but I never figured out a way of really motivating her to read.

"I would not participate in a program like that again without thorough training and without much closer supervision . . . I'd never done that kind of tutoring before. I'd never worked with kids before . . . I was just completely unprepared . . . The program was run by people who lived in the project. I really liked the woman who ran it very much . . . She did it out of a deep concern for the fact that the kids in her community were not learning to read. But there would have to be a lot more control for me to feel comfortable doing that . . . It felt like we were repeating something that had been repeated too many times, in terms of upper-middle-class white kids going into a black community, completely unprepared . . . If I had been prepared and trained and there had been some kind of supervision . . . so it wasn't just the two of us out there and no one paying any attention from then on, I would consider doing something like that again, because I do feel like it's worth it to try and help people to try and learn to read."

As long as her work is effective and "within the boundaries of [her] political priorities," Sara will volunteer, as long as she is "economically able." Money will begin to matter more to her next year, when she graduates from college—"I have to get a job; there's no two ways about it"—and she hopes there will be funds available to create a staff position in the prison program for her. She will need a salaried job and, if one is offered, will not hesitate to accept it. There is nothing sanctified about volunteering; it is simply a way of getting "valuable" work done when there isn't any money to pay for it: "I have no qualms about not being a volunteer . . . If I thought there was anyone who was going to pay me to do this, I would be very glad to accept money . . . I would like to be paid for the work I do . . . I deeply believe that everyone deserves to be paid for their work."

But this is a "theory," a matter of principle for women who can afford to work for free, and theory should not be allowed to interfere with getting out the work:

"The theory's fine . . . everyone deserves to be paid for the work that they do . . . and if it's important work, as with social work, then society should pay for it and the burden shouldn't be on individuals . . . to bear the weight of it, and it certainly shouldn't be on women. But I do have a real problem when theory starts getting in the way of work that needs to be done . . . I always feel that people have to keep track of what's really happening on a daily basis and adjust the theory to meet those needs."

For Sara, this may mean taking any job she can, after graduation, to support her volunteer work at the prison, if she must: "If I have to work in a pizza shop for three years because I'm doing important work that doesn't pay, that would be fine . . . I think the issues of self-esteem and self-respect are probably key here . . . My family has always been very supportive of all the political work I've done . . . There's never been a self-esteem problem related to being paid. I think that probably is key. And the issue of women's self-esteem is one that we've got a whole lot of work to do on . . . and I think it would be very sad if that gets fought out over the issue of volunteerism."

It has never occurred to Sara, until I raise the question, that there might be something wrong with women volunteering. She was twelve years old when the volunteer tradition became an issue for feminists. She grew up expecting to earn her own

living, like her mother and most of the women in her community. She didn't know any full-time volunteers or any "housewives"—"I'm not familiar with that role." The volunteer tradition has never been an issue for her:

"I never thought about it before . . . It's hard for me to have
any kind of hard line on that . . . The society has certainly
benefited a great deal from women's volunteer labor in ways it
maybe doesn't deserve . . . I think that for a woman who is
stuck in that traditional role . . . the woman who is married,
who can't work because her husband won't let her, because she
doesn't feel that's right, because she can't find a job—and can
afford to do volunteer work and wants to do that . . . Part of
me is saying that there's something wrong with that whole
image of white middle-class women who have husbands who
support them giving their free labor to society. And part of me
is saying that without changing their roles, if in fact what would
happen is that they would sit home all day, that they may get
something very important and fulfilling for them out of that,
and I have a hard time denying them that . . . unless I had
something better to offer."

The ideal, of course, and what Sara wants for herself, is to be
paid for the work of your choice. "One of these days," she will
go to law school: "I'll probably end up being a criminal lawyer,
partly because that's somewhat of a mandate from the women
who I work with. There's so many who wouldn't be there if
they'd been properly represented. And they need good lawyers
. . . I would like to keep working with women in prison. To me
they epitomize everything I work for in the women's movement. It all comes together. All the issues of race, sex, class,
come together in a women's prison. All the issues of motherhood, a woman's right to have children or not, state intervention in that, all of the issues of how women should be and how it
goes about programming us to be that. It's all laid out in front of
you in a prison, by the programs they do and don't have, by the
kind of wallpaper they do or don't put on the wall. It's very clear
and the work is very exciting, in the sense that I see it integrat-
ing everything that I've worked on before, at different times
. . . It uses some of everything. I find it real rewarding and

exciting and very difficult work . . . I expect I'll be doing this for a while."

She will never get rich doing this kind of work. Sara doesn't want to be the power in the boardroom and is "conflicted" in general about the entry of women into the corporate world. Economic equality and independence are essential, she says; but she doesn't "see change coming from corporations," and it is hard for her to "feel good" about women becoming corporate executives and part of what she believes is the inequitable distribution of power in American society:

"Everybody can't move to the top because there isn't room at the top for everybody, so I have a hard time with individuals moving to the top as a solution. Because for everybody at the top there are necessarily gonna be hundreds of people at the bottom. It's built into the structure. My vision is a much more socialist vision. Ideally we have to try and find some level at which we can all survive, where my survival is not dependent on the fact that there are gonna be twenty-five women on welfare. I understand the necessity of moving into the business world if we're all gonna support ourselves. So some women are gonna have to do that. At the same time, I have a deep discomfort for that reason. We can't all fit up there at the top. I don't think we all want to, either."

A GROUP FROM SMITH COLLEGE

Irene wants to be a social worker and is considering joining the Peace Corps. Madelyn is preparing for a career in corporate finance. Helene and Leslie are pre-med students. Deirdre is a photographer with an interest in community work. Merril wants to be a lawyer. Natalie is looking for an administrative job in the nonprofit world. Carol is an English major who isn't sure what she wants to do after graduation; she only knows she doesn't want to teach.

All eight are undergraduates at Smith College. They all expect to be professional women and to marry and, at least for now, they are all volunteers, members of the college service organization. They do not see themselves as entirely representative of Smith students today: there is a lot of resistance on campus to volunteering. "People are very caught up in their work and see [it] as a distraction." "People react by saying, 'What are you gonna do? Join the Junior League?' They see it as an entry into society." "Someone who is interested in social work has to explain more than someone who wants to be a lawyer."

Irene works at a community center that collects surplus food and distributes it to the hungry. She doesn't see this as women's work—the center is staffed by men and women volunteers—but other people do, and they rarely take her seriously when she says she wants to be a social worker.

"When I say I might want to go into social work, people say 'Oh, well, you don't know what you want to do.' Especially Peace Corps. I think a lot of people look at the Peace Corps as something that you want to do if you're sort of a lost child of the sixties . . . I think a lot of people don't think of it as a profession that you could really go into . . . Like I never knew that people went to graduate school in social work . . . It makes me mad to be typecast as someone who doesn't know what they want to do. I've always liked doing social work."

Deirdre became involved in social service work in spite of herself; she volunteers at a local nursing home for course credit. She enjoys the work but struggles with her own impulse to do it for free: perhaps this is only something that has been "instilled" in her as a woman:

"I'm finding all these conflicts within myself . . . My experiences at the retirement home are favorable, and I always have a good time with the women there and had a lot of good response . . . but I'm wondering where this good feeling was coming from. Was my giving a selfless giving? It hasn't been worked out yet. But I'm working it out where I enter into it with well-defined goals that I want from the experience, what the experience has for me and what I can give to [it] . . . I'm not a martyr and I can't be a martyr, but I know that I'm giving a lot and there's a definite factor of reciprocity that has to be worked out, that women especially have to struggle for."

Everyone in this group talks about reciprocity and what they get back from volunteering—personal satisfaction or career training and skills. There is nothing wrong with "using" volunteering: "The thing I've always found about volunteer services, I never entered them because I felt it was my responsibility. I did it because I wanted to and I also regard it as really good practical experience. And I don't find that selfish, and I think now with the economy the way it is, I think we need volunteers, especially students . . . We're in a position now as students to do it because we don't have to take care of ourselves." Until they do, volunteering is a good "testing ground." It helps direct them professionally and gives them the confidence to deal with new and often frightening situations; it helps them grow up.

Helene is a pre-med student who volunteers at a home for the retarded:

"I felt that of the projects I looked at, working with retarded citizens would be the hardest for me and provide the newest opportunity, something I had never done before . . . Last year was really difficult . . . not knowing how to handle myself with them . . . And I've been able to handle myself a little better now; and in my relationships with other people, I don't see them anymore as being retarded or not normal. They're just special. It's nice to be able to walk up to one of them and talk to them on a regular level, even though you know they're not gonna be able to answer back . . . You talk to them; you just talk to them."

Merril plans to go to law school and volunteers at a shelter for battered women. She sees both personal and professional gains for herself in this work:

"It was nice to know what the legal opportunities are . . . I'm learning what the options are for women in situations like that." Perhaps, as a lawyer, she will "do something more counseling-oriented, like doing marital work with women.

"It taught me better listening and counseling skills, which have been valuable in my personal relations . . . It gave me a lot more confidence in myself . . . like, these were battered women and I wasn't. I was just a young little girl who wasn't married and had never been beaten and didn't have children, and I felt that I was being presumptuous at first and I think I

gained a lot of confidence in realizing I could . . . help someone that had gone through a situation that I really had never
been through."

Carol volunteers at a center for troubled teen-agers, not for
the sake of her career but to pay back a personal debt:

"I was on the other end when I was younger . . . I just really
felt that—there I was and I had all my problems and there were
people willing to help me, and I felt it was real important for me
to share myself now. And also because they're women. And I
just know how far I've come and if I . . . can help someone else
to do the same thing, that's really good for me."

No one in the group feels exploited by her volunteer work—
"you're not being exploited if you're getting something wonderful out of it"—and no one believes that social service work is
antithetical to social change, as long as it makes you aware of a
social problem. Although it was frustrating working with battered women, says Merril, "it made me more aware of a situation that I hadn't really given that much thought to.

"Working with these women was trying to repair some dam-
age. It wasn't solving the issue; it was dealing with some women
that had been beaten, but it wasn't dealing with the issue of
beating in general. And that was the frustration."

But the frustration is sometimes a "precursor to addressing
the larger issues . . . You have to start with the small and realize what the problems are."

Deirdre calls social work a "stepping-stone" to an understanding about social change:

"I work with older people in a retirement home. The residents there talk to me about the problems of the aging, which is
a big social problem. I would never be aware unless I read about
them, but that's not good—because you don't really read the
experiences of a 94-year-old man or a 102-year-old woman. It's
very rare that you get the chance to work in the field and find
out where this feeling hits home for them."

This has been Deirdre's first volunteer job. It has been an
"enriching" experience and her ideal now is to continue to
volunteer while she pursues a paid career doing "political"
work as a community organizer: "This experience has really

given me a way . . . to keep a balance (between paid work and volunteering) and realize how rewarding each can be."

Volunteering is "political action, social action," and it rounds out your professional life. Madelyn wants a career in "finance" and volunteers in a tutoring program for disabled children. Her first career goal had been to "work with children," possibly as a school psychiatrist:

"Now I'm an economics major, but I still feel about tutoring and children . . . working with learning-disabled children as something I want to do and something I'm still interested in, even though I'm not gonna do it for a career. I might do something like that as a volunteer activity while I'm doing something in finance or the corporate world. Volunteering is supplementing a part of me that wants to do something else. My career is satisfying one side of me or interest and my volunteering another. I don't think it's a conflict. I think it's an addition."

Madelyn is sure she will have a career in corporate finance, and there is nothing radical in this assumption. She will never be the kind of volunteer her mother was: "My father was working and she was home with me and didn't want to be out working." Educated women don't stay home anymore, and she doesn't expect to have to fight for her work rights, even in the corporate world: "Equal pay or equal rights just seem like something that should be, not something we should have to ask for, just should be."

There is a lot of confidence here about professional opportunities for women, in law, medicine, and business: "My family is very pro-woman, my father especially, I don't have that fear, 'Oh, I'm a woman, I'm gonna have problems.' If anything, it's the opposite. He's always telling me that in his business it's the women that are moving, the women that are going places, and I think that it's been really good for me to hear that. And he's brought me down there to talk to some of the women involved —the opportunities that are open to them and the things they're experiencing just floored me."

Everyone here also hopes to marry, they would "prefer" to marry, but not at the price of a career: "I would like to marry, but if I don't, I would never give up anything I was working for, for a husband." The most you do is "compromise": "I would

give up something. I would also want him to give up something," says Merril. "Last year when I was very serious with my
boyfriend . . . and I was taking 'The Psychology of Women'
and we used to talk about—'Well, Jeff, when we get married
. . . and I get pregnant, will you be willing to take care of the
child and stay with the kids half the time?' We used to talk about
the options."

Not all the men they know are quite so willing. Leslie wants
to be a doctor; she will never give up her career to marry, she
says, but a lot of men still expect her to:

"I'm from the South, so I run into a lot of traditional values
. . . When I was in high school, I was considered a feminist. I
was the only girl in high school who used to say that she was for
the ERA . . . I find that a lot of women in the South . . . they
want to say, 'Well, I'm for equal pay and I'm for equal work, but
I don't want to call myself a feminist.' And they don't want to
say, 'I'm for the ERA' because they're afraid they're gonna be
too radical. I consider myself a feminist but I don't consider
myself radical, so up here, that's okay. When I get home I have
to deal with it on a completely different level. Because all my
male friends still expect me to give up what I want if I ever
marry. And that's very difficult for me to deal with . . . I used
to get really angry about it. And I would argue [myself] blue in
the face, and I would say, 'I want to be a doctor and when the
times comes, if I have kids, I'll work it out.' But I've gotten to
the point now . . . I don't get radical and I don't attack them,
because it doesn't do any good. They get so defensive and they
just back into a corner. So I try to be very rational, even though
it's very emotional for me and I find that attitude very hard to
deal with.

"Another reason it's hard for me is that my father's raised me
since I was a little girl, and he's raised me with the idea that
'You're gonna grow up and take care of yourself. You're never
gonna have to depend on any male.' And so I came to expect
that from men . . . I have a hard time dealing with that irrational response of men, so I just say, 'Well, some day you're
gonna have to deal with it. You can't expect a woman to give up
everything for you . . . if she has a career, you're gonna have
to do some of the housework too.' "

All their parents are supportive of their career plans, but some still see them as things that can be put aside for marriage. To their daughters, a career is both a personal and a practical necessity, whether or not they marry.

"My father used to say to me, 'Well, Merril, when you get older, you can marry one of three things, either a doctor, a lawyer, or a millionaire.' It wouldn't be bad to marry any of those things, but I'd . . . like to be contributing. I don't want to be a parasite.

"One of my friends . . . her life is geared toward getting married; she wants nothing else . . . Almost every time we go out she brings up, 'Merril, do you think I'll get married . . . I'd die without it. I think I'd want to kill myself.' The thing that's so sad is that she feels that once she gets married she'll be happy and her life will be solved . . . So many people have expectations that are irrational: Once you get married, you're not lonely and you're not unhappy . . . There's still always times when you're lonely and there's still times when you're unhappy, and anyone who has expectations like that can't help but be disappointed."

Natalie is in the first semester of her senior year. She is looking for a job with a nonprofit agency or a corporation with a good "social responsibility" program, and she is worried about finding one.

"I don't think parents realize the economic situation . . . They're fine; they're making money and they have jobs. They hear about it. They read about it, but they're not out in the job market.

"I'm worried about next year, and my father said, 'Well, don't worry, you can always come home. You can find yourself a rich husband.' As if I would want that . . . To think that anyone could support another person in the first place."

FIVE

CONCLUSION

T hat they would earn their own livings and care for themselves was hardly a fact of life for middle-class women just twenty years ago. It was a rallying cry for revolution that shook the foundations of the traditional nuclear family. When the contemporary feminist movement began, the ideal woman was still seeking salvation in marriage. She had been programmed to need a husband: she was nothing and would have nothing without a man. It may be about time but it is still remarkable that, in twenty years, a paid, professional career has nearly become a conventional option for a woman. Going to work is one of the things that ideal women do. The achievements of first-generation feminists can be measured in what the second generation takes for granted—that they can only support and save themselves.

It is a pleasure talking to young, relatively privileged women who are, apparently, at ease with the prospect of independence. Perhaps this generation will not have to struggle so with "fear of success" or the much discussed dependency syndrome of their elders. Perhaps the crisis of confidence for women is passing, and with it some of the conflicts and controversy over volunteering. A woman who expects to earn her living and be paid equally for equal work can volunteer for "something extra" without fear of being demeaned or exploited, losing her professional identity or capacity to care for herself. She may even make volunteering a primary work activity while her children are young or combine part-time volunteering and part-time paid work, if her family can afford it, as long as it is not expected or required of her.

To suggest that there may still be a place for volunteering in the lives of women today, not just as a form of career advancement but for its own sake, along with paid work and family, is not to suggest that women were born to serve. The impulse to volunteer is a simply human one—that's been sexualized by our culture. Women were only trained to serve and trained to sacrifice their professional lives to the family. So it may still be a long time before the middle-class woman who has had her consciousness raised can volunteer freely, without a twinge of conscience or self-doubt or anger about her socialization and her secondary status as a woman in the workplace. Equal opportunities and equal pay, like the Equal Rights Amendment, are undoubtedly things that "just should be," but they aren't, not yet; and, for some, volunteering still feels like a knee jerk of femininity. Yet there are reasons to volunteer, to serve a cause or community, that transcend reasons of socio-sexual conditioning and job satisfaction and skills to be gained from volunteer work. The problem is not volunteering; the problem is femininity and the demands that have been made on women by the nuclear family.

There are, after all, paid working women who also work for free and career volunteers who have chosen their work and prospered, instead of being trapped or defeated by it. It is clear that many of yesterday's professional volunteers would have been paid professionals today; like most of us, they are products of their time. But it is not clear that paid work would, for them, in their time, have been more fulfilling or worth the cost to their families, and it is patronizing and presumptuous to suggest that their years at home were wasted. The "traditional" volunteers I interviewed were, with few exceptions, not the downtrodden, slightly incompetent, childlike women that feminists of my generation have imagined them to be. They were, more often, thoughtful, sophisticated working women who, by volunteering, had managed to find something for themselves within the confines of a culture in which sex roles, relegating women to the home, were narrowly defined and enforced.

They did not have it all, but neither, I suspect, will we—not all at once at the same time. At best, we will have it in stages, shifting priorities back and forth from professional to family life. Working eight, ten, or twelve hours a day, five or six days a week, doesn't leave much time to relax and play with the baby. Compromises have to be made, child-rearing deferred or career advancement slowed. The balance will be easier to find in an ideal feminist world of flextime and day care and men taking care of their babies—when the onus of "juggling" it all will not fall only on women. But there will still be conflicts between children and careers, and someone will have to give up something to resolve them. Liberation won't mean "having it all"; it will mean choosing our compromises instead of having them chosen for us. And, in a feminist world, when women are free to work for money, they should feel free, once again, to volunteer.

This does not presage a return to the old ways. New marriage and career patterns for women will shape new patterns of volunteering. Already the army of career volunteers is dwindling; the profile of the typical volunteer is changing—she is likely also to work for money, at least part-time—and the typical suburban community that has always depended on her voluntary services will have to change with her. Her town in Westchester has always "lived on its volunteers," says Ellen Covner, a part-time paid professional and part-time volunteer. Now, with so many women working at paying jobs, the community has to adjust "to reflect their needs." Voluntary associations are holding meetings on evenings and weekends, and a few fathers are beginning to participate in "traditional women's things," like PTA activities. But there is no one to organize the annual town fair, it is nearly impossible to find a mother to lead a Brownie troop, and the community is not ready or willing to pay for services it is used to getting from its women for free.

"At one point the suggestion was made that we hire someone (to be a Brownie leader). There was just tremendous reaction of 'Oh—how could you! What kind of community is this when you have to hire someone to be a Brownie leader!' And it was just voted out of discussion . . . The outrage was tremendous. I really have not forgotten how stunned they all were at the suggestion . . . Yet it was clearly a suggestion that was very sensible and might be done in the future."

Ellen agreed to be a troop leader for two years. ("They paid for all my baby-sitting. They had no problem with that.") At forty-one, with two small children, she divides her time between paid work, as a free-lance copy editor, and volunteering, at school and in activity groups for children. She worked full-time before her marriage and expects to go back when the kids are grown, but, right now, her "primary commitment" is to her children; for them she prefers to straddle the worlds of paid workplace, home, and community. It is "sometimes exhausting . . . to be all these different things at once," but as long as her children are young, Ellen will continue to be a part-time volunteer.

Middle- and upper-class women who have entered the professional world may be beginning today to find a place in their lives for volunteer work. Paid professional women are not abandoning volunteering, suggests Deborah Seidel, executive director of the Junior League, claiming that League membership did not decline or even "stagnate" during the 1970s; instead, the percentage of paid working women within the organization increased, forcing changes "in a whole system that had been built around the availability of women in the daytime." League president Ann Hoover now favors basic organizational reforms including shorter volunteer work assignments, and "lunch break" and evening meetings, to accommodate women with limited time for volunteering.[1] The Junior League, popularly considered one of the most traditional voluntary associations, (which one must still be invited to join) is slowly becoming an organization of paid professionals as well as professional volunteers. Thirty-six percent of its members now work for money;[2] nearly one half are either in the paid work force or in graduate school. Its members are also getting older, indicating that women may be starting their volunteering later, as they start their families, after they have established themselves professionally. As the Junior League is gaining professional women, says Seidel, "we are seeing fewer twenty-two-year-olds and many more thirty-three- , thirty-four-, and thirty-five-year-olds."

These women are helping to shape a still nascent, alternative image of the woman volunteer as a career woman who donates a few hours a week, on the side, to her community. A recent article in the New York *Times* heralding the new suburban volunteer portrays her as a "businesswoman [who] devote[s] one or two lunch hours a week to [a] meals on wheels program."[3] That she has returned to volunteering reflects, in part, a desire to remain connected to her community, as well as a need for the kind of personal contact she does not always find in her job. "A lot of women now . . . want to go back into direct service volunteering as a supplement to what they're doing," says Deborah Seidel. "It becomes a satisfying personal experience which they don't have if they sit in the office every day."

Paid professional women may even have something to learn or simply remember from the volunteer ethos, about the nonmaterial reasons and rewards for working and about a corporate culture that has trained men to value success above all else. The corporate world is hardly a hotbed of feminism; women have to enter it warily, says one self-proclaimed feminist ("with a capital *F*") and career volunteer:

"We've been so eager to get into this corporate world; we're so eager to be accepted by men, we're willing to accept the values that men have created. Instead of saying to ourselves, 'Well, maybe there's something wrong with those values.' I think there's something wrong with saying we only value what we pay a lot of money for. And I'm not willing to accept that. And I'm not willing to accept a corporate structure that does not deal with the problems of families in general. I don't want to see women buying into the values that men have bought into, where men worked twenty-hour days and they never saw their families. And that's what women are doing; they're doing exactly what men are doing. And I understand it . . . Women that are there now have to do it, if they're ambitious . . . But I would like to see the women's movement say, 'Look, this isn't for women, to go out and work twenty-hour days, and it isn't for men . . . It'll happen slowly . . . there isn't an alternative yet . . . But we have to demand that the corporate structure begin to value family life, that we begin to say human beings are worth something, that there is something other than this work ethic which supersedes everything else."

It will not be easy for women to keep their distance from the values of the corporate world as they make their way up within its hierarchy. The new professional woman is under tremendous pressure to conform to traditional masculine standards of behavior. Even as a corporate volunteer, in a corporate responsibility program, she may be encouraged to choose a typically masculine activity like board work, instead of a direct service job. According to Deborah Seidel of the Junior League, corporate women who are interested in direct service volunteering often complain that "corporations don't respect that as a valid corporate-time activity, whereas they do respect sitting on the board . . . There's no question but that corporations understand board work but they don't understand direct service volunteering." To succeed in this traditional, male-dominated world, you have to "tone down" your feminism, says one college woman who plans to pursue a career in finance. "It seems that women in finance . . . are entering a predominantly male profession, and the men are probably our fathers' age and the traditional roles hold for them. You can get ahead and you can always do what you aspired to, but just don't be too blatant about it because the men aren't going to accept that, and if you want to get ahead . . . you can do anything you want, just don't be too blatant about feminism . . . You have to go along with the whole corporate image . . . I wouldn't flaunt the feminist attitude in a corporate situation."

I doubt this is the way to liberation. It is, at least, a treacherous path to tread. Corporate success, if it means developing a corporate consciousness, may prove to be only a Pyrrhic victory for feminists, a senseless end to the volunteer tradition. It would be sad and silly for women to abandon volunteering in the name of feminism so that they can abandon feminism for the sake of becoming corporate drones.

This is not an argument for keeping women out of the professional and business world, only a caveat for those who enter it. Becoming a part of the economic mainstream, on their own, on an equal basis with men, is a clear and very pressing priority for women, and it is sophistry to suggest they will forfeit their souls or sexuality to success. But if there is nothing "dirty" or "evil" about money, neither is it the Holy Grail. Women will not be saved by paid work alone any more than they were saved by marriage. "A paycheck is a paycheck," a measure of what your work is worth to someone else, payment for what "someone else wants you to do," says one woman who combines paid work and volunteering. The price tag on your work simply reflects its practical value in the marketplace. Money and power, however essential, are practical commodities, to be earned and expended for a purpose in a practical world.

There is a lesson in this for aspiring new professionals and traditional volunteers, a lesson that was overlooked in the 1970s when volunteering fell out of favor and paid work was posited as the one and only path for women. There was some irony in the popular notion that a woman should seek not only financial independence but "fulfillment" in salaried work. Most paid workers will testify that most jobs only pay the rent. "Most of us . . . have jobs that are too small for our spirit. Jobs are not big enough for people . . . most of us are looking for a calling."[*] For all the flack about volunteering, this was one message that did not get across to women ten years ago—that the primary purpose of work is to make money. Most men and working-class women do not go to work to find themselves. On that magical day when we achieve equal rights in the workplace, most of us will still be bored with our jobs.

Achieving economic equality is essential and, I hope, inevitable for women, but it will not by itself fulfill them. Even a prestigious, highly paid job is rarely worth more than what it buys, rarely what we would choose to do if all our time were our own. Volunteering still has something to offer a professional woman—the freedom to choose her own work, to pursue a cause or a passion, or simply to relax in a job she can shape and control, to experiment and enjoy herself. Volunteering is a chance to do her own work instead of someone else's, and it can serve her well as she takes her place in the "real" world of men and money. Women who combine paid work and volunteering have always known that the two are not incompatible but complementary. There is no inherent conflict between paid work and volunteering, no need to abandon one to embrace the other.

[*] Studs Terkel, *Working* (Introduction), New York, 1972, p. xxix.

My own idea of a feminist work ethic is one that integrates the volunteer tradition with a new tradition of paid professionalism for women, striking a balance between love of work and money. "You have to have money to live, you have to market your skills and demand your due," observes one woman who works for money and for free. "But you don't have to be paid for work that you like, work you're invested in personally." Paid work is simply a matter of earning a living. Volunteering is "doing something that you care about."

This is why I suspect that as more middle- and upper-class women begin to earn their own livings, they will continue still to volunteer. The fact that volunteering will not define their lives does not mean it cannot be a part of it. The volunteer tradition can survive by changing, as it is today, to reflect women's changing roles at home and in the paid workplace. I do not think it will disappear. Not because of renewed public and press interest in "voluntarism"—that may only be a fancy that will pass with Reaganomics. Instead, the hundred-and-fifty-year history of women volunteering and the testimony of volunteers today confirms for me that there is a place for volunteering in a feminist world. If it is no longer a career choice for women, it has not yet been written out of the script. Volunteering can become a phase in a woman's life that accompanies child-rearing, career changes, and retirement, or serves as a sometime complement to paid work and, perhaps, a calling.

Continuing the volunteer tradition will require some delicate balancing—of what women want for themselves, their families, and their communities. Volunteering raises a diverse set of complex questions that every woman must answer for herself, about her concepts of work and pleasure, her place in the family and society, her self-worth, and the worth and power of all women as a class. It is a tradition rich in contradictions; for a hundred and fifty years it has organized and politicized women and given them work to do outside the home, while it protected the family system that put them there, under the care of their husbands. We have so many contradictory images of volunteering, as a force for the liberation or exploitation of women, for know-nothing do-goodism or progressive community service. Volunteering has, indeed, been all of these. But what it has come to represent for me, instead, is the simple belief that good work is worth doing for its own sake, for free.

Surely this is worth preserving on our way into the marketplace—the capacity to enjoy work, with or without the promise of a paycheck, the pleasure of working from the heart, not out of necessity or compulsion or for worldly recognition or reward. To do the work you love and do it well is simply joyful.

NOTES

PREFACE

1. Jane Addams, *Twenty Years at Hull House* (New York, 1961), pp. 60–75 and 90–100. (Originally published by Macmillan, 1910.)

2. "News of the Classes," *Smith College Alumnae Quarterly*, April 1981.

3. Interview with Robert Ginn, Director, Smith College Career Development Office, September 19, 1982.

One—WOMEN, WORK, AND MONEY

1. In a question-and-answer session on April 16, 1982, President Reagan suggested that high unemployment rates did not reflect a severe economic recession, attributing them, instead, to the entry of women into the paid work force. Stating that "the basic strength of our economy" would "bring us back to normal," he added: "Part of the unemployment is not as much recession as it is the great increase in the people going into the job market, and, ladies, I'm not picking on anyone, but because of the increase in women who are working today and two-worker families and so forth." See Irvin Molotsky, "Jobless Rate Tied to Big Work Force," New York *Times*, April 18, 1982, Sec. 1, p. 37.

2. U. S. Department of Labor, Bureau of Labor Statistics, 1983. See also "Expanding the Role of Women in Our Economy," Report of the Task Force on Women's Economic Issues, Rep. Geraldine A. Ferraro (Dem., N.Y.), Chairwoman, September 21, 1982.

3. According to Rep. Patricia Schroeder (Dem., Colo.), raising money is an "unbearable problem" for women candidates, partly because it is so difficult to obtain significant contributions from women voters: "A woman will write a check for $25 and think that's big, and a man will write a $500 check without batting an eye."

4. Andree Brooks, "For the Woman: Strides & Snags," New York *Times*, October 16, 1983, Sec. 12, p. 31.

5. Remarks by Secretary of Education T. H. Bell on the "Phil Donahue Show," May 4, 1983.

6. Ferraro, "Expanding the Role of Women in Our Economy," p. 67.

7. Judith H. Hybels and Barbara J. Hill, "Volunteer Work: Benefits and

Transitions," *Wellesley Alumni Quarterly,* Vol. 62 (Winter 1978), pp. 3–5.

Two—THE WAY WE SEE OURSELVES

1. The Gallup Poll (conducted for Independent Sector), "Americans Volunteer, 1981" (The Gallup Organization, Inc., Princeton, N.J., June 1981).

2. *Volunteering, 1979–1980: A Status Report on America's Volunteer Community* (Volunteer—The National Center for Citizen Involvement, Washington, D.C., April 1980). (Volunteer is now located in Arlington, Va.)

3. See "Analysis of the Economic Recovery Program's Direct Significance for Philanthropic and Voluntary Organizations and the People They Serve," A Report to the Board of Directors and Membership of Independent Sector (Washington, D.C., 1982). Noting that "reductions impact disproportionately and severely on the already vulnerable in our society," this report suggests that it is "unrealistic" to expect corporations to "leap forward to assist voluntary organizations in trouble," and that we should not look for "major" or "dramatic" growth in foundation or individual giving. It concludes that "obviously, philanthropic and voluntary organizations cannot pick up a large part of the (budget) cuts," and that "it is important not to exaggerate how much of the new load can be assumed by volunteers."

4. Address by President Reagan to the National Alliance of Business, Washington, D.C., October 5, 1981.

5. See Ann Hulbert, "VISTA's Lost Horizons," *The New Republic,* August 30, 1982, pp. 18–20.

6. Ibid.

7. Ibid.

8. See Shirley Keller, "Volunteers from the Workplace," *Volunteering,* Vol. 1, No. 2 (Volunteer—The National Center for Citizen Involvement, Arlington, Va. January 1982), pp. 9–10.

9. A recent newsletter issued by the National Council of Jewish Women reports on the awarding of CEU's (Continuing Education Units) to volunteers: "A nationally recognized unit for measuring continuing education, the CEU is awarded by many colleges, universities, and professional organizations, as well as corporations as diverse as Xerox, and the American Management Association." Elinor Multer, "CEU, Credit Where Credit Is Due," *NCJW Journal,* July/August 1982.

10. Interview with Winifred Brown, Director, Mayor's Voluntary Action Center, New York City, March 4, 1983.

11. Andree Brooks, "Among Volunteers, Change in the Suburbs," New York *Times*, October 28, 1983, p. A24.

12. Ibid.

13. Ibid.

14. Memorandum to Shirley Leviton, President, National Council of Jewish Women, September 23, 1982.

15. Gallup Poll, "Americans Volunteer, 1981."

16. Untitled report by Independent Sector (Washington, D.C.), on "highlights of the first two years," pp. 15–16.

17. Gallup Poll, "Americans Volunteer, 1981," pp. ii–v.

18. Ibid., pp. 12–20.

19. Ibid., p. 12.

Three—VOLUNTEERING IN RECENT HISTORY

1. For a history of working women in pre-industrial America, see Rosalyn Baxandall, Linda Gordon, and Susan Reverby, eds., *America's Working Women: A Documentary History—1600 to the Present* (New York, 1971) and Barbara Mayer Wertheimer, *We Were There: The Story of Working Women in America* (New York, 1977).

2. Robert W. Smuts, *Women and Work in America* (New York, 1971), p. 4. (Originally published by Columbia University Press, 1959.)

3. Mrs. A. J. Graves, *Women in America: Being an Examination into the Moral and Intellectual Condition of American Female Society* (New York, 1841), in Nancy F. Cott, ed., *Root of Bitterness* (New York, 1972).

4. Eleanor Flexner, *A Century of Struggle: The Woman's Rights Movement in the United States* (New York, 1973), p. 78. (Originally published by Harvard University Press, 1959.)

5. Flexner, *Century of Struggle*, p. 78; Wertheimer, *We Were There*, pp. 60–61.

6. Smuts, *Women and Work*, pp. 17–23.

7. Wertheimer, *We Were There*, pp. 233 and 210.

8. Smuts, *Women and Work*, pp. 19–20.

9. Ibid., p. 67; Wertheimer, *We Were There*, pp. 227–232.

10. Wertheimer, *We Were There*, pp. 227–32.

11. Ibid., pp. 212–32.

12. Smuts, *Women and Work*, pp. 19–23.

13. Edith Abbott, *Women in Industry* (New York and London, 1926), pp. 300–14.

14. Harriet Martineau, *Society in America*, Vol. III (New York, 1966), p. 147. (Originally published by Saunders & Otley, 1837.)

15. Julia Ward Howe, "Why are Women the Natural Guardians of Society's Morals?" (Address to Annual Congress of the Association for the Advancement of Women), in *Julia Ward Howe and the Woman Suffrage Movement*, Introduction and notes by Florence Howe Hall (Boston, 1913).

16. Martineau, *Society in America*, Vol. III, p. 109.

17. Carl N. Degler, *At Odds: Women and the Family in America from the Revolution to the Present* (New York and Oxford, 1980), pp. 298–301.

18. Martineau, *Society in America*, Vol. III, p. 145.

19. Nancy F. Cott, *The Bonds of Womanhood: "Woman's Sphere" in New England, 1780–1835* (New Haven and London, 1977), p. 156.

20. See Helen E. Marshall, *Dorothea Dix: Forgotten Samaritan* (New York, 1937), and Frances Tiffany, *The Life of Dorothea Lynde Dix* (Ann Arbor, Mich., 1971; facsimile reprint of 1918 edition).

21. Dorothea Dix, Letter to Ann Heath, 1838, as quoted in Tiffany, *Life of Dorothea Dix*, p. 52.

22. For an in-depth history of moral reform societies, see Barbara Berg, *The Remembered Gate: Origins of American Feminism* (New York, 1978). For an excellent, shorthand analysis of these societies and their relation to women's roles in society, see Carroll Smith-Rosenberg, "Beauty, the Beast, and the Militant Woman," *American Quarterly*, Vol. 23 (October 1971), pp. 562–84.

23. Martineau, *Society in America*, Vol. III, p. 145.

24. Ibid., p. 106.

25. For an excellent documentary biography of Margaret Fuller, on which this brief summary of her life is based, see Bell Gale Chevigny, *The Woman and the Myth: Margaret Fuller's Life and Writings* (New York, 1976).

26. Ibid., p. 211.

27. Ibid., p. 57.

28. Ibid., p. 63.

29. Flexner, *Century of Struggle*, pp. 37–40.

30. Ibid.

31. Gerda Lerner, ed., *Black Women in White America: A Documentary History* (New York, 1972), pp. 75–146.

32. Dorothy Porter, "Organized Activities of Negro Literary Societies," *The Journal of Negro Education*, Vol. 5 (October 1936), pp. 555–76.

33. Martineau, *Society in America*, Vol. III, pp. 111–12.

34. Wertheimer, *We Were There*, p. 123.

35. Catherine H. Berney, *The Grimké Sisters* (Westport, Conn., 1885), p. 183.

36. "Pastoral Letter of the General Association of Massachusetts to the Congregationalist Churches under their Care," in Gerda Lerner, *The Grimké Sisters from South Carolina* (Boston, 1967), p. 189.

37. William L. O'Neill, ed., *The Woman Movement; Feminism in the United States and England* (London, 1969), p. 33.

38. Sheila M. Rothman, *Woman's Proper Place: A History of Changing Ideals and Practices, 1870 to the Present* (New York, 1978), pp. 70–75.

39. Ibid., pp. 66–69. See also Degler, *At Odds*, pp. 317–18.

40. Frances Willard, Letter to Susan B. Anthony, as quoted in Aileen S. Kraditor, *The Ideas of the Woman Suffrage Movement, 1890–1920* (New York, 1971), p. 63, n. 34.

41. Frances E. Willard, *How to Win: A Book for Girls* (New York, 1886), pp. 55–57.

42. See Rothman, *Woman's Proper Place*, pp. 74–81, and Flexner, *Century of Struggle*, pp. 205–6.

43. Letter from Josephine Shaw Lowell to Ann Shaw, 1889, in William Rhinelander Stewart, *The Philanthropic Work of Josephine Shaw Lowell* (New York, 1911), p. 441.

44. Josephine Shaw Lowell, "Relation of Women to Good Government" (Address to the YWCA, 1899), in Stewart, ibid., pp. 435–45.

45. Flexner, *Century of Struggle*, pp. 241–47.

46. Nancy Schrom Dye, "Creating a Feminist Alliance: Sisterhood and Class Conflict in the New York Women's Trade Union League," *Feminist Studies*, Vol. 2 (1975), pp. 24–36.

47. See Rothman, *Woman's Proper Place*, pp. 112–27. For a first-hand account of the settlement movement, see Jane Addams, *Twenty Years at Hull House* (New York, 1910).

48. Degler, *At Odds*, pp. 310–11.

49. Degler, ibid. See also Rothman, *Woman's Proper Place*, p. 27.

50. Elaine Kendall, *Peculiar Institutions: An Informal History of the*

Seven Sister Colleges (New York, 1975), pp. 127–28. See also Degler, *At Odds*, p. 314.

51. Kendall, *Peculiar Institutions*, pp. 113, 107, 120.

52. Ibid., p. 144.

53. Lucy D. Slowe, "Higher Education of Negro Women," *The Journal of Negro Education*, Vol. 2 (1933), pp. 352–58.

54. Smuts, *Women and Work*, p. 21.

55. *Bradwell* v. *Illinois*, 83 U.S. (16 Wall.) 130 (1983).

56. Kendall, *Peculiar Institutions*, p. 125.

57. Jane Addams, "Why Women Should Vote," in *Jane Addams: A Centennial Reader* (New York, 1960), pp. 104–7.

58. Sophonisba Breckinridge, *Women in the Twentieth Century* (New York, 1972), pp. 14–19. (Originally published by McGraw Hill, 1933.)

59. Ibid., p. 17.

60. O'Neill, ed., *The Woman Movement*, p. 197.

61. Breckinridge, *Women in the Twentieth Century*, pp. 28–34.

62. Ibid., p. 31.

63. Grover Cleveland, "Women's Missions and Women's Clubs," *Ladies' Home Journal*, Vol. 22, May 1905, as quoted in Sherna Gluck, ed., *From Parlor to Prison: Five American Suffragists Talk about Their Lives* (New York, 1976), pp. 9–10.

64. Helen L. Grenfell, "The Influence of Women's Organizations on Public Education," *NEA Addresses and Proceedings* (Los Angeles, 1907), pp. 126–33.

65. Flexner, *Century of Struggle*, pp. 186–92, and Lerner, *Black Women*, pp. 435–38.

66. Flexner, ibid.

67. Lerner, *Black Women*, pp. 444–47.

68. Ibid., pp. 450–51.

69. Mary Church Terrell, *A Colored Woman in a White World* (Washington, D.C., 1940), p. 153.

70. Josephine P. Ruffin, Address to the First National Congress of Colored Women, Boston, 1895, as quoted in Elizabeth Davis, *Lifting as We Climb* (Washington, D.C., 1933), pp. 17–19.

71. Rothman, *Woman's Proper Place*, pp. 177–88.

72. Kendall, *Peculiar Institutions*, p. 184.

73. William L. O'Neill, *Everyone Was Brave: A History of Feminism in America* (Chicago, 1971), pp. 304–5.

74. Kendall, *Peculiar Institutions*, p. 179.

75. O'Neill, *Everyone Was Brave*, pp. 250–52. See also Rothman, *Woman's Proper Place*, pp. 181–84. For a brief history of the PTA and the college sorority, see Breckinridge, *Women in the Twentieth Century*, pp. 53–54, 80–82.

76. Breckinridge, ibid., p. 51.

77. Ibid., pp. 66–69.

78. Ibid.

79. Katherine Carr Wilson, "The Country Minister's Wife," *The Smith Alumnae Quarterly*, Vol. XIII (May 1922), pp. 263–65.

80. Alice Cone Perry, "A Married Woman's Job," *The Smith Alumnae Quarterly*, ibid., pp. 273–74.

81. The Quack, "Married Women and Jobs," *The Smith Alumnae Quarterly*, Vol. XIII (February 1922), pp. 161–62.

82. Betty Friedan, *The Feminine Mystique* (New York, 1963), pp. 345–46.

83. William L. O'Neill, *Everyone Was Brave*.

84. Charlotte Perkins Gilman, *Women and Economics* (New York, 1966), pp. 164–66. (Originally published by Small, Maynard & Company, 1898.)

Five—CONCLUSION

1. Andree Brooks, "Among Volunteers, Change in the Suburbs," New York *Times*, October 28, 1983, p. A24.

2. Ibid.

3. Ibid.

SELECTED BIBLIOGRAPHY

SECONDARY SOURCES

COMPREHENSIVE HISTORIES OF THE AMERICAN FEMINIST MOVEMENT AND WOMEN'S ROLES IN SOCIETY:

Carl N. Degler, *At Odds: Women and the Family in America from the Revolution to the Present* (New York and Oxford, 1980).

Eleanor Flexner, *A Century of Struggle: The Woman's Rights Movement in the United States* (New York, 1973; originally published by Harvard University Press, 1959).

William L. O'Neill, *Everyone Was Brave: A History of Feminism in America* (Chicago, 1969; paperback reprint, 1971).

SPECIALIZED HISTORIES:

Barbara Berg, *The Remembered Gate: Origins of American Feminism* (New York, 1978).

Sophonisba Breckinridge, *Women in the Twentieth Century: A Study of their Political, Social and Economic Activities* (New York, 1972; originally published by McGraw Hill, 1933).

Nancy F. Cott, *The Bonds of Womanhood: "Woman's Sphere" in New England, 1780–1835* (New Haven and London, 1977).

Eileen Kendall, *Peculiar Institutions: An Informal History of the Seven Sister Colleges* (New York, 1975).

Aileen S. Kraditor, *The Ideas of the Woman Suffrage Movement 1890–1920* (New York, 1971; originally published by Columbia University Press, 1965).

Sheila M. Rothman, *Woman's Proper Place: A History of Changing Ideals and Practices, 1870 to the Present* (New York, 1978).

HISTORIES OF WOMEN IN THE WORK FORCE:

Robert W. Smuts, *Women and Work in America* (New York, 1971; originally published by Columbia University Press, 1959).

Barbara Mayer Wertheimer, *We Were There: The Story of Working Women in America* (New York, 1977).

BIOGRAPHIES:

Bell Gale Chevigny, *The Woman and the Myth: Margaret Fuller's Life and Writings* (New York, 1976).

Helen E. Marshall, *Dorothea Dix: Forgotten Samaritan* (New York, 1937).

William Rhinelander Stewart, *The Philanthropic Work of Josephine Shaw Lowell* (New York, 1911).

DOCUMENTARY HISTORIES

Rosalyn Baxandall, Linda Gordon, and Susan Reverby, eds., *America's Working Women: A Documentary History—1600 to the Present* (New York, 1971).

Nancy F. Cott, ed., *Root of Bitterness: Documents of the Social History of American Women* (New York, 1972).

Gerda Lerner, ed., *Black Women in White America: A Documentary History* (New York, 1972).

William L. O'Neill, ed., *The Woman Movement: Feminism in the United States and England* (London, 1969).

PRIMARY SOURCES

Jane Addams, *Twenty Years at Hull House* (New York, 1910).

Charlotte Perkins Gilman, *Women and Economics* (New York, 1966; originally published by Small, Maynard & Company, 1898).

Julia Ward Howe, *Julia Ward Howe and the Woman Suffrage Movement*, Introduction and notes by Florence Howe Hall (Boston, 1913).

Harriet Martineau, *Society in America*, Vol. III (New York, 1966; originally published by Saunders & Otley, 1837).

Frances Willard, *How to Win: A Book for Girls* (New York, 1886).

INDEX